We either choose to be
accountable for our actions
or we are forced by our
own circumstances.

THE Scent OF LOVE

ALSO BY KEITH MILLER

Books
The Taste of New Wine
A Second Touch
The Becomers
The Edge of Adventure (with Bruce Larson)
Living the Adventure (with Bruce Larson)
Please Love Me
The Passionate People (with Bruce Larson)
With No Fear of Failure (with Tom Fatjo, Jr.)
The Single Experience (with Andrea Wells Miller)

Cassette Albums
The Edge of Adventure (with Bruce Larson)
Living the Adventure (with Bruce Larson)
The Passionate People (with Bruce Larson)
Faith, Intimacy and Risk in the Single Life (with Andrea
   Wells Miller)
New Wine: Evangelism as a Biblical Way of Living

Single Cassettes
Reconnection
Questions in the Spirit
Inside I Trembled
The Miracle of Intimacy

Films
New Wine: Evangelism as a Biblical Way of Living
Inside I Trembled

THE Scent OF LOVE

KEITH MILLER

WORD BOOKS
PUBLISHER
WACO, TEXAS
A DIVISION OF
WORD, INCORPORATED

THE SCENT OF LOVE

Library of Congress Cataloging in Publication Data:

Miller, Keith.
  The scent of love.
  1. Christian life—Anglican authors. 2. Conversion.
3. Evangelistic work. 4. Love (Theology) 5. Miller,
Keith. I. Title.
BV4501.2.M4799   1983   248.4'83   83–10220
ISBN 0–8499–0331–9

Printed in the United States of America

Scripture quotations used in this book are from the following versions:

The Revised Standard Version of the Bible (RSV),
copyright 1946, 1952, © 1971 and 1973 by the Division of Christian Education
of the National Council of the Churches of Christ in the U.S.A.

The King James Version of the Bible (KJV).

The Holy Bible: New International Version (NIV),
copyright © 1978 by the New York International Bible Society.

The New Testament in Modern English (Phillips),
copyright © 1958, 1960, 1972 by J. B. Phillips.

The New English Bible (NEB),
© 1961, 1970 The Delegates of the Oxford University Press and The Syndics
of the Cambridge University Press.

The Amplified New Testament (Amplified),
copyright © 1958 by The Lockman Foundation.

To
KRISTIN MILLER-PROVENCE
daughter, friend, minister, and sister in Christ
(who has kept saying, "You can do it, Daddy!")

CONTENTS

Contents

ACKNOWLEDGMENTS

I WANT TO EXPRESS my gratitude to the clergy and laity of the Anglican Church of New Zealand, who invited me to speak at their national conference on evangelism in 1981. I am especially grateful to the Reverend Michael Smart and the Reverend Stephen Brooker, who encouraged me to come to those meetings. Much of this book grew out of talks I prepared for that week. I have acknowledged elsewhere my gratitude to the Reverend Angus MacLeod, who was also a guest speaker at that conference.

Doc Heatherley at Word has been instigator, encourager, counselor, and friend during the production of the *New Wine* films and the writing of this book. Floyd Thatcher and Anne Christian Buchanan and their crew cleaned up my mistakes, "unstuck" some sticky places, and guided me through some narrow and tricky literary shoals as editors, but also as friends. Joey Paul believed I could write the *New Wine* films, or there wouldn't have been a book. And Jarrell McCracken has given me the gift of believing in me and this project even in the dark nights when I had trouble believing in either. To the rest of the Word bunch who have not only worked on this book but many of whom have offered unbelievable love and support during these past few years, I will always be grateful.

My friends Chuck and Carolyn Huffman read the manuscript and made helpful suggestions, as did my daughter Kristin Miller-Provence, to whom this book is dedicated.

And finally I want to thank my wife, Andrea, who took hours and hours from her own writing projects to type, retype, edit, and think through various aspects of this book as coproducer with me.

I am grateful to the writers whose ideas I have quoted and referred

11

to specifically—particularly Paul Tournier and Scott Peck—and to those whose ideas I may have unwittingly used as my own.

There are other people who gave advice and suggestions and other kinds of help, and I am grateful to them all. Since this book is in some ways the product of a lifetime, I can close my eyes and envision a sea of faces of those who have influenced me and helped me along the way. I only wish there were space here to thank them all personally.

A PERSONAL NOTE FROM
KEITH MILLER

EVANGELISM IS a dirty word for some Christians. In many people's eyes it stands for manipulation and insensitivity, leading people into a negative hellfire-and-damnation religion, a religion which ignores the richness and creative potential in this life while pointing always beyond death for any meaning. For other Christians, evangelism is a "program" where periodically people are brought together to be confronted with the "claims of Christ." Between evangelistic programs, other aspects of the Christian life are emphasized.

But evangelism in the New Testament was nothing like either of these notions. Imagine a group of grown men and women, so happy at nine o'clock in the morning that people thought they were drunk! (See Acts 2:1–13.) Now change the scene until you can see a man being executed by his fellow citizens outside a city gate. As they are trying to crush his head with the stones they are throwing, he looks up and offers his spirit to an invisible God, and then says to this God, "Father, forgive them, they don't understand" (Acts 8:59, 60, paraphrased).

This strange combination of irrepressible joy and the ability to face calmly the most basic and fearful problems of life—even rejection and death—created an aura around the little bunch of new Christians. And this aura permeated the air of first-century Palestine. The *way they lived together* gave off a kind of haunting spiritual scent which drew people to them. And it was this unselfconscious scent of love which provided the essence of that which we have come to call evangelism.

The first Christian community around Jesus was a "pool of love" into which new converts were dipped to be healed and made new. The sharing of their message was inseparable from their ongoing life together. The idea of an "evangelistic program" would not even have

13

made sense to the New Testament Christians. "Evangelism" was the gospel message simply overflowing from their adventure with Christ and each other. They were announcing the kingdom of God as they were in the midst of living in it.

The purpose of this book is to examine the life we Christians are offered, the kind of life which gives off the attracting scent of love. Then I want to talk about the doorway to that kind of life—Christian conversion, another deeply abused and misunderstood term. Then we'll look at what sort of church it would take in our kind of world to produce a "pool of love" and give people an opportunity to get in it. Finally, we'll ask how the converted members of such a church would pass the cup of faith in a realistic and sensitive way to a world starving for God.

The idea for the movie series on which this book is based (*New Wine: Evangelism as a Biblical Way of Living*) came in 1981 when I was invited to speak to the first national conference on evangelism held by the Anglican Church of New Zealand. In preparing to be the keynote speaker, I had to go back through my whole life and think through what evangelism had come to mean to me. The other speaker during that week was the Reverend Angus MacLeod of Christ Church, New Zealand, who was to do the morning Bible studies. As he spoke, I realized I was in the presence of a remarkable and sensitive teacher. I don't know what that conference did for the others who attended, but it changed my life.

During the preparation and delivery of my addresses, and while listening to Angus MacLeod and talking to some of the wonderful Christians in New Zealand, I realized that up to then I had not wanted to write about evangelism, because I knew that for many people it has either become an embarrassment—the way it is sometimes carried out—or a source of frustration—because it doesn't work like it apparently did in the New Testament. But while attending that conference I felt I had to come home and do something to witness to the fact—which I saw so clearly five thousand miles from home—that evangelism doesn't have to be the ineffective or manipulative thing we have sometimes made it.

I was deeply moved by Angus MacLeod's biblical presentations and asked permission to use some of his unpublished material in the movie series, which he graciously granted. Some of that material is incorporated in this book in parts of chapters 22, 23, 26, 36, 37, and 39. Since I have blended the content and style of Mr. MacLeod's material into my own, any errors or faults in those chapters must be laid at my doorstep. But I am very grateful to my friend, Angus, for his help in this venture.

As I began writing the book manuscript, I realized that there was a lot in the films that needed to be clarified and expanded. So this book is much broader than a transcription of that material. But I have tried to maintain more of a speaking style than is usual in my books— even to the point of including some stories I would usually only tell verbally.

If you have read my earlier books (*The Taste of New Wine*, etc.) some of the material—particularly part of the story of my own conversion—may be repetitious. But I felt I had to risk losing you by doing this in order to *do* what I am recommending regarding the sharing of our stories. And although this book is in some ways the developmental flowering of seeds I first discovered and wrote about years ago, much of the material in this book appears here for the first time in my writing.

The dream I have in writing this is that you and I may take a walk together for a few hours in God's story, and in Jesus Christ and his gospel may share again the scent of his love.

I

SHARING
THE TASTE OF
NEW WINE

1

The Citadel of the Soul

WAY DOWN INSIDE each one of us there seems to be a secret part of our lives that we keep walled off from the rest of the world, even from the people with whom we live. It's a place where we experience our most poignant fears—of not being loved by somebody close to us (our children, our wife or husband, our parents), of not having enough money or not being sexually adequate (or fulfilled), of failing in our vocations or finding that life is not what it promised to be.

But this same secret place where we hide our fears is also where we keep our most private and fragile hopes and dreams. In a sense, these are even more difficult for us to talk about than the fears, because if we tell these hopes and dreams and then fail to achieve them, we have no comfortable private fantasy into which we can retreat when things are not going well. As a result, many of us play it safe and never try to actualize our dreams or even tell them to another soul. We keep our fears, our secret longings, and our flickering hesitations buried inside us.

But like a lightning bolt in the middle of the night, there sometimes comes a moment when we realize we're going to die—that we may never do the things we've dreamed of.

Several months ago this sudden awareness happened to me. I was shaving, and I noticed my hands in the mirror. I saw some brown spots on them (which a few years ago I would have called freckles). The skin was wrinkled, and my hands looked like my father's hands just before he died. I realized I am growing old. As I stood there looking at my hands, I became starkly aware once again that I am going to die.

Shortly after that morning, I went to the funeral of a dear friend who had committed suicide. She was much younger than I. After the

19

funeral, I realized, "I've got to make some decisions about the way I'm going to live the rest of my life. If I have any dreams to fulfill," I thought, "I'd better get at them. Life's going by very quickly, and there may not be much of it left."

So I began to think about what people like me might do when we realize that life is going by, and that we are afraid to try the dreams God has put in us. Realistically, how does God help us to risk changing our lives in mid-course and coming to grips with our hopes and our fears?

All this may not seem relevant in a book about "evangelism," but these are the inner problems people all around us seem to be facing. And the promise of the gospel is to free us from the real fears of death and life and to show us how to live creatively in God's image. So it seems imperative that to effectively evangelize other people, we need to learn to express the gospel in relation to the real questions they (and we) are living.

In this book I'd like for us to confront these questions by looking inside ourselves. I'd like for us to "pull back" our faces, as one pulls open a doorway, and to look into the citadels of our souls—at what we are as persons and as Christians. What's the basic story line of our lives? And where are we in it? How are we living? How are we giving and receiving love as members of Christ's body, the church?

I'd like to look with you at the Bible and ask some questions like "How does *God* want us to live together, to love and to help each other find meaning for our lives?" And also, "How do we give to other people around us the life that we find in Christ?" And "How do we as ordinary churchgoing Christians evangelize people outside our churches?"

I want to start this trip together by taking a look at the notion of "story"—especially the idea of "walking in God's story."[1]

The Notion of "Story"

The Bible is not a "theological" book in the same sense that other books about God are theological books. The late Canon Theodore Wedel spoke of the Bible as a story, a drama. I like to think of it as a drama in three acts. The Old Testament is act one; it shows God the Father's creating the world and then, after man's fall, brooding over the course

---

1. I am indebted to Dr. James Wharton for the description of the Christian life as "walking in God's story."

of history. The first four books of the New Testament are act two of God's story, the accounts of God's coming to confront and comfort mankind personally through the life, death, and resurrection of Jesus. Act three starts in the book of Acts and continues through the rest of our New Testament. And in one sense I think it is valid to say that act three of the biblical drama goes on right into the present, that we who live in the last part of the twentieth century are also living in act three of God's story.

One reason it's sometimes difficult for us modern readers to understand the Bible is that we are not trained in the art of story. With our logical minds we try to grasp the New Testament and begin to shake it and pull it apart, hoping to pick out the kernels of its meaning. But it doesn't seem to me that the truth of story works that way.

The Hebrews, who wrote most of the Bible, had a very different approach to truth than we do. They knew how to "walk into" a story in their imaginations and to ask their listeners to follow them so the truth of the story could *grasp them*. And Jesus, instead of inviting his disciples to study with him, asked them to follow him as he walked in God's story. This is the method of the biblical storytellers. And I believe that life, as it was meant to be lived together in Christ, begins not as we *think* abstractly about Christianity or *study its doctrine,* but as we learn to *step into* God's story in the midst of his people, and to let it take hold of us at deeper and deeper levels. As we enter the story, we learn to open ourselves to God with our sorrow, sickness, sin, joy, and hope. Then, hesitantly, we discover how to begin sharing the specifics of our lives with each other—until eventually we can tell our stories to people "out in the world" who are crying out for a life with hope. When they hear the fear and joy and hope in our stories and can *identify with us,* then they are often ready to listen carefully to God's story.

Somehow, we Christians seem to have lost this art of "living into" God's story, and because of our fear of appearing inadequate we are often insulated against the pain and failure in each other's stories. In our churches we freely involve ourselves with many good and inspiring activities. We sing hymns, listen to sermons, take part in communion, and study Scripture; we attend choir rehearsals and committee meetings and covered-dish suppers. But where, in the average congregation, do we have a chance to sit down and share our stories with one another? And do we ever consciously approach people outside the church with the purpose of getting to know their stories and sharing ours with them? Retirement homes are filled with people waiting for somebody to want to hear their stories. So are executive office suites and suburban homes and artists' studios. At some level we all seem to want to tell people who we really are, and yet we're afraid to for fear they'll be bored or reject us. So we skate around each other on the surface data of our lives.

But it is as we learn to tell our inner stories as Christians that people outside the church can often take the first step into God's adventure through our lives, and we can become living doorways into the family of God. Strangers can come in and touch the person of Christ among us, and we will have begun to evangelize them.

As we tell our stories, some things happen which transcend logic through the alchemy of faith. There is a magic about sharing the real adventures of our lives. After we've told each other some of what's inside the citadels of our souls, we can somehow trust each other more and understand what's really being said in ordinary conversations or church committee meetings. We can relax and not be so afraid, as we find newly shared areas of meaning on which to meet at different and deeper levels of life.

So before we begin this search for the truth about the way God wants us to live, before we start examining this adventure of learning to love each other and to share the life he's brought us, I'd like to tell you a little something of my own story.

2

What I Thought Was a Peculiar Childhood

FROM THE TIME I was a little boy, I lived basically three lives.

First on my agenda was to keep my mother's approval. She was my one-woman cheering section, and her love for me appeared to have no limits. It seemed that in her eyes I could do no wrong.

My second "life's work" as a child was to try to get my daddy to love me, but I was convinced that he loved my older brother, Earle, more than anything or anyone else. So, from the time I was a young boy, I was determined to win my daddy's love through competing with my brother. This presented a number of problems because Earle was five years older than I and a terrific athlete. (My dad loved "men's men.")

Third on my agenda as my life developed was to do something for me, to find out what I was like and what I wanted to do with my life. But this area got pretty well left out because I felt that first I had to please my mother and father and to be the best son they could imagine. I was one of those kids people hate when their mothers say to other mothers, "Oh, I'm sorry you're having trouble with your son. Little Keith has *never* given us any trouble. He's a *model* child. I guess we are just lucky." I was a classic people-pleaser.

I loved my older brother and followed him around, watching him like a hawk. I realized later that it wasn't so much that I worshiped him (which I felt like I did), but that I wanted to see how he did things so I could beat him out and get my daddy's love. But I didn't know that then.

My attempts to compete were sometimes pitiful. (If you have children or brothers or sisters, you probably understand this.) For instance I remember that when we were running across a field and came to a creek, he'd jump across it and I'd jump *in* it. I was just too little to make it across. But that never even slowed me down. I remember we had bicycles with no chain guards in those days. If you didn't roll your trousers up on the right leg, the chain caught your cuff and just wound you up on the street. And so I'd watch Earle carefully. He'd roll his pants up three notches, and I'd roll my pants up three notches—clear to the crotch! He was an unusually fine athlete, so my challenge became to try to become even better at sports than he was.

When playing football, I always tried to tackle players twice my size as fast as possible, in order to get it over with. Inside, I was afraid that I'd get hurt, but I needed to do well to please my father. It seemed that if I was aggressive I could hide my fears better.

I said this in a talk for the first time somewhere in Michigan. When I finished speaking, a man who had won the Canadian heavyweight boxing championship back in about 1950 came up to me and said, "I won the Canadian national championship and nobody ever even knocked me down. I was so terrified that people might find out I was a coward inside that I whipped everybody." And those of you who are men know that many of us were trained by well-meaning parents not to cry or be afraid. I don't think anyone ever actually *said* that to me, but I grew up feeling it. I knew that, because I was a male, I must *never* appear weak or inadequate.

My mother also told me that if I wanted to get along in the world and really do well, I should "be nice to people and learn their names." So I learned almost everybody's name in a high school of 3,500. There are a few I may have missed, but they didn't make the yearbook. And I won just about every office for which I was nominated, because in some cases I was the only name on the ballot that many of the other kids recognized. No one knew how much time I spent getting to know people.

Finally, in my senior year in high school, I was elected king of the school. Now, that may strike you as strange, but our school in Tulsa, Oklahoma had a king. I remember sitting backstage waiting to go in and be crowned at the annual variety show. As I sat there alone in a room behind the curtain, I realized with a real sadness that if I went out in the world and won everything there was to win, I still wouldn't be happy. I thought, "What a tragic secret about life."

Death and Questions About Life

In 1945, near the end of the second world war, I graduated from high school. My brother was a bomber pilot in the Army Air Force.

Fifteen days before the war was over, I was sitting in a crowded Friday-night movie with a date when I heard an usher walking down the aisle calling my name. I'd never been paged in a movie, and I felt a strange warning bell go off somewhere in the back of my head. The theater manager said that I was to go home at once. I couldn't imagine what was the matter. But I went home.

Some friends of my parents met me at the front door and said, "Your brother's been killed." I just stood there, and a cold feeling of anguish went all over me. I looked for my mother and dad, but they were off in the back bedroom together. They were just devastated.

The house was full of strange people. I looked around and, numbing my feelings, immediately took over as host. I made sure everybody had coffee, and introduced people to others whom they didn't know. I was being "the man." But after they all left, I remember going out on the back porch. It was a clear cool summer night filled with stars, and a high white moon was shining. I remember looking up through tears which wouldn't quite come and saying, "Why? Why Earle? He was such a good guy! Why not me?" And then I had a strange thought, "Somehow I've got to learn about life. I've got to learn what life means, what it's all about, so I can tell people. Because no one seems to understand how to live. And if someone doesn't tell them, then people like Earle who die young will never really get to live life.

And so I began to watch people. At nineteen, I began to try to figure out what made things go in the world of adults. Yet I always tried to look as if I were cool and didn't care about such heavy matters.

My mother had a nervous breakdown over my brother's death. She later got cancer. My father had a heart attack, combined with ulcers. Separately, both of them began to tell me the feelings which had been bottled up inside them—the hurts and hopes.

I came to realize through my talks with my father that if my mother had done several things differently in their relationship his life would have been changed. I realized then that he'd been waiting thirty-five years for her to understand what these needs were, and yet he didn't have the courage to tell her, for fear she'd think he was foolish.

As I talked to my mother, the same thing was true about her hopes and dreams. I thought, "My gosh, as close a family as we are, what must it be like 'out there' where people *aren't* close? People must be dying for some intimacy, some time apart without the children, an attentive listening ear. Couples living together, each partner wanting some simple thing the other could give, and yet . . . afraid to ask."

(I would be willing to bet anything that at least one of you who's reading this book and is married was lying in bed some night this week wanting to reach over and tell your husband or wife, "Please, just hold me," or "I want to tell you how afraid I am,"—or "how lonely I am" or even "how much I love you." But possibly you were afraid you'd feel silly or be rejected and feel worse, and you didn't reach over.)

After high school I was in the Navy for a year, and then I came back and went to the University of Oklahoma. One night I was on the way to a fraternity party at Enid, Oklahoma, with some kids from Tulsa. A boy whom we hoped would join our fraternity was sitting in the back seat with me. He was a lifelong friend of mine named Bob, a wrestler, and a very powerful and bright young man. A couple I'll call Bill and Sharon were in the front seat and it was Bill's new car. Sharon had wanted to drive, and he'd let her. So Sharon was driving ninety-seven miles per hour down a little ribbon-strip highway. The Oklahoma highways are probably better now, but then the two-lane slab often stood up about four to six inches above the shoulder.

As we were speeding down the highway, the outside wheels slipped off the slab. Well, by the time most kids are fourteen in Oklahoma, their daddies tell them, "Listen, if your wheels ever slip off the slab, *don't* try to turn the car suddenly back on the highway. Slow down and ease back onto the slab." Sharon had evidently missed that lecture altogether, and she tried to whip the wheels back onto the highway, and the car careened and tumbled down a hill—270 yards. As it rolled over five-and-a-half times it bounced past a house, where a farmer counted from his front porch (as he told us later).

When the car stopped, it was on its side and I was face down on the groundward door. I opened my eyes and through the dust I saw a pair of legs. I thought, "Oh, no, Bob's been cut in two!" Then the legs began to move and I realized he'd been thrown face first through the rear window of that '47 Plymouth. When he pulled himself out, he turned around and smiled. And his face just seemed to fall apart from the impact. Blood went everywhere, and in my humility and friendship I said, "Boy, I hope all that blood's yours."

Then I tried to get up on my hands and knees. I remember that, as I tried to pull myself up, my head just nodded slowly, and I quickly dropped back down. I knew my neck was broken. I said to myself, "What happens to you when you break your neck?" All I could remember was that you died.

I wanted to get out of that car to die, and so I asked Bob if he'd help me. Holding my head straight with both hands, I stood up, and he pulled me out of the car. I don't know how I held my face because I'd pulled some ligaments and later had to relearn to use my right arm. I remember seeing people standing around watching and taking pictures, but no one would help because they didn't want to get involved.

Bob put me down on his overcoat beside the road and covered me with my own. Sharon's neck was also broken and she was cut up pretty badly, so the ambulance took her first. I was lying beside the road for about an hour. And, as I lay there, I thought I was dying. In my imagination I saw my family. I thought about God and I began to pray. I started to say, "Listen, God, if you'll get me out of this I'll really make you a hand somewhere."

But then I remembered that my daddy had told me, "Son, don't ever make a deal you can't promise to keep." I realized I had nothing to offer God. So I just said, "Well, here I am." I remember feeling a kind of peace about dying, and I thought, "What a shame it is to find out there is peace about dying at this stage in your life."

I got over the broken neck, and I also got over the feeling of peace. But from that time on I was really focused on finding out what life means. The search I had started when my brother died really intensified. But, of course, nobody knew this except me.

3

And Where Is God?

WHEN I RECOVERED from the broken neck I went back to the university and married a lovely person. She was a yearbook queen. Now people would surely think I must be special as a man. On the inside, however, I still felt like the little brother who couldn't make it—even though I was president of "his" fraternity and had lettered in "his" sport (basketball) at the university. But I don't think many people who knew me then were aware of the extent of my insecurity.

After graduation from college I went to work for a major oil company. From the beginning I worked hard and was very ambitious. But I began to realize that though I wanted desperately to be on a fast track to "success," I had never before looked down the road to see what "success" might mean.

And as I traveled through the desert country of south Texas, buying oil leases and curing titles, I began to think again about the meaning of life. And I started to wonder about God. I thought about the silent power of God in the world, and I wondered, "What does God have to do with the way we live out our lives?" After much thought and soul searching I decided I'd go to seminary and try to find some of the answers to my questions.

I'd gotten along fine with the people at the oil company office. I liked those men and women and I hoped they liked me. But they didn't really know what to do when I told them my decision. They had a social procedure for sending people off to another office when someone was transferred, but they didn't have a way to send people off to a theological seminary! Since they couldn't think of anything else to do, some friends did what they knew how to do well—they just threw a blast to send us off. Well, I remember about two o'clock that morning my old boss put his arm around my neck, leaned over in my face,

28

looked blearily at me, and said confidentially, "Buddy, you'll *never* make it!" That was about the nearest thing to a prayer I got as I left the oil business for seminary.

When I arrived in New Haven, Connecticut, 1300 miles from home, I had a whole fistful of questions, like "What do you tell parents about Christianity when they have just lost a son in a plane crash? What do you tell somebody who's just found out she has cancer and has six months to live? What do you tell a proud independent man who develops ulcers and then has a heart attack after having been very active in business, and who suddenly has to sit around and feel useless and helpless? What do you tell people about situations like that?"

I kept asking these questions at seminary. But they were the wrong questions, apparently, because I kept hearing professors say, "Wait a minute, this is a graduate school. We're studying theology (history, liturgics, etc.) in this class, not psychological counseling."

I understand that the seminaries need to be graduate schools if we are to have an educated clergy. The Bible, church history, theology, and the social sciences are vast and complex subjects. But I had also gone to that school to find answers and directions regarding some very personal questions about the inside of life—questions I was actually living through with my family. In that seminary, at that time, my deepest questions seemed out of place and naïve.

Academically I did pretty well in seminary—as hard as I studied, an orangutan would have done well! But I thought, "There must be a way to walk into people's homes, sit down with them and get to know them. And somehow, as a person shares his life with people in these informal situations, there should be a way to make them hungry or homesick for God." Because that's what I saw happening in the New Testament.

I saw that the first Christians were excited about the healing atmosphere of the life they were living together. They were excited about the kingdom of God, and the kingdom touched them at the point of their own needs, their own lives. The new Christians had no seminaries nor training in either theology or logic; they simply shared reports of what was happening to them. "Why can't we do that now?" I wondered. "Why *don't* we do it?" I didn't know. We certainly didn't discuss such things in seminary. And I made the lowest grade in my entire school career in homiletics class—the class in which we learned to write and deliver sermons—when I tried to speak on a personal level.

After four terms at seminary I began to get very anxious. I felt as though I were in the wrong place; at any rate, I was sure I was not minister material for the church. Finally, I decided to leave. I felt terrible leaving seminary. It was hard for me to quit, because I'd never failed at anything before. Of course, this wasn't an academic failure, but it was a failure to finish what I'd set out to do. And I had the awful feeling I was turning my back on God. But inside, I *knew* that the questions I had were legitimate and that there must be people somewhere who wondered about God and life the way I did.

When I'd gone to seminary, the oil company had said I could come back to work if I wanted to, so I went to them and said, "I need a job."

They said, "Fine. We'll send you to Tyler, Texas." That was where I had spent the summers during my seminary years. I'd rather have gone to Siberia! How was I going to face all those people and tell them I'd quit seminary? I couldn't explain to them that, inside, my soul was like Michelangelo's tableau of warriors, the various parts of me twisting and struggling for release and rest.

I had anxiety attacks night and day; I sweated clear through a suit one afternoon. I don't know if you have ever thought you were going crazy, but it is a very frightening feeling. And it's not something you just go up and tell the people around you. But I thought I was losing my mind. I burned my journal for fear someone would read it and have me committed. I'd give anything to have that record now, so I could trace my struggle through those months, but I burned it because I didn't know what was happening to me.

One August afternoon I checked out a company car and just took off, driving as fast as I could. I left Tyler and headed east toward Shreveport, Louisiana. We didn't have air conditioning in company cars in those days, and it was hot and muggy. I remember driving through the tall pine forests of East Texas and seeing the dark trees flicker by.

Finally I pulled off on the side of the road and began to cry. Now, when I was growing up, I'd felt that a "real man" didn't cry—and besides, I'd always been a very optimistic person. I'd believed a good night's sleep would cure almost anything, and in those days I thought two martinis and a good night's sleep certainly would. Yet all of a sudden I didn't have any hope. I felt like I was alone in the bottom of a deep well. I thought about God and I looked up at the billowing white clouds and said, "God, I give up. If there's anything you want in this stinking life, take it."

I didn't know anything about Christian conversion or making a personal Christian commitment of my life to God, but at that moment I just didn't have any agenda for my life. I remember thinking, "Well, I might as well use my life for something. Maybe God could have a use for it." And I turned from my past toward God.

I'd like to tell you that lightening struck the hood of the car and our Lord appeared, but that didn't happen to me. What happened instead was that I realized I'd surrendered and somehow given God permission to come into my life, to take my future. Inside I'd always felt as if I were a kid wearing life like a suit two sizes too big, kind of hoping I'd grow into it. And suddenly my life fit.

After I offered God my future, I began to cry again. But this time they were tears of relief from the struggle of a lifetime. At last I realized it was all right for me to be me, and not Earle Miller, my brother. And somehow in that moment of commitment I knew I'd made contact with the Meaning of Life. Some time later, I started the car and headed back home, but I didn't know what to do next.

4

A Loner's Christian Life

AFTER COMING HOME from the encounter beside the road, I didn't
tell what had happened to me. I'd never known anyone personally
who claimed to have been converted. All I knew was that I felt a
great hope about life and a deep sense of rightness and closeness with
God. And I had an insatiable desire to learn about him.

I spent four years studying the Scriptures and reading the lives and
works of the great people in the church's history who had made a
personal commitment to God in Christ—people like Augustine, Thomas
á Kempis, Pascal, Brother Lawrence, and William Law. I read the
stories of these people's lives, one right after the other.

Since I hadn't been led to make a commitment through the evangelistic efforts of any particular Christian group, I had no pious language
or schema with which to describe what had happened to me. Every
Christian group which has an evangelistic bent seems to develop its
own highly distinctive "religious sound," with pet scriptural or theological expressions. But not having a particular religious sound or distinctive
way of talking about what had happened to me, I couldn't seem to
communicate with other converted Christians. And I felt that some
of them were uncertain about the validity of my encounter with God—
because I didn't describe it in the right phrases. I was often very lonely
for someone who could understand what had happened to me.

During the years following my conversion I prayed and read the
Bible and the lives of the saints. I began to wonder, "How can a land
man in the oil business live as a converted Christian in our kind of
world?" But I didn't tell anyone what had happened to me on the
roadside or the thoughts I was thinking.

At one point I was transferred to Oklahoma City, Oklahoma, by the oil company for which I worked, but we lived in Norman, from which I commuted twenty miles. In a local church I taught an adult Sunday school class on the Bible as it related to the problems of Christian living. Since trying to live as a Christian was my own personal pilgrimage, I decided that the best way I could teach the class was to share the struggles and directions I was finding. And I would try to deal with as many of *their* actual problems as they would reveal.

But people were not used to that approach and were reticent to discuss the real difficulties they had found in trying to be Christians. So I finally asked the class members to write anonymous questions. Later I began asking participants in seminars and other groups I dealt with to submit anonymous questions concerning their most pressing problems. And over the next few years, I actually got more than four thousand such questions. I began to write and speak to the issues they raised, feeling it would be better to deal inadequately with real concerns than beautifully with hypothetical ones.

But as I read the anonymous questions from that first Sunday school class, I was floored. The questions concerned everything from doubts about the existence of God to descriptions of unnatural sex acts. People wanted to know what God, through the Bible, might have to say about their secret problems. And they wanted to know how they—people who had disturbing, unsolved issues and doubts in their own lives— could be Christians with integrity in their life away from the church.

God in a Business Office

After several months of exploring the Christian adventure with my adult class, I began to think, "Okay, if I'm in an oil company office in Oklahoma City during the week, I ought to try to be a Christian there." But I had no idea how to be a Christian in an oil exploration office.

One morning I went in to my office and said silently to God, "Okay, Lord, today I'm going to be your person in this office." Thirty minutes later I couldn't even remember that God was there. I had intended to pray all day, but by nine thirty that morning I'd forgotten all about praying. It was then that I realized I must find a way to remind myself of my commitment to Christ so I could change the thought and behavior patterns of a lifetime. And I began to learn some things about trying to do this.

For instance, a few days later I said to myself, "Every time I walk down the hall to get a drink of water, I'm going to say a prayer for the people here in the office." So I began to pray for people. But very quickly I realized I didn't know enough *about* them to pray intelligently for them. I didn't know their problems, pains, hopes, or dreams. So I began to *listen* to them, asking questions at coffee breaks. (Well, I don't know if anything happened to those people because of my praying for them, but my health improved tremendously from drinking all that water!)

Over the next few months some of those men and women started drifting into my office one at a time. Those sophisticated business people came in and just sort of opened themselves and let me see their inner lives. And I soon realized that there were enormous personal problems, loneliness, and searching among people in the oil business.

Several years later I had met some other Christians in the oil business through my good friend Bill Yinger (who encouraged me and helped me more than he knows). Through Bill I was hired by another oil company and subsequently became that company's exploration manager. And one day when the vice president in charge of our office was overseas, I said silently, "Okay, Lord, I'm going to get involved with any of these people who want to pray about this business." I didn't think we ought to meet together on company time, but I thought, "I'll have a meeting with them before work and we'll find out how to be Christian business people."

Among the men and women in that office were a Buddhist, a Jewish fellow, all kinds of "believers," and some who did not claim any kind of religion. But I went to their offices to invite them and, since I was a manager, they listened to me. I said, "We're on a pretty fast track in this business, and I'd like to pray about what's happening and what we're doing here together. I'm a Christian. I don't know if you are or not, but if you'd like to pray together, I'm going to come early, at seven thirty, and have a little coffee. If you want to come, fine. If you don't, no sweat." That was Friday, and I said, "We'll start Monday—for any of you who'd be interested." (I had a conference room next to my office which would give us privacy.)

All that weekend I kicked myself all over the house. I said, "Why'd you do that? You're a stupid fool," (not that I have any pride, you understand). I often have what at our house we call "cringers." For instance, sometimes I have said something at a party that seemed "real clever" at the time, but when I've gotten home and remembered what I have said, I will grimace and shake my head, saying, "Oh no, *why* did I say *that?*" And so I was cringing all during the weekend about having been so vulnerable at the office. What if no one came? I'd feel terrible.

But on Monday I went in early, and of the fourteen people in that office almost all showed up. We began to talk together and share our feelings. After a few weeks the secretaries began to pray for the business and for the executives in our office, and the executives began to pray for the secretaries and for each other. We learned that we were all just persons who were struggling to live the best way we could in our circumstances.

After six months, people from other companies used to walk in the office and say things like, "What kind of a deal do you have here? These people are sure friendly." We didn't necessarily say anything about Jesus to visitors; we just loved them. I kept a journal through all this time and was amazed at the way *my* life changed. I felt more a part of the lives of the people with whom I worked.

Later I began to get invitations to speak at Christian meetings. I remember my first invitation was to speak at an annual meeting of businessmen called the Layman's Leadership Institute. I was supposed to give a "testimony"—and I didn't know anything about that. In those days, as far as I knew, we didn't have "testimonies" in the Episcopal church.

When I got to the meeting and picked up a program, I saw that I was going to "witness" between a man named R. G. LeTourneau and Billy Graham. You talk about panic! I was green as a gourd and very frightened, since I'd never been to a meeting where businessmen "witnessed."

There were several hundred men at the meeting, and I was afraid I would fail miserably because I didn't understand this form of communication. And in my pride and insecurity I prayed, "Oh, Lord, let me say something intelligent—and something that may help someone out there to find you."

There were only two Episcopalians at the meeting, and the other one was from Canada. I remember when I finished telling basically the story I've written here, an old man with white hair and penetrating blue eyes walked up to me. He said, "Son, are you sure you're not a Baptist?"

I said, "No sir, I'm *not* a Baptist."

He said, "Son, you sure?"

I said, smiling, "No sir, I'm *positive* I'm not a Baptist."

Shaking his head, he looked bewildered and said, "Well son, you sure have a Baptist heart." (It took me four years to realize that was a compliment!)

A Conference Center for Helping People Find God

About two years later I was asked to be a director of an experimental conference center called Laity Lodge. A man named Howard Butt, Jr., and the Butt Foundation were building it. I had met Howard at the Layman's Institute, but I didn't know then that he and his wife, Barbara Dan, were to become very dear friends in Christ. When I was asked to be director of Laity Lodge, I had only been to one religious retreat-type conference in my life (a parish-life weekend which an Episcopal church had put on years earlier). And I hadn't liked that conference too well. But I accepted the position anyway and we moved to Leakey, Texas.

After much thought and prayer, I said to the other staff members at the lodge, "Let's don't make this feel like a 'religious' center. Let's pretend that this is our weekend place in the country. And when people come, let's meet them just as we would if they were visiting in our home, and let's treat them as if they were coming for a social weekend with us." I didn't know how to do the "religious conference" thing. And, anyway, I wanted the people who came to Laity Lodge to think "life" and not "churchy pious thoughts."

I said to the guests who came, "Let's just sit around and talk about what's most important in our lives and what God may have to say about living. Those of us who led the conferences reflected on the Christian life by telling our own stories. We talked about the biblical accounts of the gospel of Jesus Christ, and gave people a chance to make a commitment of their lives to him.

It was amazing to me. People's lives began to change. They began to try to commit their whole futures to God in Christ while we were together, and they took it very seriously. By the end of the first summer I realized that there was something worth grasping in this "beginning to walk in God's story together through sharing our own stories." We were, I realized, engaged in an authentic biblical form of evangelism—an evangelism which led very naturally into trying to live all of one's life for God and for his people. Here at last was a way to live as a Christian that didn't smell religious.

I recalled that Jesus' severest critics and accusers had said to him, in effect, "The problem is that you're not *religious* enough." He seemed comfortable with prostitutes and with other people who were considered disreputable by the Jewish leaders and who had lots of troubles in their lives (see Luke 5:33). These nonreligious people liked Jesus and felt at home with him. And I'd seen that frequently non-Christians today don't seem to like most of us Christians the way the people in Jesus' day liked him. As I reflected on that I began to see that Jesus was not judgmental the way we often are, and that we sound so religious that people raised outside a Christian community simply can't identify with us.

And so I wondered, "Is there a way to live this Christian life that is *human*—outside of a conference or church meeting context? Wouldn't it be great if we could learn to *live* a life that is committed to Jesus Christ—without having to *be religious* all the time?!"

5

Testing the Hypothesis That Sharing Our Real Stories Is the Way to Go

I COULDN'T FIND ANY BOOKS to give to people that dealt with the actual inner conflicts and difficulties one has after becoming a Christian. The writers of the available contemporary literature at that time seemed to assume that once a person makes a serious commitment to God, his or her only problems are learning how to read the Bible and pray. It seemed to me that the moral of most of the books I read was that "real" Christians don't have problems with moral issues and relationships. The common thread was, "I *used to* have horrible problems. But since I accepted Jesus (bless the Lord and give *him* all the credit), I don't have such struggles anymore."

Well, my friends who got converted at Laity Lodge and I had a lot of problems before we became Christians, and we also had problems *after* we got converted. I just couldn't bring myself to give my newly converted friends a book which implied that the truly committed Christian is relieved of all his or her problems simply because he or she has made a commitment. If they read that and believed it, they'd all quit the church. They'd feel their commitment must not have been valid because they still had to struggle with the ethical and moral issues of life in the business and professional worlds.

As I read the story of the apostle Paul in the Bible, it seemed to me that he *never ever* got over all his pride and some of his other problems. And I remember feeling very relieved when I noticed that in the New Testament. So I wrote a book to hand to those new Christians who wanted to be God's people but also wanted to honestly face their failures and needs. In the book, I told my story and showed how it had merged with God's story. I wrote, in effect, "Since I became a Christian, I love God very much. I love the Lord Jesus Christ with my whole heart, but I still have problems. I'm still selfish, I'm still greedy, I still want to be inordinately successful, I'm still resentful, I have lustful thoughts. Yet I love God with all my heart, and I'm finding hope!"

I wrote this book and sent it to a New York publisher. Their first reaction to the manuscript was, "This book is too personal." They evidently didn't think people would want to read it. I couldn't really blame them, since I hadn't read a "Christian book" like it either. But they were still considering the manuscript.

At about that time, after I'd spoken at a meeting, a man, named Jarrell McCracken walked up to me and said he'd like for me to write a manuscript and let him publish it. I told him I'd written a manuscript and that a publisher was looking at it. He said, "We'll do a better job than they would. Ask for the manuscript back."

And I said, "I didn't know you were in the book publishing business, Jarrell."

He said, "Oh, yes."

I asked, "How many books have you published?"

He said, "None, yet. Yours will be the first." And so I wrote to New York and asked that my manuscript either be accepted or returned. When it came back, I gave *The Taste of New Wine* manuscript to Jarrell McCracken at Word Books. It was one of their first two book publications.

To our amazement, the book sold more copies than any of us could have imagined. All of a sudden, I realized a secret: people identify with our *struggles* in the midst of our hope and joy as we live out our stories. We are brothers and sisters, *not* at the level of our piety and religious achievements, but in our insecurity, pride, and fear. Because we are so afraid that our failures may "destroy our witness," we Christians tend to leave out of our evangelizing efforts and of our testimony many of the agonizing problems we have inside. But when we do this, we lose the point of identification with the unconverted: their felt need for *hope in the midst* of problems.

Success and the Beginning of Failure

After *The Taste of New Wine* hit the market, I continued to speak and study and began to write more books about trying to live as a Christian. Soon I was traveling all over the world to speak. I remember one night I woke up in Tokyo, Japan with a disturbing idea.

My basic message in those days was that if you give your life to God, the way to begin living out your faith was to go home and start being his person there. Somehow, I believed, if you live for God in the world in which he has *already put you,* he will create an atmosphere, through your faith, in which people may smell something of the aroma of Christ, and sense his caring love, and want him in their lives, too. I was convinced that this "living in your own everyday context" was the basis of an effective witness for Christ.

But here I was in *Tokyo, Japan,* advising people to stay *home* and witness to the people around them. There was nothing wrong with that in itself, but that night I realized with a shock that unconsciously *I* had been using this traveling for Christ as a way to avoid some problems which were developing in my own personal life back home. This awareness grew and I realized I had some real problems to deal with.

Have you ever seen a Tom and Jerry cartoon in which the mouse hits the cat in the head with a sledge hammer and the cat's face just cracks apart? Well, my life started feeling like that. My wife and I went through several years of counseling and wound up with a divorce in 1976.

It is painful and threatening to mention my divorce. But to tell my story honestly, I've got to tell you that I failed and was divorced. And I think divorce is one of the major tragedies in life, especially in a Christian's life. It certainly was at our house.

Up to that time I had been a "fair-haired Christian boy," and had written several books about trying to live as a Christian family. After the divorce I wanted to go hide and never come out again. I felt I was a failure—I *knew* I was a failure. You can't pretend you haven't been divorced, the way you can pretend you don't have bad thoughts or you're not a bad father.

But in the midst of my own personal chaos I also began to learn some things. For the first time in my life I began to get a sense of who I really am—just a person, a little boy inside who wants to live and work and find love and do as well as he can. I saw that I can't fix everything up for everybody and I can't always "make it all right."

Paradoxically, this awareness of my real weakness and inability to be the "Knight in Shining Armor" was the beginning of a more realistic understanding of myself and just how much I *really do need God.* And as I realized and faced my own failure, I wondered how many other Christians who've failed in their lives need him as I do. I saw that the most effective evangelism has always met men and women at the point of their deepest needs, when they have discovered that they cannot control their own little kingdoms—that they need God for any hope of fulfillment and meaning.

In the aftermath of my divorce I began to learn about grace in a whole new way. I saw that I had been naïve about the subtle strength of both sin and selfishness in my own life. I also experienced profoundly the depth of God's forgiveness and willingness to give us brand new starts when we repent, confess, and try to make restitution. But I also saw in a new way the consequences of sin, and I realized that if I were to have any kind of Christian ministry after the day that divorce was final, it would have to be a gift from God.

As I was preparing for the film series on which this book was based, I looked back over my own story—the happiness, the growth, the sadness, the pain. And I realized that with all the joys and failures I've described here, I've been preparing for twenty-five years to speak now about the love of God and the message of Jesus Christ. I want to talk about these things as they concern a certain way of *living and sharing* our real lives and the gospel message, a way of living which can very naturally draw other people into Christ's family.

Can God Pick Up the Pieces If We Share Our Real Stories? Can He Change the People Around Us?

But when one talks about "living and sharing our *real* lives with *other people*," the question which immediately comes up in many people's minds is, "How can we dare to share our lives intimately with each other in the church?" Before I became a Christian, my fear was (and often still is), that if I commit my future to Christ and become vulnerable by sharing my real self with other Christians, they won't understand. I'm afraid they'll see my imperfections and sinful pride and walk away from me. Or, if I tell the people closest to me that God is changing *me, they'll* still be as they were and will reject me for changing.

I think that, though many of us repress it, almost all of us have a deep fear that, if we let people walk into our lives and see us where we really live, they'll reject us. We're afraid that if we reveal who we truly are, we won't be loved.

But I've come to believe that, if we begin *slowly* and carefully to create safe situations in the church where we can reveal the broken fragments of our lives to one another, God can use those broken pieces as part of a beautiful mosaic as he fits us closer to himself and each other. That's why I began this book by telling you something of my life, so you can see whether knowing my personal story as the writer helps or hinders in understanding what I have to say about the message of God's story. And besides, I *do* believe God can "change the people around us." In closing this section I want to tell you a true story about why I think so.

At Laity Lodge, some people came to the early conferences who weren't prepared to become Christians at all. They'd been dragged there by spouses, parents, and well-meaning friends. Some people came out of curiosity, because it was such a cheap weekend in an incredibly beautiful setting.[1]

One man came whom I'll never forget. Jack[2] owned his own company after having been in the military for a number of years, and he stood like a tough marine sergeant. I thought, "I hope this man doesn't want to see me after hours on this retreat!", because he seemed very hostile. He'd been a boxer, a professional athlete, and evidently liked to "party" a lot.

Jack's wife was also at the retreat, and she privately said to me, "We've got four kids, and when Jack comes home at night he's so fierce he's liable to backhand one of them. So, when he comes in, I send them out in the backyard."

But sometime during the weekend this man "heard" what somebody was saying about the way God can change a person's life. And at the end of the conference, he said, "I want to be a Christian. I want to get converted." He talked to one of the staff, who told Jack how to make a beginning with Christ, and suggested a few things he could do to begin learning to live for him.

We suggested to Jack that he not tell anybody about his decision to become a Christian, that he just be quiet and kind of ease into a new way of living. We knew he wanted to do God's will and to love his Lord and the people around him the way Jesus Christ might. He was going to start by praying, by reading God's story in the Bible, and by trying to love his own family.

About a month later he came back and told us the following incident. He said that, about a week after he'd come home, his twelve-year-old boy had knocked on his study door one night and said, "Can I come in and talk to you?" This kid had been in real trouble. He was evidently

---

1. Located in the Texas hill country near Leakey, Texas. For information about conferences, write Laity Lodge, P.O. Box 670, Kerrville, TX 78028.
2. Not his real name.

almost an isolate at school. He lurked around the halls, and nobody chose him to play on any of the teams. He had almost no friends, and lately he'd been caught stealing in the neighborhood.

Well, Jack could not remember his son ever having knocked on his study door before that night. So he said, "Sure, son, come on in."

His son came in and said, "Uh, daddy, uh, what's *happened* to you?"

Jack was very embarrassed. He was quite a tough guy, and he didn't know how to talk about his new faith without appearing foolish. But he said, "Well, son, I just . . . well, I don't know how to live my life very well, and I . . . uh . . . I heard some people say that, if I gave my life to Jesus Christ, he would help me learn to live and to love people better."

And then he sat there in a long silence. Finally, his son said, "Daddy. . . . do you suppose I could give my life to Jesus, too?"

Jack told us later, "I'd never heard anything like that." He said he stood up and they looked at each other and then they embraced, which they hadn't done in years. "And that night," Jack said, "my boy started being happy."

About a week later, Jack had to go to New York City on a business trip. He said his son had never liked to meet him at the plane when he got home from trips. But as the plane pulled up to the gate (it was one of those planes where they roll a ramp up to the door), Jack looked out the window and saw his son hanging with both hands onto the chain at the waiting area. And when the ground crew got the stairway up to the door, the boy ducked under the chain and came running toward the plane.

Jack was sitting on one of the first two seats, and so he was the second person to come out. When he came down the stairway, his son ran up and said breathlessly, "Daddy!" and hugged him and buried his face in his dad's chest. Then he looked up and said, "I'm so glad to see you." And then he said, "Daddy, do you know what God's done?"

Jack said, "No, what, son?"

And his boy said with an expression of almost awe, "Daddy, *God's changed every kid in my class!*"

Hearing Jack tell that story, I knew for sure that if we step into God's story and learn to share our stories through his kind of loving, God *can* change the people in our lives.

II

WALKING
IN GOD'S STORY

INTRODUCTION

Sometimes Life Seems
Unreasonable

THERE'S A BEWILDERING QUALITY about much of life—especially with regard to personal communication. We don't talk much about the difficulty in communicating with God and the people around us. But sometimes it seems so strange to me that an idea can be perfectly clear to one person and utterly mystifying to another. At home, I sometimes get angry or impatient when my family fails to understand what seems obvious to me.

The different presuppositions we bring to life make communication, especially about important things, very difficult. And nowhere is this more true than when we try to share our faith. Some years ago I was talking to a friend about the confusing nature of life, and he said, laughing, "While we're on the subject of confusing things that happen in life, let me tell you a story."

It seems my friend knew a man named Gene, who was a consultant in New York City for one of the major oil companies. Gene lived in Connecticut and rode the commuter train in to New York every morning.

"On these commuter trains," he said, "you really don't know many people's names, but after a while you recognize their faces."

One day, the man who sat four faces down from Gene started to get sick, turning almost green and staring down into his lap with a grim look on his face. Gene noticed and began to watch him. At each station, the train got more and more packed, and as it went down under Manhattan Island the crowds of people at the stations were larger and larger. Just as the train came to the most crowded station on the whole run, the nauseated man's moment came. He began to claw his way through the crowded aisle until he got to the door. When the train stopped, the crowd in the station surged forward. And the train door was right

47

in front of an impeccably dressed man on the platform in a bowler hat. As the door opened, the sick guy just barfed all over the man in the bowler hat. Then the door closed—and the train began to move out of the station.

Well, Gene was just fascinated. He looked out the window to see what the man in the hat was doing, and saw that he was just standing there, frozen in shock. He raised his hands, palms up, shrugged, and looked up to the heavens. Gene could read his lips as he said, "Why *me?*"

There's a lot that is confusing about life . . . and about communication. And there is also confusion and mystery about a lot of the content in the Bible. In this section, I'd like to do two things. First, I want to suggest an approach to Scripture that may make it a little easier to understand. Second, I would like to look at the Bible story itself through the lens of intimate relationships.

6

A Mystery about
Understanding the Bible

IN THE THIRD CHAPTER of John there is a story about an important man named Nicodemus, "a leader of the Jews" who came to see Jesus one night. Nicodemus was a very sensitive, thoughtful person, and he and Jesus apparently had quite a conversation. Here is my loose paraphrase of what went on:

"Rabbi," Nicodemus said, "we know you come from God, because nobody could do the signs you do without God."

And Jesus said a very confusing thing to him. "Nicodemus, you must be born anew before you can enter the kingdom of God."

But Nicodemus, not understanding, said, "Wait a minute. Do you mean I've got to go back into my mother's womb as an old man to be born again?"

And Jesus replied, in effect, "Nicodemus, I'm talking about a 'gospel' that is so different from the religious rules and sacrifices and the way you've been raised to understand God's will that you can't even *see* the kingdom of God from where you're standing. Your whole perspective, your whole mental set, everything you've been taught—yes, Nicodemus, all of this—has to *die* before you can see the truth. I'm not talking about religious rules, Nicodemus. I'm talking about the fact that God wants to give you a *whole new experience of life.* It's so different from the religious life and the program you're committed to that to understand it you will actually have to *think* differently. Because unless your perceptions are born again, Nicodemus, you couldn't even see the kingdom and the people of God if they were all around you."

Two Ways of Knowing

What Jesus seems to be saying is that there are *two ways of knowing the truth:* the way Nicodemus knew it (and he was evidently a very well educated and wise man), and the way Jesus meant for it to be understood. I'm convinced that Jesus came to give us a way to think about "truth" which is essentially different from the way most of us have been educated to think.

I'm also convinced that what was true of Nicodemus is also true of many of us in the church today. We simply can't begin to assimilate the gospel that Jesus brought unless we change our entire way of perceiving it. Our education may have been very fine, and yet the way we have been trained to think has somehow blinded us, as the Pharisees' and Nicodemus's ways of thinking blinded them. As a result of this blindness we often can no longer be caught up in the story of the Good News of Jesus in the Bible, and we have no idea, therefore, how to share it with other people. We don't understand "born again" thinking and are even embarrassed by such a term, because it seems strange or illogical.

But if we think about it, we can see that the idea of different *ways* of thinking is not that far from our experience. Seeing the ways different kinds of people come to conclusions tells us that there is apparently more than one way of knowing, of understanding or perceiving the truth. There is the way of the scholars and researchers who examine the objective data, relate the data to existing categories, see the logical consequences of any proposal, and then use reasonable criteria in deciding whether or not to accept a proposal or hypothesis.

But there is another kind of knowledge, too—the earthy, intuitive knowledge of the person "on the street," for instance, who may be a salesperson, an entertainer, a gambler, a street evangelist, a great statesman, or an entrepreneur. When presented with a proposition or situation, this type of person moves into it, imagines it is true, "tries the truth on," as it were, in his or her imagination, and feels how it relates to other things on the stage of his or her life. This is not a logical process. It is an intuitive process of "being grasped by" the symbols or pictures generated by the proposition. Finally, a conclusion seems to emerge. Often people who think this way are enormously successful in making sound decisions, though they might never be able to present a logical explanation of *how* they arrived at the particular conclusion on which they subsequently acted. Some people call this common sense.

Another example of the fact that there are two kinds of knowing can be seen in athletics. During the "skull sessions" leading up to a football practice, the players listen to a "chalk talk." On a blackboard the coach draws each player's assigned action during the play, using an O or X for each position and continuous lines to indicate direction and movement. As a player, you are one of the circles or the X's. By paying attention to the directional lines the coach is drawing, you see where you are supposed to take a certain number of steps one way and then run through the line between two specific players. You memorize your part of that play as diagramed. And you think, "I know the play. I've got it."

But then you move out onto the playing field, and all of a sudden everything is different. It's a whole new *kind* of knowledge, because there are people running at you. "Out there," you're not an abstract O or an X on a blackboard. Rather, you are immersed in a mass of moving bodies—many of whom are trying to knock you down or fill the opening through which you are trying to go. When you take two steps to the right as the diagram indicated, there are a whole bunch of people blocking your way! You're dealing with the same basic underlying knowledge of the play, but if you are only familiar with the diagrams the chances are very great that you can never play football. The translation from *intellectual knowledge* about a play to a *participating knowledge* must be made before a team can make the play work. Both kinds of knowing are necessary.

Medical and Psychological Findings

A few years ago, psychologists began to discover that there actually is a biological basis for these two kinds of knowledge. One of the great discoveries of modern physiology is that each of the two halves, or hemispheres, of the human brain processes information in a different way. The left hemisphere deals with abstractions, logic, reason, numbers, statistics, language; it is verbal, analytical, and linear. The right hemisphere is nonverbal and deals with the concrete, spatial, intuitive, poetic, dramatic, and emotional aspects of experience. It is nonrational and holistic.[1]

Ideally these two different kinds of information work in concert with each other. The left brain of a football player grasps the abstract logic of the play during the skull session, and the right brain translates the play into the real situation out on the field. It's like learning to dance; I can memorize the steps from a book or by watching someone else, but when the music starts, sooner or later I must "forget" the steps and let my right brain blend me into the music.

The trouble is, for quite some time our mainline education systems

---

1. From a technical point of view, this discussion is simplistic. Current research indicates that the hard-line distinctions we make between right- and left-brain functions must sometimes be qualified.

have been designed primarily to cultivate the logical, analytical, left-brain mode of thinking and have virtually ignored the right-brain mode. This has had some strange and sad effects. About fifteen years ago, a man named Sperry and his associates at California Tech did some research, which I read about in a psychological journal. These researchers discovered that children lose an amazing amount of creativity between the ages of five and seven years. What happens to children during this time? They start to school. And most schools emphasize left-brain thinking and ignore or discourage right-brain thinking.

I believe the natural way the brain functions is to receive some information, perhaps in the form of language, from an outside source—say, a teacher. The one receiving the information takes it into his or her mind and assimilates it with what is already known in the most creative, imaginative way possible. This process, which involves the right brain and the left brain working together, is more obvious in children than in adults (in whom the left hemisphere often has come to dominate).

So let's imagine that little second-grade Jimmy is deep in that process of assimilation. He's sitting in the classroom, listening to the teacher. The teacher says something to the class and Jimmy looks out the window, forgetting about the teacher and assimilating the new truth he's heard. The teacher sees him staring out the window and says, "Jimmy, quit looking out the window! You look at me!" And Jimmy realizes, "If I'm going to get any love or acceptance around here, I've got to look at the teacher and stop this dreaming." So he learns to respond to and focus on the teacher. Unfettered, creative dreaming and assimilating go out the window.

Of course, not all kids staring out classroom windows are assimilating what is going on! And not all teachers and schools discourage right-brain thinking. But it is true that creative dreaming, art, music, drama, storytelling, creative writing—the kinds of activities that exercise and develop the imaginative, perceptive, integrative faculties of the right hemisphere—tend to be neglected in our educational systems. They have been moved to the educational precipice, sometimes pushed over into oblivion, as those systems have moved toward a quantitative way of viewing and evaluating life and the world—even relationships!

Of course, there are people in every generation—artists, thinkers, creative scientists, and business people—who seem to defy the left-brain bias of our culture and to use both halves of their brains to full advantage. They seem to develop the right hemispheres of their brains almost in spite of their left-brain training. (Interestingly enough, many of these people—like Einstein—are now considered "geniuses" but did very poorly in school!) But the majority of us leave school with the left hemisphere almost completely dominating the right in our thinking. Now, I don't want to be misunderstood. I'm not anti-education; I have three degrees in different areas. And I believe there is enormous value in educating the left brain. Our scientific and scholarly achievements based on the left-brain, analytic, linear approach are almost unbelievable. Besides, the dreams and images that originate in the right half of our brains often must be translated or organized by the verbal, rational left half in order for us to communicate or to put our dreams into action!

But the point is that, although the two sides of the brain were designed to work together, in our culture and our educational systems the left side has been highly developed and the right side almost ignored. The result is a one-sided approach to existence—a well-developed ability to analyze and criticize and categorize but a dwarfed capacity for dreaming and creating, for looking at the whole picture, for understanding the emotional, "illogical" aspects of our existence.

We are, for the most part, a society of left-brainers—and this includes Christians as well as non-Christians. That leaves us at a disadvantage, especially when it comes to understanding our faith. For the Judeo-Christian faith as it is transmitted to us in the Bible is given to us largely in right-brain images: parables, songs, poetry, drama, and stories about historical events! So the living truth of the Bible is often very elusive to a highly educated, left-brain, person. We find it very difficult to quit "thinking about"—analyzing, dissecting—Christianity and to "step into God's story" by committing our lives and being "born again"—a right-brain image.

Again, I don't want to cast aspersions on biblical scholarship; I know it's very important. But I do not believe one can step fully into God's story with half a brain—even the brilliant left brain of a scholar! We are told to come to him "as a little child"—and that means with both halves of our brains, bringing him our feelings, our commitments, and our imaginations as well as our analytical processes. Until we grasp this fact that it is our "whole brain" inner child who leads us into God's kingdom, I believe our attempts at evangelism will continue to flounder, especially in churches where the education level is high.

What about Learning from the Bible?

There are people who think the Bible is "logical" and that logical truth can be extracted from it the way scientific truth can be extracted from nature. But that's left-brain thinking. Theories on brain function indicate that the left brain, if it is in control, screens out and represses anything that doesn't agree with it.[2] And the left brain insists that all "truth" must be logical. It is this left-brain tendency, I think, that has confused so much of our biblical understanding.

I believe that much of the Bible was meant to be understood through a process different from what is usually considered "logic." The biblical story was written not to be outlined and analyzed, but to be experienced and internalized. When we read one of Jesus' parables this way, for instance, we don't start by listing the three main points. Instead, we immerse ourselves in the story, absorb what is happening and make an intuitive leap to grasp the truth the parable contains. When arrived at this way, the point of the story can be highly motivating in the learner's life, whereas learning facts *about* a parable is seldom motivating.

But instead of reading the Bible as story, left-brain scholars over the years have tended to make logical systems out of what they have unraveled from the biblical content. From these systems the church has then laid out certain doctrines or explanations as "the Truth," with the result that many people have come to feel they don't have to read the Bible in its original story form. And when this happens, when understanding the principles and doctrines extracted from God's story is considered more important than *experiencing* the story itself, the story dies as a source of living truth and inspiration for any generation.

Let me illustrate what I mean when I say the Bible can't always be understood through "logical" thought processes. Just recall for a moment the following examples of biblical advice:

1. *If you want to be first in your group, the leader, you've got to be the slave of your followers—even wash their feet* (Matt. 20:26, 27 and John 13:1–15).

2. *If you want to be exalted, humble yourself* (Matt. 23:12).

3. *If you really want to be wealthy, give all you have away and become poor* (Matt. 19:16–22).

4. *If you want to find your life, lose it* (Matt. 10:39).

These biblical truths are not logical from a left-brain perspective! Try telling a presidential candidate that to get elected he or she needs to develop a true servant mentality. Or try telling a multimillionaire that to become really rich he or she has to give all that money away. Or tell a cancer patient that the way to keep on living is to die.

---

2. For a brief explanation of the findings on right- and left-brain function, see Thomas R. Blakeslee, *The Right Brain: A New Understanding of the Unconscious Mind and Its Creative Powers* (New York: Anchor Press/Doubleday, 1980).

From a left-brain perspective, these are irrational bits of advice. I believe that's why many intelligent and well-educated people have rejected the Christian faith. They say, "This biblical stuff is ridiculous. Look at all this paradoxical gibberish." But generations of Christians who have become involved in God's story from an *experiential* standpoint have found that these "illogical" statements are *true*. By left-brain definition, for instance, it's a logical impossibility for a slave to be his or her master's leader. And yet this is the common experience of converted Christian leaders—they find that they become true leaders only when they offer themselves as servants to their people. And they learn that becoming a "slave" to Christ opens the door to an amazing experience of freedom!

The same principle is true of many church traditions. Non-Christians (and some Christians) often point to the church's architecture and liturgy and say, "What good is it to continue using antiquated symbols like hymns, stained-glass windows, and candles?" And they point out the logical inconsistencies in wasting time and money on such things.

But the hymns, the stained-glass windows, the candles and crosses and liturgy and sacraments are *not meant to be logical* in the usual sense of the word. And Christians over the centuries have found that these things are profoundly "true" in a right-brain way. The traditional symbols and sacraments of the church open the trap door to our unconscious minds and take the truth of the gospel below the level of the merely rational into the deep essential fabric of our lives, where our crucial decisions are made and where left-brain logic cannot go.

Although we all use both hemispheres of our brains in concert (and although in many ways I'm trained to be a left brainer from the word *go*), I believe our preoccupation with "logical" learning has kept us from seeing many of the truths about God and his story—truths which need to be "born again" into us.

For instance, how are we to get inside the right brain "mystery" of the Scriptures and discover how we are to live with each other and with God?[3]

---

3. I realize that throughout this discussion I am doing the very thing I've been saying we've overdone—using left-brain language and principles even to describe right-brain phenomena. But since the right brain has no ability to use "words," all verbal communication must necessarily be translated through the left brain. I'm just trying to indicate that certain ways of using words (stories, parables, emotional vignettes, and so on) are often more effective in getting in touch with the motivating center of the average person than logical formulations of doctrine and didactic instruction—though both are very important for maturity in the faith.

7

A Look at God's Story through the Lens of Relationship— Act One

HOW DID GOD MEAN for us to relate to each other and to him from the beginning? What is this strange story we've been asked to walk in with Jesus and his family, and to tell to the world? It has helped me to realize that from the beginning of the Bible we are looking at a kaleidoscope of poetic right-brain images which point to an exciting view of healthy relationships.

Let's look at the biblical story of the drama of God, Act One. The author of Genesis (which means "beginnings") starts by telling us some basic truth about God and about life. I'd like for you to read the following as if you had never read anything in Genesis before. Just let yourself go into the story and see how the truth touches you:

"And the Lord God made man from the dust of the ground and breathed into his nostrils the breath of life. And man became a living person" (Gen. 2:7, paraphrased).

As one's mind wanders far back down the highway of history, the road soon becomes a winding trail and finally a footpath, disappearing into the mists and the myths of antiquity, toward the beginning of human life as we know it today. But whatever happened on the outward stage of history when the first human became a person, an absolutely astounding event took place somewhere *inside* a human brain.

Imagine a dark and silent universe, filled with moving, shifting cortical atoms, oblivious of themselves and of the one in whom they moved. And then suddenly into that meaningless night came a lightning bolt! Some cataclysmic shock! Or perhaps only something as simple as the flipping of a switch, or the breathing of a breath. And for the first time on earth there was a new dawn: self-awareness, the awareness of one's own life and death, of the ability to perceive and grasp one's hopes and dreams and the meanings of one's behaviors and creations. And this was an ability that only God and human beings were to have.

56

Into Adam the clay God had breathed something of his *own person!* And with that breath came the awesome capacity for voluntary human relationships, for love and hate and the conscious struggle for power which seems to be a part of every human relationship at some level.

Look again at that early scene in God's story, way back through the mists of time. The next thing the writers recorded about human life was that God created a very close personal relationship between a man and a woman—marriage. They were to have such exclusive loyalty and commitment to each other that the author says, using right-brain terms, that they would become "one flesh." As the story developed, this very first relationship, with its close involvement between two people—the relationship which we call marriage (and family)—became the model for the ideal spiritual community life.

Look at that first man and woman in the garden and see how the story unfolds. As a part of that first relationship between two persons was born simultaneously a relationship between them and God. And at that moment, I think, the essential nature of authentic and fulfilling relationships became apparent.

The Birth of Intimacy

Look at the story from a right brain perspective. Adam and Eve, it says, were walking in the garden where God walked. They were naked and they were not ashamed (Gen. 2:25). I used to wonder, "Why did the writer put it that way? What did the writer really mean by the words, "they were naked and not ashamed?"

The Hebrew poets were apparently right-brain thinkers. What could it mean to a Hebrew poet to say they were "naked and were not ashamed as they were walking with God in the garden"? I believe it means they were *hiding nothing* from each other or from God. They were intimate. God evidently made us for open, no-hiding relationships with each other, and with him. Imagine the peace of being fully known by God and each other—and being loved anyway. It would be paradise. And that is precisely the way the Garden of Eden is described.

Sin, the Destroyer of Intimacy

At this point enters that irrational bent we human beings have for spoiling all our relationships. It's a self-destructive tendency we have towards fouling our own nests in order to try to get what we think we want for ourselves, and it usually involves the desire for some kind of unconscious or conscious power or control. We call this tendency "sin."

Remember how the story goes? God said, in effect, "Now, listen, you can have everything in the world. You can drill for oil, you can have your groceries, you can swim in the river, you can make love, and you can talk to me—whatever you want. Just don't eat of the fruit of that tree over there."

But what Eve did, the story says, was talk it over with the snake, and he convinced her she could take power from God by disobeying him. She went and did the very thing she had been told not to do; she ate the fruit out of the tree and gave some to Adam.

Adam and Eve were ashamed when they had done this—and they were afraid. They had broken their relationship with God. So what did they do? The Bible says they made clothes and covered themselves. What would that mean from a right-brain perspective? I think it means they hid their real selves from God. Intimacy was gone, and the implication was that all relationships from then on would be fouled up.

God called to them: "Come out, Adam and Eve, come out!"

And they said, "No, thanks." Adam and Eve's mistake was that, in their pride, in their shame, they hid from God and from each other and so missed out on intimacy. The Bible tells us that we were made to be creative coinhabitors with God of a beautiful, emotional place, a place where intimacy and no-hiding relationships with God and with each other are the norm. But our sin was that we tried to take over the power position of the relationship. We hid our motives and our true feelings and so found ourselves alienated from God and from each other.[1]

Much of the rest of the Old Testament is the story of God seeming to call down the pages of history, "Adam and Eve, come back. I love you. We can have a loving relationship." All through the Bible God seems to be continually trying to heal broken relationships caused by his people's dishonest relating with each other and with him. God's kind of religion, it seems, always has to do with healing brokenness and bringing people back into loving relationships.

But from the time of the first man and woman, we seem to have

---

1. The Bible says that when God, shaking his head, sent Adam and Eve out into the world, he made them some appropriate clothes. The authors of Genesis realized that if one is going to go out in the world without God, one needs privacy and protection. So the result of sin is separation not only from God but from true intimacy with other persons.

continued to run away from the very thing that would make us happy. We hide our true selves and our true condition from God and from each other. And consequently we are condemned to sit together in isolation—sometimes even in the pews of our churches.

I believe the Bible is saying that God wants to heal us and to make us happy. Yet we run away, try to take over God's place in life, and as a result we get into trouble. God tries to leave us free to choose to come to him so he can free us in a deeper way. But in our pride we respond again and again, "No, thanks, we can handle it, God."

For example, the Old Testament writers tell us that God instituted a series of rituals through which the Hebrew people could come to him for healing and reconciliation. He set forth a system of sacrificing turtledoves, sheep, goats—various animal sacrifices—as powerful sacraments through which his people could regain a sense of freedom from guilt and a reconciliation with him. The purpose was to call the people back into a right relationship with God and each other. But over the years his people seemed to turn the whole system into a legalistic method they could control—a system through which *they* could *buy* their way back into God's approval with religious works!

(Today we Christians sometimes do the same thing. We attempt to use even good things he has given us to do, like the memorization of Bible verses, church attendance, serving on boards and committees, witnessing, even tithing—more and more "controllable" things—to try to win, to control God's love and approval in a strange spiritual barter system.)

The Hebrew people in the Old Testament developed more and more controllable ways to use religion to bring back their "righteousness" and to heal the relationship with God "legally." They tried to do religious duties without having to stand naked before him and each other. And they tried to separate their secret greedy and unfair behavior toward other people from their worship of God. But their attempts to avoid facing the consequences of their "legalistic dishonesty" was evidently not pleasing to God at all.

God's Anger

Many people have said to me, "But why does God get so angry in the Bible?" Well, he evidently was angry, for many reasons (see Amos 4, Hos. 5, Mic. 3).

One of the specific things that really made him angry was when his people tried to get righteous by "going to church," while at the same time they were making themselves powerful by taking advantage of the poor. God didn't like that a bit. According to the Bible, God's got a real thing about poor people. He's for them (see Amos 2:7, 4:1, 5:12). This concern runs through the whole biblical story, and many of us have missed it. The reason, I think, is that it is not logical from a left-brain perspective. God *should* be prejudiced in favor of the religious . . . *us!* But unfortunately the facts are he seems to be prejudiced toward the poor.

The Hebrew community's intimacy with God was broken when his people oppressed the poor—even when the religious services and sacrifices were all in order. And so prophets like Amos came along from time to time to say that such oppression made God *very* angry: "This is what the Lord says: 'For three sins of Israel, even for four, I will not turn back my wrath. They sell the righteous for silver, and the needy for a pair of sandals. They trample on the heads of the poor as upon the dust of the ground and deny justice to the oppressed!' " (Amos 2:6, 7, NIV).

But there's another way to look at God's anger. Haven't you ever been angry with a small daughter because she wouldn't do what you knew would make her happy? Your anger in this case is really a sign of your love and concern. But from the *child's perspective,* you, the parent, are simply *very angry* and may do something terrible to her. The child can't really understand why you seem so upset—since young children can't grasp the negative consequences their unwise behavior may bring them.

Similarly, I believe that, although God was trying to save the Hebrews through the prophets, the prophets seemed to be saying only, "God is angry!!" But when one reads the end of almost every prophetic book, the author says in one way or another in God's behalf, "Look, if you'll repent and come back, all I really want is to love you."

There are people still running today from what seems to be God's anger. But the bottom line of God's message in the Bible—Old Testament and New—is not "I am angry," but, "I love you. I want to be intimate with you." And in our guilt and fear, many of us miss the fact of God's offer of grace in the Old Testament and see him only as a distant, angry ruler/judge.

The Need to Get Right with God

Whatever else they made of it, the religion God had given the Hebrews was always an enterprise of healing. But they added on to it and codified it in more and more detail until they had a system whereby *they* could heal every angry rift or separation their bad behavior might cause between them and God. They could also "get right" with people after breaking God's rules regarding relationships.

What they did in essence was make the sacrificial system into a left-brain barter market. It was logical that if a person offended God, God would be angry and would demand a "payment" of a commensurate size. So the priests weighted the various sins as to their importance to God and the offender gave an animal or other sacrifice of that relative value. Then God would "feel all right" about the sin and forgive the offender.[2]

Lamb of God

But with all the sacrifices made throughout the year, the people still weren't *sure* they had covered all their sins. They had a right-brain feeling that God might want something more. And they had developed a way to deal with those sins which had not been specifically taken care of each year. They got two little animals—goats, usually—and symbolically they put on the head of those goats all the sins that for any reason hadn't been handled individually in the community during the year. Then they slit one animal's throat and sent the other out into the wilderness to die (see Lev. 16). It was a vicarious sacrifice, and the animal was called the "scapegoat."

But in the sacrifical system as a whole, the animal which was most often thought of as a vicarious sacrifice among the Hebrews was a lamb. And as time went on the seers of ancient Israel looked for a *person* from God who would be "the lamb of God," and who would take away the sins of the people of the whole world (see Isa. 53:7, John 1:29). When this one came, God would no longer be angry and distant, but would be close to the common person again, as he had been in the Garden.

---

2. From a right-brain perspective there was an awesome truth behind this system. But when it became legalism, separated from the people's behavior, it was an offense to God. See Amos, Hosea, Micah.

8

With Whom Was God Still Intimate?

AS THE BIBLE STORY GOES ON, it seems that only the outstanding *leaders* (for instance, Abraham, Moses, and David) had relationships with God that were intimate. Apparently, the common people didn't usually experience the immediate "personal" contact with God any more, except through their priests or leaders. But the surprising thing is that these leaders were often *not* the most honorable men and women around. The logical left half of the brain would say that anyone who would be chosen as an intimate by God would be a totally pure and honorable person. For instance, anyone who is a real spiritual hero would certainly not be a liar or a coward. He or she would be a well behaved, strong person with impeccable moral character.

But according to the Bible, God evidently has had other criteria for choosing those through whom he will work. For example, consider Abraham, a man who was chosen by God to be the father of the faithful of all times, the classic example for all generations of what faith is (see Gen. 17:1–7, 22). But Abraham really had some problems.

At one time he and his pretty young wife, Sarai, were moving down to Egypt. He said something like this to her: "Listen, I understand the king of this country really likes girls. If he sees you, he'll have me killed and take you into his palace. So why don't you just tell him you're my sister and then he won't kill me." Great, honorable man?

So he went to Egypt and that's what happened. When the king saw Abraham coming down the road with this good-looking wife, he said to his servants, "Go find out who that is." The king's servants caught up with Abraham, and they asked him who the girl was. Abraham answered, "She's my sister."

Then the king said, "Okay, bring her into my house." Then the king put Abraham in business, and gave him cattle and a fresh start. And that's evidently how Abraham got his wealth in Egypt (see Gen. 12:10–16). Now, I've paraphrased this story but I think that is basically what happened. And according to our standards Abraham's behavior was hardly that of a courageous and honest person of God!

Take another example—Moses, the Hebrew nation's greatest hero of the faith. He was "the man of God." According to the Bible, God said to him in the wilderness, "Moses, I want you to lead these people out of Egypt and their slavery there."

But Moses said, "I can't speak well, Lord. I . . . stutter. Send Aaron. He's a *great* speaker." Moses kept trying to get out of doing what God wanted him to do (see Exod. 3–4).

Gideon and Saul are two other examples of "heroes" who tried to get out of doing a heroic thing for God (see Judg. 6 and 1 Sam. 10:17–22).

And finally, consider David, the great messianic model hero. David was an ancestor of Jesus (see Luke 1:26–33), a man "after [God's] own heart" (see Acts 13:16–23).

But as we look at David's story in the Bible, we can see that David was hardly the kind of person we would imagine God choosing—one who acted "after God's own heart." One day when David was king, he looked out of his window and saw a beautiful girl bathing. David asked who she was, and learned she was a married woman. Her husband, Uriah, was one of Israel's loyal soldiers who at that very moment was at the battlefront, fighting for David. But David sent for Bathsheba anyway, and slept with her.

It wasn't long before Bathsheba learned she was pregnant. When she reported her condition to David, he thought it over and sent for Uriah from the front line, giving him a message something like this: "Uriah, I'm going to give you a leave. I want to get messages from the front." So, when Uriah got home, David sat him down and said, "Here, Uriah, have a martini. Now, tell me what's going on at the battle." So Uriah gave him a full report.

Then David said, "Now I tell you what. Go on home and sleep with your wife. Spend some time with her and then go back to the front line. Thanks a lot. You're doing a *great* job."

And Uriah said, in effect, "Oh no, sir. I wouldn't do that. All my buddies are out there fighting and dying, and here you're offering me special treatment by allowing me to go home and sleep with my wife. It wouldn't be fair to my buddies. I'll just sleep on your front porch." He was much too honorable to go home and sleep with his wife when his friends were risking their lives for David and the kingdom.

So David said, ". . . Have another martini!" But Uriah slept on David's front porch that night, and for several days refused to go home and sleep with his wife, though David got him drunk in an attempt to influence him.

David thought about his dilemma some more. Then the next day he said to Uriah, "I want you to go back to the front line and give this letter to Joab, the general of the army."

The letter said, "Joab, this guy is hero material. I want him to attack a machine-gun nest and capture it single-handedly. And if he should capture the first one and survive, give him a second chance." So, in effect, David had Uriah murdered, and then he took his wife. (Note: This was my rather loose interpretation of what went on. For the story as it's told in the Bible, see 2 Sam. 11–12.)

David's story further reveals that he was one of the least effective fathers in history. One of his sons raped one of his daughters and another son murdered the son who did it. Then his son Absalom attempted to steal the kingdom from his father and then tried to sleep with David's wives and concubines. And I don't think David handled any of these situations in a way a modern family counselor would call "well" (see the stories in 2 Sam. 13–18). All of this seems to indicate that David was just not a good father, yet he is referred to as the prototype for Jesus!

What qualities did all of these leaders—imperfect as they were—have which would cause them to be close to God? Why would God have a special relationship with people like that? Evidently it was because they were *honest* with God, and *culpable.* Nathan the prophet went to David and accused him regarding his sin with Bathsheba: "You are the man." But instead of having Nathan killed (which many rulers of his day would have done), David heard God confronting him through Nathan's words, confessed, and said, "I have sinned." He remained open, intimate, with God.[1]

An Awesome, Frightening God

In Old Testament times, the common people were often scared to death of God. He was very awesome and distant. The word *holy* meant

---

1. I am not of course indicating that God condoned or approved of any of these sins. I am just saying that he apparently valued confession, intimacy with God, and integrity more highly than pious and errorless performance.

"property of God." But anything which was the property of God was like electricity. The belief at this time was that you didn't touch a holy thing because God might "shock" you and kill you (see 2 Sam. 6:6–8). So only the priests handled the holy things, and only they went into the Holy of Holies in the temple—into the presence of God. Unfortunately, though, this sacrificial worship system with its set-apart priests and holy objects was a far cry from the kind of intimate relating with God Adam and Eve had experienced in the Garden.

But then the eighth century prophets came and said to the people with their intricate sacrificial worship, "No! God doesn't want your sacrifices as much as he wants straight, no-hiding relationships from you. And he especially wants you to give up cheating the poor and worshiping false gods!" (see Hosea, Amos, Micah).

It seems to me that the prophets were trying to say, "*Real* morality is not based on legal rules or sacrificial appeasement. God's kind of morality springs from a notion of intimate relationships in which you can repent, confess, and be forgiven when you have sinned against God or another person."

God was continually trying to get his people to repent and receive his grace. He wanted to forgive them and get on with a loving relationship. But in their pride the Hebrews would not admit they were greedy and proud and wanted to control God and other people. They kept on trying to manipulate and control God through their "sacrifices." Finally their religion was so controlled by the religious heirarchy that one could be healed only at the temple in Jerusalem and only in certain prescribed ways. They closed the "local churches" and had a monopoly on sacrifice and healing at the temple.

And then the prophesies came true. The prophets had said, in effect, "Keep acting this way and God is going to punish you by sending the Russians, who are going to come in and destroy your nation" (except they said the Assyrians). And sure enough, in about 721 B.C., the Assyrians came and took about ten-twelfths of the country's leadership away. And then in 586 B.C. the Babylonians came and took the people in Jerusalem and Judah away into exile.

"Exile" was part of the way some of the major nations built their empires in those days. Let's say the Assyrians set out to take the states in the United States of America one at a time, and they captured those of us who live in Texas. To put us "into exile," they'd take the leaders from Rio Grande, Texas and move them to New York City. Then they'd take the New York leaders and put them in, say, Tempe, Arizona. They knew that to foment a revolution, you've got to know the territory.

So if you take the leaders and switch them around, you won't have any effective revolutions. That's the theory. So the Hebrew leaders were sent to Assyria and Babylon.

During the exile, as the Hebrew leaders were taken away, the temple was destroyed. Look at what this did to their religion. When the temple was destroyed, they could no longer be healed through the temple's sacrificial system. And since the temple was the only place they were allowed to conduct their sacrificial rites, it looked as if their religion had been destroyed.

But they could still read the pieces of the law they had taken with them. These "scraps of parchment" had God's story written on them. The Hebrews had always loved to repeat the story. And now, although they couldn't go to the temple, they could memorize the story and the rules. So for many people, "keeping the rules" got substituted for the sacrificial system and for walking with God intimately.

During the exile, the Hebrews invented the synagogue, which is perhaps the greatest teaching institution in history. Everywhere there were ten male Jews, they could read the law and pray. But without the awesome fiery healing aspect of the temple, religion for many Hebrews became a left-brain head trip of laws and rules, because they could no longer be healed. They became "the people of the Book."[2]

---

2. This is of course a simplistic picture. Evidently among the Hebrews there was always a faithful remnant (however small or secret) who loved their Lord and said their prayers with a great sense of intimacy.

9

Jesus and the Unfolding of the Plot— Act Two

BUT A DREAM HAD BEEN BORN in the midst of all the pain and separation of the Hebrew people, a dream that seemed to seep up out of the ground at night like a mist. All the people—both the common people and the scholars—had a piece of the dream. And the dream was that God was going to step back onto the stage of history through a special person who would bring back God's kind of love and openness and justice and peace. This rule would be called "the reign of God, the rule of God," or as we translate it, "the kingdom of God."

There were three threads of tradition indicating how God was going to bring about his Kingdom or reign.

Some Hebrews thought God would send them a political ruler, like David, who would take over the government and would whip the other nations into shape. Then he'd bring in "the kingdom," which would be a central political force in world history. Another group, equally as significant, thought God was going to send a "suffering servant," like the one portrayed in Isaiah—a humble person riding on an ass. A third group thought God would send a superhuman being who would come on the clouds of heaven and would change things with a power beyond human comprehension.

But when Jesus came, all three groups missed him, because he didn't exactly fit any of their preconceptions. And yet, in a strange sense, he was the fulfillment of the dreams of *all* the seers of ancient Israel. He had a big kingdom, a worldwide kingdom—bigger than David's. He was a humble man who backed away from political power and rode into Jerusalem on a donkey. And yet he was also more than human; he performed God's healing in their midst and rose from the grave after his crucifixion.

But by the time of Jesus, the left-brain enterprise of following rules

and laws had created the Pharisees, who just couldn't understand the
story any more. The intimate healing aspect of their religion, which
was its core, seemed to have almost disappeared by the time Jesus
came. And when Jesus showed up on the scene, he saw that his people
had designed their worship and relationships to *look* real while masking
or hiding their true motives and behaviors. This provoked Jesus to
say to some of the finest and most religious elders, board members,
vestrymen, and deacons among the Jewish people something like,
"You're whitened sepulchers. You're honorable on the outside, but
inside you're full of rottenness and you stink. You pretend to love
God, but you're incapable of loving either God or each other. You're
interested in the outward show of conformity to the moral rules, but
you don't even take care of your own families!" (see Matt. 23:13–36).

True Morality

"Badness and goodness," Jesus said, in effect, "don't result from
outward religious behaviors. They come from within the heart, and
that is where God is going to meet us, judge us, and forgive us. In
your self-protecting religiosity, you are no longer walking with God
in his story" (see Matt. 15:1–20).

"And when someone breaks a law [the law was tough then, as you
remember], you say, 'Stone him to death according to the law.'" But
then Jesus told them a totally unexpected thing—that God was *not
interested in destroying the sinner!*

What? They were amazed! It was a watershed moment in history!
All people and all religions had agreed about one thing: the sinner
should be destroyed. Because of two thousand years of familiarity, it's
hard for us to see how radically different this message of Jesus was—
that God wanted to treat sinners in a different way than they had
been treated before. Even though God's love and grace was evident
in the Old Testament, this revelation of the specific nature of that
love's application to sinners was startling. And to illustrate this, Jesus
told parables which described a way of handling sin and broken relationships that did not hinge on the use of power and punishment.

Remember the story of the Prodigal Son—the runaway son who
had squandered his father's money, behaved immorally, and certainly
deserved to be punished and rejected (Luke 15:11–72)? But when that
young man finally came home with nothing and with no excuse, he
was received by his father with open arms. Someone once said to me,
in effect, "The father's not being *fair* to the older brother." And that's

true from a logical perspective. But, using a right-brain image, Jesus was saying, "God is like this. He saves us when we don't deserve it. He doesn't want to humiliate us and grind us down when we have failed."

God not only doesn't want to destroy the sinful person, he evidently wants to *restore* that person to a *better* or *more intimate* relationship with himself (and with the person sinned against)—better because, having been forgiven, the sinner knows and understands a revolutionary secret about life and relationships.

This is the secret: Because of our basic sinfulness, God has a *right* to destroy us. But instead, he gives us a *whole new life.* And when we receive forgiveness and new life, knowing that strict justice would have brought condemnation and punishment, then we are often motivated for the first time to love God and to be good and moral *out of an overwhelming sense of love and gratitude instead of out of fear.* This notion of grace—of undeserved forgiveness and love—brought the possibility of a transformation of practical morality into human history.

The practical consequences of restoring intimacy into our relationship with God and with people are profound. We can now be honest about our failures and sins because we've been forgiven and made new and righteous in God's eyes. We no longer need to hide our true selves in order to be considered God's "righteous" people.

Jesus was talking about our actually living in the open relationships which God had intended from the beginning. In this kind of relationship, the emphasis on punishment under the laws would not be necessary because there would be repentance and confession, forgiveness and new chances. And our gratitude and love would give us the motivation to try and try again to heal our broken relationships with God and each other and to become an honest, continually renewed, intimate people.

Jesus lived out this message of continually renewed intimacy. As we see him in action, walking along the dusty roads of Palestine, Jesus was a very intimate man. He broke the rules to be intimate. We've blocked this out because our left brain says, "No, he wasn't; he couldn't have been because he was God." But as we open ourselves to the Bible's story, we see a great many examples of how Jesus related to people intimately.

For example, a Hebrew rabbi was not supposed to speak to a woman in public; I understand that this applied even to his own wife or mother. Yet, Jesus talked to the woman at the well, who was practically a prostitute. He broke the rules in order to relate to her.

And when they talked, he didn't say, "Madam, how is your Sunday school class?" Jesus was gentle with the woman, but strong. What he said was, in effect, "Lady, your problem is not religion. It's sex. You've slept with so many men, you don't know which one to rightly call your husband" (see the story in John 4:7–38). That is a rather intimate discussion for a man and a woman who are not even supposed to be speaking to each other!

Over and over again, Jesus dealt with people's most intimate problems. When someone would ask a left-brain or legalistic question about religion, Jesus would go beneath their surface logical query and respond to the emotional, right-brain dilemmas which lay behind the question.

For example, the rich young ruler came up to Jesus and said, "I've kept the law and done all the necessary religious things. What must *I* do to be saved, to inherit eternal life?"

Jesus penetrated to the very core of the man's problem when he said: "Go sell your business and give the money to the poor" (see Luke 18:18–30). He knew where the man's *heart* was, what he really worshiped more than God. His love for his business was bigger than his love for God. But rather than giving the man a left-brain sermon on the fact that he was being separated from God by the love of his business, Jesus gave him a choice to make—a choice which made the right brain truth self-evident to the young man.

Another example of Jesus' being intimate took place when the disciples asked him to teach them to pray. Remember at this time God was considered to be awesome, distant, electric. In fact, God was so scary that a *priest* could go into the Holy of Holies, where God was supposed to be, only once a year.

And before *he* could go in they would tie a rope around his leg in case he had a heart attack. Then they could use the rope to drag him out, because it wasn't safe for anyone to go in after him. This is the awesome God of whom they were speaking when they asked, "Lord, teach us to pray" (see Luke 11:1–4).

But Jesus said, in effect, "All right, bow your heads." Then he looked up and said, "Daddy." (He used the word, *Abba*, the word a child would use in approaching a loving father.) *Daddy!* This was revolutionary, and the religious authorities were scandalized. Now we can begin to see why the religious leaders wanted to kill him.

But there are those today who say, "You shouldn't take away the awe of God with this 'friendliness' angle you are teaching." Now, I don't believe for an instant that Jesus was trying to take away the sense of awe. Instead, he was lifting up a right-brain paradox: This awesome majestic God who made everything in the universe wants to be intimate with us as a father—as a *daddy.*" Wow!

In one way of speaking, it seems that in the life and teaching of Jesus we see God opening his chest and revealing his hopes and dreams, the inside of himself. Through his story he was showing us his dreams for a relationship with us. He was opening his heart to us just as we might open our hearts to somebody we love and want to be close to. Jesus was, in that sense, God's offer of intimacy, of his tender personal self, to the tender personal self in each of us.

It was as if, in Jesus, God came walking vulnerably out from behind nature to reenter an open, personal kind of relating, the way he had planned it in the beginning. But God's people said again, this time to Jesus, "No way. This whole business is too threatening. Besides, it's not 'legal.'" And they killed him to shut God's mouth in his call for open, vulnerable relationships.

But just before he died, Jesus said to his disciples, "I've got to go because this personality that you see in me is going to be all over the world. It's going to be released to be among you when I can't be with you. Everywhere people are going to be able to relate to this personality, this Holy Spirit you see in me."

His disciples were afraid (as we are afraid) to come out of their personal inner caves (where we crouch and hide and hope somebody will find us). And Jesus said that the Holy Spirit would come in a way so intimate that he would actually *come inside us* and communicate with us in our isolation. The Spirit would, he suggested, teach us and take us by the hand, leading us out into God's sunlight where we could take the hands of other people also coming out of their caves of hiding. And it would be this vast company of timid cave dwellers coming out of hiding that would constitute the church of Jesus Christ, the kingdom of God. And one of the miracles of the church is that as we walk together in his story, we can learn from Jesus' personality, from his intimate Spirit, how to live and to reach out to lost and lonely people everywhere and tell them this good news. And with his Spirit in us, communication would be open and intimate.

A New Commandment

Then Jesus made a revolutionary statement. He said, in effect, "Besides honesty and justice, which you've always known God wants, I have a new commandment for you from him." And he commanded the disciples to love each other—and even their enemies—the way he,

Jesus, had loved them. Here was a whole new dimension of faith. God had always loved us and wanted us to be honest and fair with each other. But Jesus was saying in a new way that we must *love each other*, not just be righteous. (Then, as now, many of God's people had become very "righteous" but were not loving.) So Jesus commanded us to love—which he said had always been the first (*and* second) great commandment anyway (see John 13:34 and Matt. 22:34–40).

The End of Act Two: Jesus' Death

Jesus' death and resurrection brought about an atonement (at-one-ment) between God and his people. In some right-brain way, Jesus had become the scapegoat for all the people with God. Remember, that's what the scapegoat idea was all about—vicariously to take care of all the remaining sins of the people, to create again an at-one-ment with God. Jesus was in that sense our scapegoat and our sacrificial lamb rolled into one. And the church still speaks of him in the liturgy as "the lamb of God that takes away the sins of the world," because he continues to take away our sin and separation and to renew our intimate communication with him.

10

Down through the Years to Now—
Act Three

WHEN JESUS DIED on the cross, his disciples thought all was lost. After having left everything and followed him for three years, they must have been devastated when they saw him dead. Imagine them on that black Saturday after the crucifixion—hiding clustered in some closed room or rooms, not knowing where to go or what to do. The tears of frustration and the anger at having fallen for Jesus and his Good News must have been awful.

Then came Sunday morning. And with the incredible discovery that Jesus was *alive* came the dawning of a whole new idea—a whole new era. In the Resurrection they saw God's signature scrawled across the life and message of Jesus—no one but God himself could have authored that life.

Over the next days and weeks a mind-exploding hope was born in the little group of disciples—a realization that God really had come on the stage of history in Jesus' life to institute his kingdom, to bring justice, peace, and new life. But they didn't know what to do about it all.

Then came Pentecost, when they were meeting together with several hundreds of believers and inquirers about the kingdom. And the Holy Spirit—the personality, the spirit they had seen in Jesus—"descended upon" them (see Acts 21). Suddenly they received the power to communicate intimately across racial, national, and linguistic lines. It was as if the people in God's kingdom were made new and given one heart—just as God had intended in the beginning.

Communication with God seemed very different after Jesus' death and resurrection and the coming of the Holy Spirit at Pentecost.[1] This

---

1. Thought of by many Christians as the "birthday" of the Christian church (see story in Acts 2).

was because the Holy Spirit, the personality of God that was seen in Jesus, was to be with the church and with each of us intimately forever. What a staggering idea! God will be *present, communicating with us intimately,* not just at the temple, not just through the great mediators, but constantly within each of us and in the midst of our family, the church. It's an amazing idea that not just the words of God, but his actual presence, is with us wherever we may be.

Stop a Moment

If this is true, then the personality of Jesus, the Holy Spirit, is in the room with you now as you read—wherever you are. To help in grasping this new kind of intimate communication, here is an experiment which will use the right hemisphere of your brain. First, take a moment to relax. Close your eyes and consciously relax your shoulders, your arms, your legs, your ankles, and your feet. Now, imagine that God Almighty, who created everything we know and understand, is actually present trying to communicate with you. Stop and just be aware of his presence. If it is helpful, imagine Jesus sitting in a chair across from you, looking at you with love and understanding in his eyes.

Put the book down on your lap for a moment and listen. If God Almighty is not in some sense here with us in this room (whether we "feel" his presence or not), then we of all people are the most deluded—for this is his promise to us.

We become aware of God's presence when we take time to be silent, to listen. But we also experience him—perhaps most often—in community with other Christians. This is true because his presence is not just in silence or in words; it's in touches, in love, in forgiveness, in the Eucharist or Holy Communion, in the reading of his story in the Bible. It's in smiles, in sacrificial service for other people, in understanding them. God's presence is a touchstone of living meaning as we walk in his story and give his love and help to the poor, and to people who are trapped in all kinds of ways.

Can We Dare Risk the Pain of Rejection?

The call to "walk in God's story" is a call to risk putting aside sham and deception—with the help of his spirit and his people. It's a call to learn the difficult art of being open with God and with each other, so we can find and bring to others the intimacy of God's kind of love. But most of us have gotten so far from what God intended that the idea of simply being ourselves and expressing what we are seems crazy to our logical minds. We're sure we'd be rejected by everyone we met!

To most of us, the idea that we might really consider starting to be honest with everybody in our life about our feelings and our relationships is terrifying. Most of us have had too much history of being hurt and rejected. So often we say, "Yes, I want to be open, Lord. I want to be your person," but in the privacy of our own hearts, it's a different story. "Not me, Lord. I'll be nice but not open. My past is too painful."

There is a true story which helped me to see that God can really use our past, whatever it is, to help us step into his story with the beginnings of new courage and openness. Some years ago I moved to the town of Kerrville, Texas and, after a time, started a small sharing group.

The group spent the entire first meeting just getting acquainted. Since it is so hard for most Christians to get below the superficial social level with each other, we decided to spend that "get acquainted" time talking about the past. (Many people find talking openly about the past less threatening than talking about the present.)

I remember saying, "Okay, now, we'll take turns. As we go around the circle, we're just going to tell a little bit about ourselves as children. First, where did you live between the ages of seven and twelve?" (That seemed like a safe question.)

And so people took turns telling where they had lived as children. One woman said, "I didn't like anything about my childhood. I didn't like my town, my family, or anybody." Although she was a wealthy and privileged person, it was obvious that she was bitter and cynical about life.[2]

The next woman in the circle, whom I'll call Alice, started to pass. (We always let people pass on these questions if they wanted to because to some the questions seemed very personal.) But then she said, "No, wait. I want to tell you. I was raised in an orphanage in West Texas. I was not an attractive child and my parents hadn't wanted me, so they had delivered me to this 'children's home.'

"I'll bet no child ever wanted to be adopted more than I did. Every

---

2. When I have used a story about someone, I have disguised his or her identity, or I have asked permission to use the story.

time somebody would come to the orphanage to look at the children, I'd run out and jump up and down in front of them, and try to get their attention. I was so eager—almost hyperactive—that no one ever wanted me.

"But one evening the matron called me in and said, 'Alice, somebody wants you to come live with them.' I began to jump up and down with excitement, but she said, 'Now calm down, Alice. It's only a trial visit.' But I *knew* it would be permanent.

"My new foster parents took me to this little town in West Texas. And the house I lived in was the biggest house in town! It was one of those 'almost antebellum' houses with fourteen-foot ceilings. It was big and old and a little run-down on the outside—the paint was peeling and a few things like that. But it had a big entryway and a stairway that curved up to the second floor just like in the movies. I thought it was the most magnificent place in the world, and it was *my* house.

"I ran home from school, or skipped real fast, every day just to make sure the house was still there. I was the happiest kid you could imagine. But one day, about six weeks later, I came skipping home and rushed through the big old door. And there in the middle of the front hall was my old cardboard suitcase with my coat thrown over it. At first I was confused, but then I knew . . . they didn't want me."

Alice stopped for a minute; the silence hung heavy in the room as she stared at the floor. Then she said, "You know, that happened to me seven times before I was thirteen years old."

But the rest of us in the group didn't even hear that last sentence. We were still back in the hallway looking at the little girl and her battered suitcase and trying not to cry.

Then she evidently saw what was happening to us and shook her head. "Oh no, don't!" she said. "You see, I *needed* my past. It brought me to Jesus Christ!"

If we step into God's story, if we learn to share our stories and communicate without hiding our true selves, I'm convinced that, whatever our past is, whatever our fears, he'll use them to bring us closer to Jesus Christ and to his people.

III

THE POWER
OF CHRISTIAN LOVE

INTRODUCTION

Does Christian Behavior
Release Real Power?

EARLIER, I SUGGESTED that if we think about things logically, with only the left hemisphere of our brains, we often miss the most important truths about God and living. Love is one of those things that can't quite be assimilated when analyzed by the left brain; prayer is another. Both love and prayer require some experience of their object in order to become "real."

For a long time I felt there was no real power in prayer. We Christians work like crazy, and then pray—evidently hoping that prayer will add a little extra spiritual "juice" to our efforts. But our behavior seems to indicate that we think the real "gasoline," the real power, comes from the effort itself. Many of us have, at one time or another, secretly accepted the idea that although prayer is good and Christians should pray, God doesn't *actually* change things in the real material world because of prayer. It is just a sort of coincidence when what actually takes place correlates with what has been prayed.

For a long time I believed that praying was a good thing to do because it let God know that I loved him. But I felt it wasn't reasonable to think that prayer could change anything very significantly in the physical world. I wasn't *sure* of this, but I also didn't *depend* on prayer regarding such crucial things as my vocational future.

But some years ago, I changed my mind drastically about prayer. One afternoon I was sitting in my living room preparing a talk to be given at a ministers' conference on prayer. I was very nervous, because that particular day I was feeling so low that I wasn't even sure I believed in God, much less prayer. I thought, "I can't possibly tell those ministers how I'm feeling, because they are all committed servants of God and they probably don't have these experiences—or if they do, they are probably able to handle them easily."

While I was sitting in the living room sweating this out, one of my daughters, seven-year-old Mary-Keith, came in from school. She was in the second grade. We had moved, and for the first time she had encountered the physical fitness tests that President Kennedy had instituted in the schools. Mary-Keith had just been through the tests for the first time that day. She was crying. Being a loving father, I put down my papers, took her on my lap, and said, "Honey, what's the matter?"

She said, "Daddy, it's the chin-ups."

Being trained in Rogerian psychology (and not having any idea what she meant), I said, "Would you like to talk about it?"

"Well, Daddy, I didn't do too well on the chin-up test where you pull your chin up to the bar and see how long you can hang."

"How long did you go?"

"Eight seconds."

Realizing she had never done anything like that before, I said, "Well, that's not bad. A lot of people can't even hold themselves up on a bar like that at all."

"Yes, but Susan did twenty-four seconds—and Bobby loves Susan!" Bobby was their common boyfriend in the second grade, and I realized this was a serious problem from her perspective.

Being the kind of "fix it" daddy that I am, I said, "Okay, I'll tell you what we're going to do. I'm going to put a bar up in the backyard between two posts. I used to work out on a high bar, and I'll show you how to do some exercises which will strengthen your arms so you can stay up there a long time. And then you may be able to hang up there longer than anybody in your class. When is the next test going to be?"

And she said through teary but hopeful eyes, "Tomorrow."

Tomorrow! It was looking pretty hopeless. But then I saw my notes on prayer, and I said, "Let's pray about this." And I said a very sincere prayer, something like this: "Dear Lord, help Mary-Keith on the test tomorrow to do the best she possibly can. Help her to learn something from this experience, and to give it all she's got. In Jesus' name, Amen." I thought that was a pretty good fatherly prayer. And then I said, "Now, honey, when you get up there tomorrow to do the chin-ups, why don't you pray?"

She said, "Okay," and then she ran off to play.

The next day when she came in after school, I was still working on my talk. She came running in and sailed past me, happy as a lark. I grabbed her as she went by. (Obviously, she had forgotten about *our* problem.) I asked, "Honey, how did it go today?"

She said, "How did what go?"

I said, "The *chin-ups*—how long did you hang on the bar?"

She said, "Twenty-five seconds."

"Twenty-five!" I was astounded. "How did you do it?"

"I did what you said, Daddy. I prayed."

I reached for my notes and a pencil. "What did you pray?" I was going to get *this* prayer down.

She said, "Well, Daddy, when I got up there, and started getting real tired, I whispered to God, 'Let me beat Susan! Let me beat Susan! Let me beat Susan!' "

Now, I'm not recommending this as a model prayer. But that day as I sat there listening to my little girl, I realized that we were not dealing with a "spiritual" problem. We were talking about a problem in physics—mass and energy. This little girl in a twenty-four hour period, without any additional training at all, simply by saying some words inside her head that nobody else even heard, *increased her physical performance in the real world by over 200 percent!* And I realized that often we don't even begin to understand what can be released physically through what is inside of us, because of the words we say in prayer.[1]

In order to fulfill our potential as we walk in God's story, I believe we've got to understand that there is a kind of energy, a kind of power, available to us as Christians that people in the left-brain, logical world do not understand. That power is released not only by prayer but also (primarily) by loving. Jesus used the power of God's love all the time, and said that "the man who believes in me will do the same things that I have done, yes, and he will do even greater things than these" (see John 14:12–23, Phillips). And that same evening he commanded us to love each other as he loved us. He said that, if we do love others like that, our love will be the recognizable sign that we are his people (John 13:34–35).

If Jesus' commandment to love others as he loved us is the agenda of life in the kingdom, and if evangelism is God's message overflowing from this life, then it seems crucial to learn how to love in God's way before we go out evangelizing. This is because it is the experience of that love which has always carried with it an energizing power to heal and save the broken and lost people in the world.

But what is Christian love?

---

1. Not to mention prayers which pertain to people and situations outside our own bodies!

11

The Focus of Christian Love

WHEN I FIRST TRIED to love other people as a Christian, I didn't know anything about it. I didn't know what to do. So I found myself trying to imitate what I saw other Christians doing.

Using "Religious Language" As Love

But as I watched the Christian bunch I got in with, it appeared to me that the way some of them loved people was by using religious language. It sometimes seemed as though they would run up to people and kind of spew it on them. My non-Christian friends were really turned off by this and resented being "assaulted" with religious terms.

And in their constant talking about their new "religion," some of these Christians appeared to use the Bible as a way to show off their knowledge of the faith. They would quote it all the time. They didn't just say, "Good morning." They said, "John 3:16"—just the reference. But I knew that if I came into the office where I worked and said, "John 3:16," my friends in the oil business would think I was talking about the restroom on the third floor.[1]

I understand that quoting the Bible is necessary and helpful, and I do it. But to me, as a new Christian, it seemed like you could just walk up to some of these people, punch them in the navel, and a scripture

---

1. I am walking a fine line here because I know from my own experience the happiness and growth which come from memorizing and quoting from passages of Scripture. But I see no place in the Bible which indicates we are to use Scripture and religious terminology as a way to display our knowledge and expertise—especially to non-Christians. And I'm saying here that I find it helpful when I can restrain the urge to let people in on "how much I know" (see Matt. 23:5).

verse would come out of their mouths—like a payoff in a slot machine. It seemed phony.

Of course, I did meet some Christians whose use of Scripture appeared natural and deep. And I have met many for whom the Scripture is so much a part of their lives that it is not at all like an added thing they push at you. But I've been intrigued by the fact that, for the most part, our Lord only used Scripture when he was teaching or when he was dealing with Satan. Both Mark and Matthew say that when he spoke to the common people he just told stories: "He did not speak to them without a parable" (Mark 4:34, RSV; see also Matt. 13:34).

When I was in the oil exploration business in Oklahoma City, a religious-talking, evangelizing Christian had been trying to corner me. One day I saw him coming down the street with a handful of tracts, and I quickly ducked into the door of a shop. I just stepped in and pretended to be shopping, and I watched him out of the corner of my eye until he went on down the street. When he was gone, I looked up and found that I was in a shop which sold very personal women's underthings. I thought to myself, "This is how far people will go to avoid a Christian they think is a fanatic." And I realized *that's* why some Christians avoid traditional evangelism.

What I'm trying to describe is an attitude on the part of some Christians which seems to say, "I've got it, you need it, and I am going to talk to you about it—whether you want me to or not." And, to compound the problem, some Christian leaders use guilt as a motivator to encourage new converts to go out and confront people with the "claims of Jesus." But unfortunately, this approach seems to ignore the feelings of the people being witnessed to. I did this for some months when I first learned a way to lead people to a commitment to Christ. And I must confess that sometimes I was more interested in alleviating my own guilt and need to be a good witness than I was in the needs of the people I was confronting.

I suppose there is no way to avoid mixed motives in witnessing to people. But I have learned the hard way that *working off my own needs and guilt* by confronting people with the gospel sometimes can be very ineffective. Although it's a gross oversimplification, that's what I call the "vomit approach" to loving and witnessing. You come out of a church meeting like a rodeo rider out of chute four and let the next person you see have it! Now, doing that may make *you* feel better; after all, you have witnessed to what you believe. But sometimes it doesn't do a lot for the recipient. I'm pleading here for *loving* the other person first—before talking about the gospel—so that the words we use later may release their healing power in his or her life.

The Magic of Listening

What I gradually came to believe was that *just* saying words—even very true and holy words—is not what is meant by loving people as a Christian. At the office, I had learned some things about a kind of preparatory loving I had seen Jesus doing in the New Testament—a kind of a "tuning in" to the person who is with you, a sensitivity that makes what you may say later about God much more authentic and understandable.

In fact, I began to learn that talking was *not* the most powerful way to get people's attention. Much to my surprise, I found that *listening* is a much more effective way of giving my presence to somebody when I am with them. It's as if my listening attention were a spotlight that God has given me to focus. I can focus my attention in the past, I can focus it out in the future, or I can focus it into the lives of the people around me.

By personal experience I know that, when somebody really gives me his or her attention, that person draws me gently out of my cold tight absorption with myself and into the healing arena of the "in between"—that space that exists only between the two of us. It is like magic. In such an exchange with another person we often find ourselves moving into the area of the personal, and the situation changes. When I am listening to somebody this way, even in a crowd of people, I've noticed that I am often watching them and listening as if no one else were there. I imagine a glass bubble is around the two of us, and that only we are sharing this special moment of attention.

I have become convinced that what we call the *agape* love of Christ rides down the beam of our attention into people's lives. And this seems to be true whether we are involved with a wife, a husband, a child, or a stranger being encountered for the first time. In a way, I think this focusing on the other person is a taste of the greatest kind of love there is. For in a strange way we are giving people our *lives*, a second at a time, when we give them our undivided attention.

As a counselor, I have talked to many people who have said in different ways about an estranged mate, "I don't expect him (her) to do a lot for me. I just want him (her) to know that I exist. I want his (her) *attention!*" A single such contact in which someone feels heard and understood—and loved—is very powerful.

Years ago, when I was director of Laity Lodge, we had scheduled Elton Trueblood to speak at a weekend conference. That weekend, a young woman came from hundreds of miles away just to be at a conference where he was speaking. None of us knew this young woman; she had heard about the conference from a friend and had driven the long distance by herself.

One of the things we did that weekend was to divide into small groups, and one of the small-group activities was to go around the circle and answer the question, "What is the most important single encounter you've had with another human being (not counting members of your family)?" In one group, after a few people had responded, it became the young stranger's turn.

She looked up and said, "Well, when I was a child, maybe ten years old, Elton Trueblood came to our city to speak. My daddy was an elder in the church and in charge of the program, and so the speaker was to stay in our home for several days. At the dinner table during that week, Dr. Trueblood would ask the adults questions and then listen attentively to their answers. But then he would turn to me and ask me a question, and he would listen to my answer with the same care he had given to the adults. Then he would ask me another question about what I had said! He did this all week long. He treated me as if I were an intelligent, sensitive, mature Christian. And that week I made up my mind that I was going to spend the rest of my life becoming one."

The young woman's story is a vivid illustration of the fact that we may become what people see in us when they love us enough to listen and pay attention to us. All of us long for others to see the positive things we sometimes see in ourselves. Christ did this often. He would have a brief encounter with a person and that person's life would be changed. I realize now that some people can't believe *God* is interested in them because they have never known *people* who are. And when we listen to others and give them our undivided attention, I believe we are preparing the way for a possible encounter with the One who loves us all, and who hears each of us as if we were the only person in his universe.

12

How Do You Keep Loving When No One Cares?

As I THRASHED AROUND in those early years, trying to learn how to be an authentic, loving Christian, I found myself rejecting the models I saw around me in the church. And I found I was cutting off all the people who had been the "audiences" to whom I had played my life. The people in the oil business didn't seem to be interested in what was going on in my Christian life. And I couldn't identify with many people at the church I went to because they thought I was off balance. (I was bubbling over with excitement over what I was learning about "the Christian life.") And I began to feel very isolated.

One morning I woke up lonely and sad, and I said to God, "Lord, I guess I've cut off all my audiences. Nobody seems to understand me."

And it was as if a Voice said to me, "Why don't you play your life to me as your audience? I am everywhere. I'll go with you through your days and nights." And that was when I began to discover how much peace and strength could come from beginning to try to play my life to God instead of to people.

At that time one of my best friends was a man named Bud Wilkinson, who was the football coach at the University of Oklahoma in the 1950s, when they won over forty games in a row. It is commonly accepted that he is one of the greatest college coaches of all time.

I was taking some notes about Bud, hoping someday to write a book on his life. And I noticed an unusual thing when I watched the football practices. I had the strong feeling that if he were to say, "There is a bus coming down the street. I want some of you men to go tackle that bus," every player on the practice field would rush to be the first one to hit the bus.

Now, I knew we didn't have that kind of motivation in our church, and I knew I didn't have it personally. So I kept watching to see what might account for the enormous drive Bud's teams had.

When other teams cracked under pressure, Oklahoma's players would just keep coming. After being tackled, for instance, they would scramble out of the mass of bodies to get back to the huddle and run another play. Sometimes Oklahoma's players could get back and begin another play before the other team was even at the line of scrimmage. And when the pressure would build almost to the breaking point and the crowd would be roaring, the other team would appear to get rattled, but Oklahoma's players never seemed to lose their composure. They would just keep moving.

As I probed around to discover the secret of Bud's success, I learned that he made extensive use of game films. All four quarters would be carefully filmed. The coaches would watch the films on Sunday after Saturday's game and mark good and bad plays with circles. On Monday, they would bring the team in and run the films. If a player had made a mistake, he could see it on the screen. But if he'd made a good play, the team could also see what the player had done. This routine of reviewing game films provided a strong reinforcement and motivation, especially since the players knew that their coach—whom most of them held almost in awe—was seeing in detail everything they might do or try to do.

All of a sudden, I realized why it might be that these players didn't get rattled under pressure. They were playing the game for Bud Wilkinson. They knew that, even if it rained or snowed the day of the game and the crowd in the stands missed the line play, on Sunday Wilkinson was going to see what really happened.

The Oklahoma University players were playing the game to a different audience! And it suddenly occurred to me that whether or not it was true for that team, it was an important truth for my life. If I could learn to play my life to a different audience—to God, not to the people around me—then, whether I fouled up or succeeded, I would know God was with me and I wouldn't be alone.

This realization gave me an enormous release from compulsion and tension. It was a very restful thing. And I began to try to live with God as my audience from my first waking moment. I found I could be more loving because I was aware that he was with me. And I discovered that there is a lot of power released in the world through the seemingly inconsequential loving acts we engage in when we begin to play our lives to God as an audience.

About that time I heard a story which helped me understand this strange power that can be released when we play our lives to God. It seems that there was a New York businessman who got converted. This man determined that he was really going to be a loving Christian. But even with all his enthusiasm it seemed he just wasn't succeeding.

One day he was really feeling sick of himself. So he looked in the mirror with determined eyes after he'd finished shaving and said to God, "Lord, I'm going to be a loving Christian all day if it kills me!" So he began his day by rushing over to Grand Central Station to catch a train to Boston. He was rushing through the station with his briefcase in one hand and an overnight bag in the other, almost late for his train and trying not to swear. All at once he heard, "All aboard!" and he realized the train was just about to pull out. He started running, but just before he got to the train, he felt his suitcase hit something. He looked down and saw a small boy who had been carrying a large jigsaw puzzle. Now dozens of puzzle pieces littered the platform.

The boy started crying. The train started to move. And just as the man was getting ready to make a run for it he remembered his promise to God. So he set his bags down, patted the boy on the head, smiled, and said, "I'll pick it up for you." While he gathered up all the pieces of the puzzle and put them all in the box, the little boy was watching him intently. When he had finished putting the lid back on and handed him the box, the boy looked up with a kind of wonder and said, "Mister, are you *Jesus?*" And in that moment on the train platform, the man realized that, in a sense, he had been.

There's an amazing power in lovingly touching people's lives where they don't expect to be touched. And this was what I was learning in "part one" of my adventure to try to love people: I was learning to let my urgency to "talk" subside as I first tried to listen and care for them in the present moment, to take the focus of my life from the distant horizon and to center it on the people close to me. I was also trying to play out my life to an attentive Lord who walked with me through my days and nights.

It was then that I realized I had a life full of people I cared about. I was investing myself in these people, and for a while I had strong feelings of love for them. Then, over the months and years, as I started speaking regularly at Christian meetings, my life got *full* of people. And after a while it seemed like there were *too many* people. My feelings of love for them subsided. I got tired and discouraged, and I just didn't *feel* loving.

Then came "part two" of my adventure to try to find out how to love people as Christ loved them.

13

The Relationship Between
Christian Love and Warm Feelings

ONE DAY I REALIZED that the "honeymoon" with God was over. I saw that a lot of the Christian life is not warm feelings of excitement and neat stories. Much of it is just plain discipline and hard work, like anything else that's real in life.

Now, I had been used to that in basketball and business; I knew that if you want to change your ability to play the game you have to pay a price. And my experience told me, "That's what you're going to have to do in learning to live for Christ and learning how to love people."

But I guess I had been expecting magic in the Christian life. Because of who Jesus Christ is, I had expected life with him to be something very different from all my other experiences of life—as if he were going to use "white magic" to help Christians. Now, as I read my Bible, I began to understand that Jesus rejected the use of magic a long time ago (see Matt. 4:1–11). I began to see that he ordinarily uses the same laws and rules everybody else does—he just knows more about the way the mind and body work and the "laws" and "rules" of nature, having been the only one around when they were invented.

But realizing these things didn't keep me from being bothered by the fact that, even though I was *helping* people I'd never even thought about before I was converted, I was still losing some of my fresh *feelings* of unselfish love for others. As a matter of fact, I was getting sick of people. It's difficult to talk about that as a Christian. Christian speakers are not supposed to say, "I never want to see another group of people!" But I felt that way. And I would catch myself smiling and saying to a crowd, "It's good to see you. I'm glad to be here with you," when at one level I *wasn't* glad to be there at all—although I *was* grateful to be a Christian. I began to say to myself, "This is not feeling very good."

The lack of loving feelings really worried me because it made me feel like a hypocrite. So I prayed and read, and when I had the chance I asked some of my Christian friends about my "problem." Some of them confessed they really didn't feel loving toward people all of the time. But even that wasn't much comfort to me, because I knew that Jesus had *commanded* us to love. As I continued to struggle with my feelings, I wondered, "Am I really a hypocrite for reaching out and doing loving things for people when I don't feel like it?"

Then one day something happened that helped me understand how Christian love works. I was sitting on my front porch, thinking about this whole business of loving people for Christ's sake, and my mind was in a sort of dream state. I was absorbed in my own fantasies, but I was also half-aware of my little girl, who was riding her tricycle down the driveway.

All of a sudden, I heard a sound and looked up. A big truck—like a moving van—was barreling down the hill. I saw that a large bush was blocking my little girl's view of the truck, and that she was headed right out in the street. All of a sudden I realized that she was going to ride *right out in front of* that truck!

I didn't have any time to reflect. I put my hand on the porch rail, vaulted it and ran toward the street. Just as I got there, I realized, "Good gosh, I can push her out of the way, but *I'll* never make it." But I didn't stop; I dove and pushed my little girl out of the way. And I felt and heard this terrible "crunch" as that truck ran over me. . . .

As I indicated, it was just a fantasy. But I went ahead and played out the rest of it. I could see the funeral. There they were, lowering me into the grave. All of these people—my friends and family—were saying, "You see, he really *was* a loving Christian. What a guy! He gave his life for his daughter." (I have a vivid fantasy life.)

Then as I continued to sit there on the porch, thinking about what had happened, I saw the same scene starting to replay itself. But instead of my daughter on the tricycle, this time it was the mean little boy from down the street.

Now, I like kids. I *am* a kid in many ways. But I didn't like this kid. Just the day before, when I had tried to catch him to talk to him about throwing rocks at my little girl, he had given me a nasty sign with his finger and run away—I never did catch him.

But now, in my imagination, I saw *him* coming down the driveway. I thought to myself, "What if he really were riding on that tricycle?" Then the fantasy continued. I heard the truck coming, and the nasty kid was heading down the driveway toward the street. And I didn't know whether to say, "Sic 'em, truck!" or what. All of this flashed through my mind in a split second.

But then all of a sudden, even in my fantasy, I *could not* let that kid get killed. I vaulted the rail, ran into the street, and pushed the tricycle out of the way. And of course I was killed.

As I sat there thinking about these two scenarios, the question popped into my mind, "Which one of these acts was the greater act of Christian love—saving my own daughter or the kid down the street?" What a question! After all, any pagan would die for his daughter if he had the guts. But I didn't even like that other kid. I had *no feelings of warm Christian love for him at all!*

It was then that I began to get excited. Maybe Christian love, the kind God wants us to live out, is not what I thought it was. Maybe it's something more than those warm loving *feelings* for the unlovely I'd longed for and prayed for and felt guilty when I didn't have.

I went back to the Bible to see what it said about Christ's kind of love. I turned to the thirteenth chapter of 1 Corinthians, that marvelous classic passage about love. The apostle Paul pointed out there that love is more important than all the other spiritual gifts we may receive. In fact, he said, without love the other gifts don't mean a thing.

Then I asked myself, "Where can I see this kind of love in action?" And I thought about Christ's gift of himself and reread the story about his last hours before the crucifixion. Jesus had come to Jerusalem, no doubt with the realization of the personal danger he was in. He came and wept over the city, the people of God, and realized he was coming to some kind of climax in his life and ministry.

Then I read that strange scene in the Garden of Gethsemane at night (see Matt. 26) in which Jesus left his three most trusted friends and went off by himself and prayed. I thought, "Now, here I'm going to see it. Here is real love in action—Jesus approaching the act which changed the world's conception of what love in the human context is like. Why can't I feel the way *he* felt about loving people?"

I read and reread that very moving account. And as I read it the third time I was shocked to realize that Jesus was evidently *not* filled with warm feelings of love at that moment. As a matter of fact, he prayed three times asking *to get out of* the most loving act in history. He said, in so many words, "Let this cup pass from me. I don't want to go on, God." And he sweated blood, the scriptures say—his agony was so intense.

Then, when Jesus did agree to go ahead with what was before him, he didn't muscle his feelings around and say, "Now that I feel good, warm feelings about dying, Father, I'm ready." Even after he had bowed to his Father's will, Jesus didn't especially *look forward* to what was going to happen. He apparently went out of *love* for *his Father,* not because he *liked the course he was to take!*[1]

Jesus apparently based his decision to face the crisis of his life not on a warm feeling about the results of the action nor its benefits to others, but on his loving obedience to his Father's will as he could determine it. If this is true, then Christian love is not based on the feelings that I'd longed for. When I realized this, the Lord's *command* for us to love made sense to me. And my studies in psychology and my own experience have since confirmed that this view of love is sound. While we cannot *control* our feelings, we can more nearly command our *concerned actions.*

But what about those wonderful warm feelings of love which are so invigorating? Don't they have any place in Christian loving?

---

1. I am aware of the controversy over the source of several of these verses and that my use of this scene bypasses the whole question of what Jesus in his humanity actually knew in the garden about the ultimate value of the next day's actions. For a brief but excellent scholarly treatment of the human-divine question regarding Jesus, see John Knox, *The Humanity and Divinity of Christ* (New York: Cambridge University Press, 1967).

14

Cathexis or Genuine Love?

RECENTLY I READ a book called *The Road Less Traveled,* by M. Scott Peck, a psychiatrist.[1] His insights on love in that book have changed my thinking significantly.

He says there are two aspects to what we call love. He called one "cathexis" and the other "genuine love."

Cathexis

According to Dr. Peck, cathexis is an attachment. It's the way we invest energy in persons who have caught our attention in a positive, attracting way. When we see somebody we like, we send out an energy which affixes itself to them. This just happens, without any effort. And as energy flows out and attaches itself to the person or thing we're attracted to, we say, "I just *love* him or her," or "I *love* your dog" (after only knowing the dog a few minutes), or "Why, I am *in love* with this attractive woman! I want to spend the rest of my life with her!" (when we've only met the woman once).

"Falling in love" is a perfect example of cathexis. It is effortless. There is nothing in it that has anything necessarily to do with a *mutual* relationship or with genuine intimacy. We don't even have to know someone's name to fall in love with him or her! It happens all the time. It's one of the most powerful human experiences. People have gotten married, thrown away their careers, destroyed existing marriages, and given up huge inheritances on the basis of a single experience of cathexis.

Cathexis is, in fact, what most people I know call love. And if we

---

1. New York: Simon and Schuster, 1978.

don't have these strong feelings of attraction for another person or for God, we think we don't love them. This mistaking of cathexis for genuine love has led to many tragedies in marriages, long-term dating relationships, or attempts to live life walking in God's story. This is because when the strong feelings subside, we think the love is all over and often are ready to call the whole thing off.

Genuine Love

If the strong feeling we usually call love is only cathexis, then what is genuine love? Peck defines genuine love as "the will to extend oneself for the purpose of nurturing one's own or another's spiritual growth."[2] Of course, there are other aspects of love, but this definition seems to fit Jesus' commandment to love—"A new commandment I give you, that you love one another; even as I have loved you" (John 13:34, RSV)—and the admonition of Paul in which he summarized the whole law as to "love your neighbor as yourself" (Rom. 13:8–9, RSV).

Modern psychology validates this whole idea by stressing the fact that there is just no way we can love others in a healthy manner unless we have a wholesome regard for ourselves. And this means spending time and effort on our own spiritual development. And when I speak of *spiritual* growth, I don't mean just *religious* growth. Spiritual growth involves the whole personal side of ourselves that God has given us to tend and cultivate.

When we spend time reading the Bible or praying and come to a meaning of some kind that we think will help us, we are extending ourselves for the purpose of nurturing our own spiritual growth. But we are also nurturing our spiritual growth when we are learning to be strong and free persons, to stand up for our values and for ourselves. And it is an important part of our spiritual nurture that we find our own potential and freedom. This is evidently part of the way God wants us to love the world and ourselves.

Some people say, "I don't think I *should* pay any attention to myself or to my potential. I don't want to be assertive or stand up for myself too much in my family. It sounds selfish." Well, of course it would be selfish to assert yourself *at the expense of others.* And yet Jesus' whole ministry pointed to the fact that God wants us to be whole persons. James, the apostle, pointed to this goal of wholeness when he wrote, in another context, ". . . that you may be perfect and com-

---

2. *The Road Less Traveled,* p. 81.

plete, lacking in nothing" (1:4). And in Matthew 5:43–48 Jesus intimated that we are to perfect the potential God has put in us so we can love as God loves.

What I'm saying is that, in the long run, we can't nurture anybody else in a healthy way unless we nurture ourselves. And then, when we do begin to love others, we love them by attending to the conditions which further their growth as persons, whether we are talking about a wife, a husband, a child, or the poor people in our community.

When I create a condition in which my wife, for instance, can find and fulfill her potential as the person she was made to be, I am loving her the way God loves her—even if her freedom and growth may make me uncomfortable or frighten me.

Some of the things we do for other people—things we call love— are bound up with cathexis, in that they have a large self-serving component. With cathexis the lover always expects a payoff—big or small, subtle or heavy. Sometimes I do "helpful Christian things" for people so they will think I am a fine man, or a good Christian. The payoff for me is when I imagine them telling other people "what a great person he is." Whenever I find myself "loving" people this way, I know that there is a heavy element of cathexis in my love.

Love As Christian Evangelism

But from the Christian point of view, the commandment to love has a new meaning beyond cathexis. If I love people, I'm going to extend myself for the purpose of seeing that they have the opportunity to develop as God meant them to develop. And because it is Christian, this love would also include extending myself so they might discover a new relationship with God and with other people.

So *evangelism,* which includes the message that we *can* have a new and fulfilling relationship with God and with others, *is a way to love people.* As a Christian evangelist and witness, and because of what God has done for me, I want those I contact for God to find their potential under him.

This means that evangelism is not just a fire brigade campaign to rescue people from a fiery pit. Rather, it seems to me that evangelism is a natural response of our love for God as we move toward people to nurture their spiritual growth, hoping this will create conditions in which they may discover and develop a deep and intimate relationship with God and other people.

What Love Is Not

Peck's concept of cathexis and genuine love is very useful because it gives us a yardstick by which we can measure our attachments and relationships and even our Christian life. It gives us a helpful way of determining what is *not* love.

Loving a painting or a dog, for example, is not genuine love. Some people get very disturbed when they hear this—especially the part about dogs! But, as Scott Peck says, the only school we send dogs to is obedience school, and that is hardly for their spiritual growth.

"Falling in love" is (by itself) cathexis, not genuine love. Wanting the person we love just for our own maintenance and gratification and not for their spiritual growth is the kind of "love" that often ruins marriages.

Now here's a shocker: Falling in love with Jesus is not genuine love. Please read this carefully. If the love of Jesus is *only* a strong emotion and *does not call us to extend ourselves to nurture our own and other people's spiritual growth, then I am convinced it's not genuine love, but only a form of cathexis.*

Usually new converts who "fall in love with Jesus" mature and begin to learn about their faith and how to relate to God and love others. But people in the church sometimes get turned off when new Christians just "love Jesus" and never change their lives or learn to love other people. Such "Jesus lovers" don't grow, they don't move into other people's lives, they don't sacrifice anything. But when they are confronted or criticized, they seem to say, "How can you judge me? I love Jesus!" And it is hard to fault someone spiritually who says he or she loves Jesus.

Now, I'm not trying to condemn anybody. And I certainly think we should love Jesus! I'm just trying to say that I don't think feelings of "being in love with Jesus" which do not lead to changed behaviors constitute genuine love.[1] When the going gets rough, those people are often gone, unless their initial attraction changes to a deeper kind of love.

---

1. Someone asked me, "If Peck's description of love is Christian, then does it mean that if we truly love Jesus we are to extend ourselves for *his* spiritual growth?" My answer to that question is that he has given us human representatives to receive the love we want to give him: the hungry, the thirsty, the strangers, the naked, the sick, and the imprisoned (Matt. 25:40—"Truly, I say to you, as you did it to one of the least of these my brethren, you did it to me," RSV). So as we extend ourselves for the spiritual growth of the poor and despised, it would seem that we are loving Jesus.

15

The Purpose of Cathexis

I DO THINK that God has given us the experience of cathexis, the strong pleasant feelings of love, for a particular purpose. Although my hope is that such feelings will last forever in a good relationship, I believe cathexis is particularly important as the first stage of genuine love. In other words, the strong feelings of being "in love" motivate us to get into a relationship with God or another person so that we can discover whether or not real love is going to develop. Since the fear of genuine closeness is so great, it takes these strong feelings of attachment to get us close enough to *try* love.

It is only when the initial strong feelings subside that we can discover whether or not genuine love is going to develop. This subsiding of feelings can be a terrifying experience, for instance, in marriage. Many divorces take place because couples don't understand that for most people the initial almost overpowering feelings of being in love must go through a metamorphosis.

The Terror of Losing the Feelings of Love

After Andrea and I had been married for a little less than a year (and I had been very much in love with her), I woke up one morning and realized I felt dry; I had no "deep emotional feelings" for her. I liked her and I thought she was a fine person, but the strong, highly charged feeling was gone. I panicked and said to myself, "Good Lord, maybe our romantic love is over!" And I began to get very tense. I even avoided conversation time with her for a day or two.

But in our relationship we are committed to being very open about our feelings, whatever they are. We feel that in a truly intimate relationship in Christ, God can help the partners handle any truth. But it is

97

almost impossible—even with God's help—to resolve a difficulty which is hidden or about which we are being dishonest. We'd had a number of frightening but revealing experiences of working through some threatening personal revelations. But this was a real test of our commitment to openness.

I put off talking about my lack of feelings for days because I was afraid it might ruin our relationship. But finally I said, "Andrea, I love you. As a matter of fact, I love you more than I ever have, and I don't understand this. But I don't have the same exciting, stimulating feelings I've had ever since we started going together." (Now remember—this is a guy who hasn't been married even a year, and he's telling this to his wife!) I asked her, "Have you ever had any 'dead feelings' like this?"

And after a few seconds she breathed a sigh of relief and said, "Whew! Yes, and it scared me to death. I'm having them right now and I was trying to figure out how to tell you." It had frightened her, too.

We decided to walk hand in hand through that experience, to see what would happen to us. We had never known anybody who had talked frankly about this "dead feeling" experience with each other—even though we know now that most couples go through it.

After we had gotten our fearful feelings out in the open and had assured each other of our love and that we were glad to be married, we both relaxed and felt a great wave of relief. During the days which followed, as we walked through this time together, we felt much closer. And to our delight and surprise, the strong feelings of love came back (although we've discovered that we have to face these times of numb or arid feelings periodically).

But talking about such a "dry spell" is a very scary thing to do. Because what if the other person responded to your confession by saying, "Well, no, I still have the great feelings of love all the time." You'd just want to die! It takes a lot of understanding to receive this kind of communication.

But the fact is that, sooner or later, *everybody* who has fallen in love evidently has an experience similar to the one I have described. Sooner or later the strong initial feelings of cathexis must change. So the bad news is that it's a scary thing to face, and the good news is that the relationship moves to a deeper, more comfortable level, and the warm feelings will probably come back.

It was a great relief to me to know that love and deep relationships don't depend on the feelings always being strong. So if you're experiencing this deadness in a marriage, don't just assume that love is gone.

You may find it helpful to begin to talk about it, because if you succumb to your fear and push the other person away, it is evidently possible (eventually) to send the feelings of love away forever. On the other hand, talking about the experience can allow those feelings to creep quietly back, because "electric" feelings are a by-product—a secondary aspect—of genuine love, not the primary thing itself.

What About the Love for God Disappearing?

I had a similar experience with my faith. After an exciting new beginning with God, for months I felt elated about life and about my relation to him. But then one day I didn't feel so excited. And when the strong feelings diminished, I wanted to withdraw. I didn't want to see my Christian friends or even pray to God. This dead feeling lasted for days.

One morning I woke up and I said, "God, I don't like you, I'm sick of this Christianity, and I'd like to fly away to Mexico and hide." I didn't even get up and put on my clothes. I just knew lightening was going to strike me right there in the bed. But it didn't.

And that day I realized with a great sense of relief that every sensitive Christian must have these dry periods and that God can handle them! I saw that a lack of goose bumps does not mean we don't love God. As a matter of fact, that's one of the things God has come to do—to help us confess and deal with our real feelings which frighten us. Then the feelings—positive and negative—can add color, richness, and wisdom to our relationships with each other and with him. When I realized these things about God's love, I felt a deep gratitude to him that he loves us and accepts us just as we are—with all our feelings . . . or lack of them.

But now the question arises, after we *face* our flickering feelings, how do we *deal with them* in a practical way?

16

The Stuff of Genuine Love: Work and Courage

In *THE ROAD LESS TRAVELED*, Scott Peck goes on to say that, after cathexis subsides, genuine love always requires two things: *work* and *courage*.

Work

It takes work to give your undivided attention to people, to spend time with them. You have to put everything aside and concentrate on the loved one. When cathexis is there, it's easy. You have strong, warm feelings and can listen to or care for somebody all night. These strong feelings can keep you listening and loving even at the end of a hard day. But later, after cathexis is gone and you're tired, sometimes you would rather read or watch television than listen to somebody (or even make love to them—and that applies even to someone you love very much!).

So, after cathexis subsides in a relationship with a mate, with a friend, or even with God, then genuine love takes work. Then, quietly and unexpectedly, the work of listening or loving in other ways will often renew the early feeling level of the relationship.

Sometimes it's really hard for me to give up my own comfort and my immediate pleasure to pay undivided attention to anybody, even God—maybe especially to God. Love takes work.

Courage

But the second thing genuine love requires is courage. If we love someone, we invest ourselves in that person's life and begin to help him or her become all they can be. And a deep feeling of attachment can come into the relationship. In fact, often we love the people upon whom we pour our attention and energy more than we love those who help us.

But here's the rub: even though it may make us feel good to love someone, it is also scary. It's scary because they may reject our help and let us down, or they may back away and desert us—and eventually they may die and leave us. All of us evidently feel the fear of loss or rejection at some level, if we are really vulnerable to other people. And when we risk becoming involved in genuine loving attachments, we risk this pain and possible rejection. This sort of caring is frightening. It takes courage to love.

So work and courage, not Hollywood feelings, are the ingredients needed to fulfill Christ's commandment to love. And warm feelings are a gift which may or may not accompany an act of love.[1] If this is true, I realized once more, then God's kind of love is not dependent upon the feelings for which I had longed and prayed. I saw clearly that love is a "willing" which results in an *act* of the kind that God wants performed in someone's life, including my own—an act which will lead to health, wholeness, and spiritual growth. And, at the same time my act of loving will help fulfill the love God has for that person, or for me.

But wait a minute! Won't this "unfeeling love" seem cold and impersonal and be resented by the one you help? In other words, if I don't *feel* love when I do something loving, won't the person being loved think my action is a cold act of selfishness—a working off of my own need to look loving? Here is a situation in which the right brain/left brain distinction is very important. Logically, this should be true; help given without accompanying feelings of love should be experienced as something other than love. But in actual experience it is usually not true.

How Then Does Christian Loving Feel?

Christian loving seems to work something like this: first, I determine to love someone for Christ's sake. My primary motivation for this kind

---

1. One of the difficulties in this discussion is that there are different kinds of "warm feelings" in different kinds of relationships (with God, in marriage, in friendships, with the poor, etc.). But different people also apparently have different capacities to experience "warm feelings." Some people seem to feel them all the time and others almost never. But what I am saying here is that we can still love God or the people to whom we are relating—warm feelings or not.

of love is gratitude to God and desire to do his will. But the *act* I *do* is actually *for* (focused on) *the person I'm helping.*

If I give somebody some food, for instance, that person *receives food from me.* The act is aimed at that person, and, from the recipient's perspective, if the *intent* is loving, she or he feels loved—even if I don't have caring *feelings* during the transaction. It's a paradox. When we give a person our attention, our effort, and concern or material things, he or she will probably feel loved—unless of course we evidence a superior or condescending attitude. For instance, if I am pretending to feel loving, my phoniness can often be seen. But I'm not talking about faking it. I'm suggesting that if I really want the best for the person I'm trying to help—even if I don't *feel* loving—the help will probably be received as love from me.

The late Gertrude Behanna was a dear friend and remarkable Christian communicator who had a significant influence on my life and work. One day while we were talking about this matter of love and feelings, she said something like the following: "I had the darnedest experience on a recent trip. I was exhausted, and I had been sick at my stomach for several days. But this particular night, when I got up in front of a big meeting to give my pitch [as she called her story] I just felt terrible. I looked at all those people and thought, 'I really don't want to be here, Lord. And besides, these people look like a group of self-satisfied fat cats on a fence!'

"But I got up there and told my story. As I talked, I felt numb, as if I were on some kind of automatic pilot, and I had no enthusiasm or positive feeling for what I was doing. I could hear myself talking as if I were some stranger. When I was finished, I started to leave the stage. But a young woman came up with tears in her eyes and said, 'Mrs. Behanna, I have never felt or seen the love of Christ in anyone's heart and eyes the way I saw and felt them in yours tonight.' "

Now, Gert hadn't been up there speaking because she had warm feelings for the people or even because she thought it might make her feel good. She had been doing it because of her love of Christ. But apparently people had sensed her love for Christ at some unconscious level and had felt loved themselves.

How does Christian love feel, then? If you had asked Gertrude Behanna that particular night, she'd have probably said, "Tired."

Actually, sometimes these "unfeeling" acts are more powerful than acts that come from feelings because no payoff is expected. Say, for instance, that a husband listens to his wife because he is feeling romantic and knows that, if he does listen, she'll "let" him make love to her later that evening. That's not nearly as great an act of love from the wife's perspective as if there were no payoff involved. (Of course, the situation would be the same if reversed.) I've had people tell me in counseling situations, "I just want him/her to listen to me when he/she doesn't *want* something." That's one reason psychiatrists are paid seventy-five dollars an hour; they listen with focused attention and caring. And although they are being paid, it's an up-front transaction and the clients feel sure they aren't going to "trade their listening" for something else later.[1]

---

1. Since no one's motives are pure, obviously there is always a component of self-interest in human loving. But anyone who has ever felt that he or she is only listened to and tolerated because of what he or she may give in return will understand the power of a nondemanding act of love.

17

The Power of
Specific Loving Acts—
Some Examples

AS I SAID EARLIER, when we first asked people to come to Laity Lodge and tell their stories, I knew very little about Christian conferences. We had outstanding and well-known "speakers" who attracted people to the meetings. But we decided that since our purpose was to help people learn about living their lives for God, it might also be fascinating and helpful to have ordinary people who were new Christians report what was happening to them.

So we asked people who were converted at a conference to come back a month later and report what had happened. We didn't ask them to give what was then a standard "testimony" such as "What Jesus Did to Solve My Problems," but we asked them simply to tell what they had experienced—good and bad—as a result of trying to put their futures in God's hands. If Christianity didn't work for them, or if nothing changed, we told them just to say so. We wanted to get at the truth about this business of trying to live as a Christian. And since most of those people did not come from traditions in which public witnessing by lay people was practiced, they didn't have stereotyped forms in which to couch their "testimony."

The first person who came back to speak was a young woman I'll call Ann. She was a pretty Junior Leaguer, had a beautiful family, and was very articulate. When Ann got up in front of the conference, I thought, "This is going to be an interesting experiment."

But I was uneasy. What if she had had a very negative experience? What would the people think, and how would we handle the rest of the conference? I was standing in the back of the room with a very austere and skeptical-looking man who was a very respected Christian businessman and board member of a large theological seminary.

The young woman walked up to the front of the room and said,

"Well, nothing happened." When she said that, my worst fears were actualized. I had scared feelings and very untrusting thoughts like, "Oh no! Why did I ask *her?* Why didn't I make sure she had had a positive experience?"

But Ann went on, "I'm sorry. I wish I could tell you something exciting happened to me because I gave my life to Jesus, but in my case nothing happened."

I said, from the back of the room, "Why don't you just describe your month." (I was desperately reaching for something to do, and stalling for time until I could think of what to say or do next. In my inexperience, I felt sure the conference program was failing.)

Ann's brow furrowed, and then she said something like the following: "Well, I guess my husband and I were having a pretty rough time when I came up here last month. After I made a commitment of my future to Christ, I decided I was going to spend some time just listening to Ben talk about his business, which I haven't been too interested in. So I just started listening to him. And this week we've decided we're going to take a trip together—just the two of us—to play and spend some time without the kids. We haven't done that in a *long* time. I guess maybe you'd say we're getting along a little better in several ways.

"And my kids—you all suggested that we listen to our kids. So I started spending some time with ours, and they're hanging around the house a lot more lately and talking to me." Ann smiled. "I guess we are getting along a little better too.

"And my mother. I've been visiting her this month 'for Christ's sake,' because I couldn't do it for my sake. My mother cried when I went to see her this past week."

Ann thought a moment. "Oh yes. I started inviting my neighbors over for coffee about two weeks ago. Some of them are pretty lonely and I've tried listening to them—though I still haven't had the courage to witness to them about my faith."

She thought for several seconds, then finally shook her head and said a little sadly and very seriously, "I'm sorry, Keith, but I can't say that anything really important has happened in my life since I committed it to God."

I glanced at the businessman standing next to me and there were tears on his cheeks. Here was this wealthy, powerful man standing back there crying. He whispered, "She's just like me. I always felt terrible because my Christian life wasn't exciting. I never got run over by a train or did anything dramatic."

I think many of us don't realize the life-changing power that comes from simply setting out to love people for Christ—even if we don't have exciting feelings. And the right-brain paradox is that this kind of loving can even change social institutions and affect hundreds of lives!

A Widow's Mite

I mentioned earlier that when I was living in Kerrville and attending a small church there, several of us started a sharing group. After we had been together for about a year, we decided that instead of just "loving God and each other," we needed to reach out to other people in the community. We wanted to find out about loving people out in the world the way Jesus did.

We decided to begin by telling each other what we were *already* doing to love people in our community. So we went around the circle, each answering the question, "What are you doing now to help people— besides your family—in this community?"

Most of the people in the group talked about the usual things—the clubs they were in, the P.T.A., the items they were making for the church bazaar, and a few other such activities. Then we came to Jane, a perky little eighty-two-year-old woman with white hair, who was very much involved in what was going on in the group. She'd been a registered nurse all her life, and we'd all been impressed with her frankness and her love for the Lord. She was one of those people who said exactly what she thought.

When her turn came, Jane said, "Well, here's what I've been doing. There's a terrible problem in this town." (Kerrville is a retirement community. There are several large facilities for older people there and many retirees living alone.) Jane continued, "I found out that there is an enormous number of people in this town who are sick and don't have even the medical care of an enema. So I've been going around giving these old people enemas, and making them feel better."

We all tried not to smile and to look spiritual. But then I saw what I was doing, and I stopped and began to listen carefully. This cheery little saint had been going around giving relief to people who never could have found this kind of free help in that community. It wasn't a pleasant job, but she did it because she loved her Lord.

I asked, "Hey, Jane. How did you start nursing people for nothing?"

Jane thought for a few seconds, then she said, "Well, when I was a young nurse, my hair wasn't white—it was red. And I guess I had a pretty fiery temper to go with it. I worked at this big hospital, and poor people used to come in to the emergency room. The hospital would turn many of them away because they couldn't show financial capability. As a Christian this just made me sick. And I finally said, 'I can't stand this, Lord.' So I began stopping the women patients who had been turned away as they left the hospital and saying, 'Why don't you just come over to my house?' "

She had a very small house which she started to fill with cots and beds and sick women. She began to take care of these sick people in the evenings when she was through working at the hospital and on her days off. The women who could get around would help the others until she got home from work.

It wasn't long until Jane had used up what little money she had on her patients. "One day," she continued, "I sat on the front step until the mail came, and I began to cry when I got a thirty-dollar milk bill. I couldn't pay it, and I couldn't figure out any way I was going to be able to pay it. Then I remembered a big Episcopal priest I'd met."

This big priest was a real character, but a very good-hearted man. Jane said she went to see him. She let him know how she had felt the Lord wanted her to feed these people and to help them get well, and then how she had run out of money. Then she told him she just didn't know what to do.

When she'd finished talking, the priest said abruptly, with a twinkle in his eyes, "How come you've got all of those Baptist, Methodist, and Catholic people in your home? Maybe you shouldn't be in the Episcopal church."

He was only pulling her leg, but she retorted, "You shouldn't talk like that! You're not going to run me out of my church. And *you* should help me!"

The big man shrugged, "What do you want me to do?"

She had no idea what to ask him, but she said, "Well, you could start by paying this milk bill!" And he did.

Years later, this priest, whom I knew, became a bishop. He went on to an amazing career of service and influenced hundreds of lives. Many people never knew that the mammoth medical center he spent a great deal of his life promoting—for Baptists, Methodists, and all kinds of people—might never have been built except for the vision he had seen in the simple obedience of a poor little red-headed nurse who was trying to love her Lord and the people around her.

God's kind of specific love can be very powerful.

IV

CONVERSION— BEGINNING THE ADVENTURE WITH GOD

INTRODUCTION

The Problem of Terminology

ONE OF THE DIFFICULTIES we Christians have in trying to communicate our faith to the "outside world" is that unconsciously we tend to speak in such an abstract, "in group" way. After a few weeks as a member of a group of converted Christians, the new convert often picks this up and starts using the phrases and words he or she has heard others in the group use—words that may have little or no meaning to non-Christians.

These "in" religious words were often originated in the cauldron of the pain and joy of real life, but over the years, as life and language have changed, they've gotten separated from that pain and joy. So we wind up with a bunch of strange religious-sounding words which don't smell or taste like today's life at all. In our enthusiasm we don't seem to realize that people outside the Christian community don't *really* understand what we're talking about. And our insensitivity to the fact that our language sounds like super-pious religious jargon makes many people doubt our basic intelligence.

Some years ago, when I was attending a seminary in New Haven, Connecticut, I heard a story about a seminarian who was a very articulate young man—bright, sophisticated, and enthusiastic. As the story went, he'd been a Big Man on Campus at a midwestern university, and when he came to seminary he proceeded to win both academic and political honors. His confidence in himself and in his abilities seemed unlimited.

This young man, like many other seminary students, was often asked to speak in parish churches. Once, about Christmas of his middle year, he was asked to go down to New Canaan, Connecticut, to speak to an affluent, well-educated congregation. The student had been asked to speak on a specific theological subject. He'd never spoken on this

111

subject before, but with great confidence in his communication skills he gathered all the books that he needed on the assigned subject and put them in a suitcase. His plan was to get on the train at New Haven, spread the books out on the seat opposite from his, compose his master-piece of a sermon, then get off the train in New Canaan and preach (a plan which—given the short distance between the two towns—would take a lot of confidence).

He was running late that Sunday morning, but managed to run down the platform and jump on the train just as it was pulling out of the station. But to his surprise, it was a holiday train, packed with people, and he couldn't find a place to sit down. With his suitcase of books clutched to his chest, he began to go from one car to the next in a state of rising panic. At last he came to an empty car. With a huge sigh of relief he sat down, spread his books out, and began to compose his sermon.

In a few moments the porter came through and said, "Pardon me, sir, this car is reserved. We're picking up some people from the mental institution at the next stop and we're taking them down to New York City for a physical Monday morning."

The student looked up with a broad smile and said, "That's all right, porter, I'll take full responsibility. I'm a divinity student."

The porter looked at him, then shook his head and said, "All right." So sure enough, at the next stop a bunch of people got on the almost empty car and began to mill all around this young man. He pulled his books in as the car filled and the people sat down all around him. The last person to get on was a man in a white jacket with a clipboard, who said in a loud clear voice, "All right, everybody, sit down and be quiet." After they all settled down around the student, the man with the clipboard began to count the occupants in the car, pointing his finger at each person. "One, two, three, four, five, six . . ." and he came to the student and stopped, not recognizing him. He said, "Pardon me, who are you, and what are you doing here?"

The young man looked up with a confident smile and said, "Well, I guess you could say I'm a neo-Kierkegaardian existentialist. Actually, I'm an Episcopal theological student from Berkeley Divinity School and I'm preparing an address on the eschatological implications and general efficacy of the redemption as expressed in the atonement."

The man in the white jacket looked at him skeptically for a few seconds, then, pointing his finger directly at the young man, continued: ". . . seven, eight, nine, ten . . ."

Of course, that's an exaggerated story, but it is true that much of our religious language is not comprehensible to "outsiders"—whether the terminology we use is the "neo-Kierkegaardian existentialist" or "Hallelujah, Praise the Lord." It is also true that simple, everyday language can be very effective in communicating the gospel.

My friend Chuck Huffman, an ordained minister, tells a story about his first assignment in a large church after seminary. He was supposed to substitute for a professional speaker before a sizable group of people at the church. He was uneasy because in this group was going to be the eminent New Testament scholar Dr. John Knox, who had been a professor of Chuck's at seminary.

The man for whom Chuck was substituting suggested that he just tell his own story of how he became a Christian. But with three years of top grades in theology in his pocket and with John Knox in the audience, Chuck was terrified. He just knew that telling his story would be ineffective and would appear naïve to Professor Knox. But after much anguish Chuck decided to go ahead and tell his story. After he spoke, Mrs. Knox came up to Chuck and said, "John will tell you later how much your talk meant to him. He can't now, because he was so touched that he's still crying."

The Communication Process

What actually happens in a communication situation is something like this: We speak a word and assume that the listener understands it precisely the way we do. But in fact, he or she hears the word and gives it a peculiar significance related to *his* or *her* past associations with the word. The listener and speaker may assume that the word has the same significance for them both, when in fact they may put *very different* interpretations on what is said because of the different ways they understand it.

Let me give you an example. I'm going to write a math problem below, and as soon as an answer pops into your mind, I want you *very quickly* to say out loud what the answer is.

$$\begin{array}{r} 9 \\ 8 \\ \hline \end{array}$$

What was the first answer that came to you? Seventeen? One? Seventy-two? Now, these answers are *7,200 percent apart,* and which one you chose depended entirely on the *sign* (addition, subtraction, or multiplication) you unconsciously put on the problem—and I originally put *no sign* there at all.

People tend to have this "sign" difficulty with the term, "Christian conversion," which is what we are going to take a look at in this section.

18

How Do We Get Motivated to Love As Christ Loved?

IN THE FIRST THREE SECTIONS of this book, I've suggested that authentic evangelism is the overflow from a way of life, a life of loving and relating to people in a sensitive, vulnerable way while walking intimately with Christ in God's story.

Christians have always felt that the *motivation* to care for people should come as a grateful and natural response to God's love. But it doesn't take a psychological research team to discover that most of us in the average church pew are *not* strongly motivated to love people in a sacrificial way or to pay the price to study and learn about the faith.

What is it then that can jar us churchgoers off dead center with enough force to motivate us into a *lifetime of learning and loving people who aren't necessarily lovable?* How can we be inspired to love and to give of ourselves and our money—which is sometimes hard to do day after day and year after year?

Loving (and especially loving the unlovely) is difficult enough because it goes against our self-centered preoccupation with our own agendas. But the difficulty is often increased by the fact that a lot of people whom we try to love and to help in Christ's name just don't *like* us! What then can motivate us to keep loving in the face of such self-centered inclinations on our part and personal rejection from the people we try to love?

Any Christian education director who's been around a while knows how difficult it is to get people to come out to a new education or evangelism program. People often won't even come and learn what's good for *them,* much less how to love and evangelize *other people.* And yet some Christians spend most of their waking hours actively

115

seeking to learn how to live for God and love other people. What causes this unusual and highly motivated behavior?

The New Testament and the church's history have indicated that there is an identifiable moment when some people change from being self-centered, protective, and fearful to being willing and even eager to go out and risk their lives loving the unlovely. And this change is brought about by an experience called "Christian conversion."

But over the years various groups of Christians have so cheapened or "mechanized" the term *conversion* and its meaning that many people in the church at large have put a very "bad sign" on the notion of conversion and eliminated it from the "thinking" Christian's consideration.

A New Look at Conversion

But I want now to take a new look at conversion, because it is so central and essential in the New Testament and in the church's history. And I believe it is the experience of conversion which provides the motivation to love when feelings of love have departed. But because of all the bad signs that have been put on "conversion," I hope you will try to set aside your preconceptions for a few minutes. Try to read and listen to the following words as if you had never heard about Christian conversion before.

Conversion in the Context of Human Development

Whatever else conversion is, historically it has been a total change of direction for a person's whole life. And if we want to understand how conversion can change the direction of our whole lives, I think it may be helpful to take a look at the way we as individuals may develop a life direction *before* we are confronted with the gospel. How does our natural development as human beings lead us to ask the questions which only the gospel of Jesus Christ can answer?

19

How We Become Afraid to Love and Be Loved

WHAT ARE THE PRESSURES in our lives as children which lead to our growing up with so many secret fears and uncertainties about our own adequacy in certain areas of our lives? Why are so many of us afraid to love vulnerably and to be loved, bewildered by our inability to maintain intimacy and "peaceful progress" toward success, yet longing for these things? No one really knows how we get this way. There are many theories, but equally brilliant people disagree hotly about personality development. I want to give you a brief, storylike right-brain picture of one way we may develop. It's simplistic, and the chronology of the "stages" is not intended to be accurate. But, as I said earlier, that's part of the problem of looking seriously at life; we have to simplify very complex issues in order to "get a handle" on them.

Dr. Paul Tournier, a Christian who is a psychiatrist in Geneva, Switzerland, has helped me profoundly with his pictures of human development. He says we're all on a search for some sort of happiness. From the beginning, a baby seeks pleasure. When we're born, Tournier says, we're natural responders. (If you have had children, you probably already know this.) If babies are not happy, they cry. When their bladders are full, they wet. They express what they feel openly as they respond to life where it touches them.

All babies have certain basic "drives," or needs—for example, the need for food and water and air. But another universal basic necessity is the need to be loved and held. As a matter of fact, some years ago researchers discovered that babies who were deserted by their mothers often would become disoriented, then sicken and die from no apparent cause, even though they were placed in hospitals where they had good nursing care.

The discovery was made that if untrained volunteer surrogate mothers

117

would come in and just hold one of these babies for about an hour a day, the baby would very likely get well. Our need for the touch of love is evidently so great that we will die or be stunted in our development if we do not receive it as a baby from someone—even a stranger.

This theory was tested with monkeys, and it was discovered that baby monkeys would also get disoriented without a mother and would not develop normally. They'd begin to evidence a kind of "crazy" and erratic behavior. And so researchers formed adult monkeys—surrogate mothers—out of chicken wire covered with terry cloth. The baby monkeys would hold on to the chicken wire mothers and begin to become more calm and "rational" in their behavior.

Conflict

As long as a human baby gets his or her needs met and is loved, all is well. But inevitably there will be conflict in a baby's life. I'm going to use as an example a hypothetical little boy named Herkimer. Let's say Herkimer is born into a happy home. Nobody's ever crossed him during the first months of his life. (He's had a very good life.)

One Sunday morning Herkimer's sitting in his high chair getting ready to eat some warm soupy oatmeal. Just at that moment, the minister's wife thoughtfully comes to call, right after church. She's wondering why Herkimer and his mother weren't there. It so happens that Herkimer hadn't been feeling too well, so they didn't go to church. (And with Herkimer, most mothers would have stayed home. Nobody really wants to bring Herkimer to church—even when he's well. He is a very free spirit.)

The minister's wife sits down next to the high chair and tickles Herkimer under his chin. And with a big smile, he says, "Coo, coo."

She says to Herkimer's mother, "Oh, isn't he a *darling!* He's *such* a cute baby!"

And his mother says shyly, "Thank you." She says to Herkimer, "That's a good boy." Then she puts Herkimer's bowl of warm oatmeal down on the high chair tray and gives him a spoonful of it. And with cheeks bulging, Herkimer turns back to the minister's wife and says, "Coo, coo," blowing warm oatmeal all over her Sunday dress.

His mother says, *"No!! No,* Herkimer! *We don't do that!"* Her face is red and very angry. So Herkimer, being a bright little boy, gets the idea right then that he won't get loved either by his mother or the minister's wife by blowing oatmeal. In the next few weeks he tries it once or twice more—with different people—and gets pretty much the same results. And then he realizes that blowing oatmeal is out forever if he wants to have the love he needs so much in life. Out of these experiences Herkimer gets the message that he'll have to *hide* some of his greatest ideas (like blowing oatmeal).

The Beginning of Hiding Our True Feelings

But this presents a problem, since Herkimer doesn't know *how* to hide. None of us do, at first. So, Paul Tournier says, we develop "personages" behind which we can hide. (The little developing consciousness inside us, which we feel is the "real us" and who does our conscious experiencing and reasoning, is called a "person.") We present these "personages," or mask-like minipersonalities, to the different important people or groups in our lives in order to win their love and approval and to hide our sins and fears.

My wife, Andrea, in a book we wrote together called *The Single Experience,* describes a time when she was single that she realized she was living four lives. One life was that of a young executive in a company, wearing Brooks-Brothers-type clothes to help her appear more businesslike. After work and on weekends, she changed out of those clothes and redid her hair to get a kind of swinging-singles look. Then for church she had another set of clothes and a different look. And she had another personality when she wrote to her parents 950 miles away. To them she was still the good little girl who was being nice and working hard.

And in addition to these four there was a person inside who wondered which one of these personages—if any—she really was.

Most of us, it seems, begin early to develop multiple personages in order to get approval from important people and groups in our lives whose values are very different from each other's—and perhaps from our own. In fact, it seems that this is the way everyone's life develops at some stage.

Learning to Hide

But back to Herkimer. He has a big problem to overcome before he can develop his protective personages—and he's got to do this in order to survive.[1] He's never hidden anything before—he doesn't even

---

1. I am not suggesting that protective personages are evil. Healthy people must maintain privacy and relate to people differently in different roles. But the Christian ideal is to relate to each person or group with integrity. For instance, I would not relate the same way to a small daughter as I would to my banker. But I can relate honestly to each.

know yet that he can hide his thoughts and feelings! A child up to a certain age thinks mother and daddy know everything he or she is thinking. After all, when mother says to a child like Herkimer, "Son, you have to potty," she's right every time!

How then *do* we learn to hide our real inner person and those thoughts we think will get us rejected by our parents and the people around us? I believe it works something like this.

Let's say that little Herkimer is older now and is about to go off to nursery school. His mother has trained him carefully. She tells him he can walk down to the far corner by the park, go across the street by the policeman, and go on to school. Or he can cross by the other policeman on the near corner, walk behind the buildings, and go on to school. Either way is okay. She walks him through both routes for three or four days, and then says, "Okay, Herkimer, you're on your own."

So with great pride he heads out of the house on his big morning, secretly trying to look like Clint Eastwood walking coolly past some dangerous criminals. (I'll never forget my first day walking by myself. I swaggered and tried to look very fierce—hoping no one could hear my heart pounding.)

So anyway, Herkimer makes it to school. When he gets home several hours later, his mother says, "Sit down, Herkimer. Which way did you walk to school today?"

Well, he figures she knows all this, and so it's very boring to him to tell her. So he says, sighing, "By the park."

"What did the teacher say?"

So he tells her about "his day." This goes on for about a week, then Herkimer gets sick of it. He wants a little privacy. So he decides to do something he's never done before. He's going to lie. He knows his mother's probably going to clobber him, but he's going to do it anyway.

This particular day he takes the route behind the buildings. When he gets home, his mother asks, as usual, "Herkimer, how'd you go to school today?"

He says, "By the park," and clamps his eyes shut, braced for the worst.

But his mother goes on, "What did the teacher say?"

All of a sudden he realizes—his mother *can't read his mind!* Look at the possibilities! He can keep a secret. Now he can live one *outer* life, which is the life he shows to the world, but he's got a whole *other inner* life where he can safely think all those neat thoughts—

like blowing oatmeal—which would cause him to be rejected. He can even think bad things in Sunday school and nobody will know.

And so he begins to fill this secret place down inside his mind with things everybody tells him he shouldn't talk about or even think about—thoughts which he considers in some way to make up his real person. Learning to keep a secret, then, becomes a major first step in developing into an adult human being on the search for fulfillment in life.

But the next step is a frightening one.

20

Choosing to Reveal Our Secrets— A Scary Step

LEARNING TO KEEP A SECRET is an important step in becoming a distinct individual, but it does *not* make a person able to be intimate and loving. As a matter of fact, being able to keep secrets may make us even more lonely and isolated as individuals, because with our secrets locked inside we can be filled with unacceptable thoughts, feelings, and guilt.

And in some ways when we learn to keep secrets, we feel we can't really receive love any more. For example, I have said to people all my life, "Love me, please, love me." And some did. But I didn't believe them, because I knew they didn't see the real me crouched inside. This real me wondered whether they would love me if they knew my secret "bad thoughts."

Finally, I realized that my only hope to receive love is to let *someone* see me as I really am—unacceptable thoughts and all. Then, if that person said he or she loved me, I *might* believe it. But I was still afraid to be open about my real feelings until a few years ago.

And revealing the inner person can be a dangerous thing for a little kid like Herkimer. For example, one day he's playing out in the yard and finds a little baby doll in the mud. It has one arm and no clothes. Clutching the doll to his chest, Herkimer walks up to the door and knocks on it. His daddy, who plays for the Houston Oilers, comes to the door and sees his son hugging this dolly.

Herkimer says, with a triumphant smile of discovery, "Look, daddy!"

The father looks horrified and disgusted and says too loudly, *"Son, put that dolly down!* Boys don't play with dollies in our family!"

Well, Herkimer, inside his little person, may have one or both of the following reactions. He can think, "Don't ever tell your secrets to your daddy. He won't love you," and he quits telling anything personal to his daddy. The second reaction may be, "This dolly is for little girls. Daddy doesn't want me *ever* to have *anything* to do with girls if he's going to love me." So he may grow up with very ambivalent feelings about women.

When a parent continually tells a child things like this while in an emotional state, why does it sometimes have such a profound effect? Of course, there are many reasons. But let's just put it in perspective. My friend John Bradshaw helped me with this. He said, "Okay, imagine Herkimer is at the door. He's got the baby doll, and when the door opens a seventeen-foot, eight-hundred-pound gorilla says, *"NO!!!"* From the perspective of a three-year-old, that is what an adult looks and sounds like." Our no's are sometimes very impressive to little children—especially if accompanied by obviously loaded emotions. When the little Herkimers in our lives perceive that love is being withdrawn because of a particular interest of theirs, they may then decide never to ask questions about that subject again.

This simply means that each child begins to have whole areas of life which are off-limits for public expression. But dealing with some of these areas is *necessary* if the child is going to grow up into a healthy, integrated person who is able to give and receive love. Subjects like death, sex, and hostility are often buried at an early age in this inner person.

Death is so fearsome to most of us that, after watching adult behavior at just one funeral, a child learns not to ask about that. Yet, as Christians, we adults say, "Oh, we believe that Jesus overcomes death, and that the dead in Christ are alive and happy with him." And then to a child we say, *"Don't* talk to Grandma about dying!"

Normal children wonder about questions having to do with death, sex, and anger all the time. And yet because of the parents' unresolved problems in these areas, children often pick up the taboo signals and don't dare talk about some of the crucial areas of life, because they feel they wouldn't be loved if they did.

Living Other People's Dreams

The search for love and for acceptance is such a major motivating force in human development that from an early age many people twist their whole lives out of shape in order to win love from the caretaking people around them. In striving to win this love, children sometimes deny *their own* feelings and questions about life and try to fulfill their parents' goals. The trouble is that, in trying to live out their parents' dreams, they often bypass God's dreams for their own lives—dreams that would make them happy and productive people.

For an example, let's go back to Herkimer again to see how this might work. Imagine that he's in church. He's four or five now. And when he stands up in the pew, which he often does, he's about as tall as his sitting daddy, who's pretty big. But imagine that Herkimer's sitting quietly between his parents one Sunday. He's already colored the bulletin with his daddy's pen, and he's put that down. Then he stands up in the pew with one hand on his mom's shoulder and the other on his dad's.

Herkimer is bored out of his skull, and he's looking for something to do to liven things up. He knows he'll get hurt if he makes any noise, but sometimes getting attention is worth a little pain. At that moment the preacher makes a very profound point, ending it with the statement, "Thus saith the Lord!" There's a hushed silence in the church. In the middle of that silence, Herkimer says loudly and clearly . . . "*A*men!"

Now he just knows he's really going to get it, because everybody turns around and looks at him. But instead of punishment, some things happen to Herkimer in that instant that have never happened before. His mother smiles and whispers across to his father, "Did you hear what Herkimer said? He said 'Amen.' "

The father whispers, smiling, "*Yes,* I heard it."

People turn around smiling and whisper, "Good boy!" And at that moment . . . a minister is born.

This child who's been desperately seeking love in all kinds of unacceptable ways starts getting love from his family for *doing and saying religious things.* Lots of Christian parents affirm their children this way. "Did you hear him pray?"

"Would you pray for us, Johnny?" And then, "Good boy." He gets a hug or a kiss for a reward.

And at age forty-five this same little boy, now grown and ordained, comes to me for counseling and says in agony, "Good Lord! I wasn't *called* to the ministry, I was *sent*—by my mother."

I hasten to add that I use this analogy because I am a professional in this field. I do not question that most calls to the ministry are valid. But I'm not referring here to ministers only. The same thing applies to bankers, to teachers, to real-estate people, to actors, and to professional athletes. People often give their *lives* to something just to please their mothers and fathers.

I spent fifteen years in the oil exploration business. I worked very hard—even got ulcers, and I did this because I wanted to win my daddy's love. This was true even though he died many years before I finally left the oil business. And I didn't discover what I had done until a few years ago—several years *after* I had left the business.

Some women tell me in counseling that they married the wrong person because their mothers got nervous when they became twenty-three (or twenty-four, or nineteen), or whatever the age limit in your community is. We as "the children" frequently make these unfortunate choices because of the deep needs for love and acceptance which are often driving us through life on a search for a way or a place to satisfy them. By the time we are adults, our "person" inside is filled with rejected thoughts and dreams and feelings, and the rejections came from people whom we loved. Is it any wonder that so many of us have so little inner self-worth, and that we have to buy things with which to "paint" ourselves pretty and successful?

To offset our inner hollowness, we polish our outer personages and present them to each other. And often we feel unloved, unknown, and lonely in the midst of large families, surrounded by material success, and in the midst of the church—maybe especially in the church. On Sunday mornings we smile until our teeth are dry. And then, when our hearts are breaking, we go away from our church meetings feeling isolated and unfulfilled because so often in church we don't talk about much that is real to us in our inner persons. We are deadly afraid that other Christians wouldn't love us if they knew our true thoughts and doubts.

And it can be very threatening to our integrity to have such a large gap between the person we feel we really are inside and the personages we think we have to show to the people around us. So we sometimes develop a way of hiding "unacceptable" thoughts and feelings and desires *even from ourselves.* Psychologists call this very dangerous form of hiding, which can be a cause of mental illness, "repression."

21

Repression and the Person
Dialogue

"REPRESSION" IS A TERM Sigmund Freud first assigned to a particularly baffling habit of the human mind. It means that we block certain very threatening thoughts and feelings from *our own* consciousness so that we aren't even aware of them ourselves. To understand this, let's say that my mind is a circle (see Figure 1, below).

Human Mind

It's about two-thirds full of "liquid darkness." The top third, which represents my conscious mind, is clear; I can "see" the thoughts and experience the feelings which come into it. But the lower two-thirds is my unconscious mind, and I have no conscious access to it, although dreams, fantasies, and costumed thoughts of which I wasn't even aware come up out of it from time to time. It sometimes seems as if these thoughts rise up from "nowhere"; for instance, names I couldn't remember at the right time just "jump up" later into my consciousness. But I am not able to *force* to consciousness thoughts which are stored in the unconscious part of my mind.

Now, the way repression occurs is often something like this. From somewhere outside my consciousness comes a thought that is unacceptable, a thought which would make me feel like a lousy person if I had it. I want to be a good person and to get love from the good people in my life. But here comes this bad thought—a thought so unacceptable that *I* can't even stand to *have* it myself—floating along like a beach ball on the water toward the boundary of my mind (see Figure 2, below).

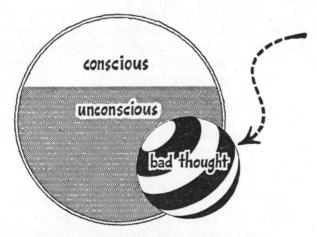

Operation of Repression

Just before it gets to consciousness, *before* I know it's coming (but my mind "knows" the idea is approaching consciousness—that's a right-brain paradox), I push it under the water into the unconscious. It enters my mind, but I never actually "see" it; I am not *conscious* that the thought is a part of my life.

Unacceptable thoughts we repress in this manner might be thoughts and feelings of greed, or sexual lust, or hostility. For instance, all healthy couples have moments of great hostility toward each other. But Christians are often trained that they should never have hate feelings toward anyone—and especially a husband or wife. So we "*repress*" honest hostile feelings and deny we even have them—though they may be obvious to everyone around us.

A man might feel hostile toward his wife, but say to her, when she accuses him of not liking her, "I *do too* like you! What's the matter with you? I didn't mean anything by that. I'm happy!" But if, while he says these things, his teeth are clenched and his hands are in fists, there's little doubt that he's repressing his hostility.

Have you ever tried to push a beach ball down under water? It takes a lot of energy. Similarly, it takes a lot of psychic energy to keep unacceptable "beach ball thoughts" down—out of consciousness. You can't even scratch your nose, much less love people well, when your energy is tied up in repression. So we often feel drained and sapped of energy "for no reason," and very isolated and alone, when we are repressing our true needs or feelings.

Wouldn't it be great if we could learn how to let these thoughts up somehow? Then our "hands" would be free to love. The problems would still be in our lives, but we could move them out of the way like a floating beachball because it wouldn't take so much energy to repress them—to deny them to ourselves.

The Person Dialogue

Paul Tournier suggests that an approach to the pain and loneliness repression brings is what he calls a "person dialogue." If we could have an honest dialogue with somebody who is open and nonjudgmental, then possibly we could feel secure enough to get these unacceptable thoughts and feelings out in the open so they wouldn't cripple us. (Sometimes in counseling it takes months or even years before some people are able to release unconscious material—so they can see it.) When we become aware of our very worst repressed thoughts, we can often see that such thoughts are a natural part of being human and that having them doesn't make us "nasty" or unlovable.[1]

---

1. It's keeping the unacceptable thoughts down, out of our own sight, that cripples us. And what both therapy and confession to God are all about is getting them up and facing them directly. This used to happen in the church. (And still does in churches which have sacramental confession or in which people have learned the secret of genuine Christian intimacy.) But in most congregations we can't risk telling our unacceptable thoughts to anyone, because we feel we wouldn't be considered righteous and would therefore be rejected. And so, we often have to pay seventy-five dollars an hour to find someone we trust enough with whom to have this sort of person dialogue. And unlike confession to a fellow Christian, the secular therapist cannot offer the word of God's forgiveness.

But often when growing up many of us don't find this kind of dialogue with another person. So at an early age we begin to hide the need for love and acceptance and forgiveness, even from ourselves. A little boy might say to himself (little girls sometimes, too), "I don't need anybody. I'll make it on my own. Don't worry about me." One child in the family, if there are several, often says to the parents, in verbal or nonverbal language, "Don't worry about me. I'll take care of myself," while inside he or she is just aching for love—sometimes feeling (correctly or incorrectly) that the parents' attention is focused on another child. And the family, taking the signs of independence at face value, may let that child take care of himself or herself. But the end result is that the child often grows up feeling unloved and rejected.

So Where Do We Wind Up?

So we are born wanting love. And many of us try to earn it by being good or doing what parents want us to. If we don't get as much love as we feel we need—and who does?—we often repress how much we want it until finally we reach the point where we no longer want love *consciously*. But we may continue all sorts of tactics to gain this critical acceptance. For instance, as I suggested earlier, we may try to guess our parents' dreams for us and try to live them out in our lives. On the other hand, we may turn to bad behavior just to get *attention,* as a sort of substitute for the love we can't earn by pleasing someone. Or we may turn away from our parents and turn *to* "full time" achievement in the world, hoping to *win* the love and approval we need by *doing* things. We may decide we're going to win love and approval from the world (or our parents) by making good grades or later by making money. (I wonder how many of you who are reading this book have made good grades, as I have, so that your parents would love you better?)

I switched to achievement early to earn my parents' love when I realized my brother had it without trying. Achievement was more "controllable" in that I could at least pour my life into work and see *some* results. By hard work I could maintain the accomplishment that would generate the approval I needed—or so I believed.

Often, our need for approval is so great that we become workaholics (I did) in our scramble to earn acceptance and approval. Other choices people make when they get to be adults and realize they don't feel loved at a deep level, but can't face it, are to use alcohol, pills, sexual adventures, or divorce to escape looking at their needs.

Some of these people have never heard of God. Others have been raised in the church all their lives—but have never felt loved. But no matter how people seek to escape their feelings, the day often arrives when they become acutely aware of feeling lost and unloved—they realize they are truly miserable. They see that life is going by and they don't know what to do.

Imagine a generation of people like this, hiding behind successful-looking faces with their loneliness, their dreams, fears, guilts, hopes, resentments, frustrations, and anxieties stuffed in the basement of their person where nobody can see them. And the harder they try to find fulfillment, which is supposed to bring feelings of love and acceptance, the more they begin to know that they cannot find such fulfillment on their own.

If one reads the papers, even in times when the economy is good, it soon becomes apparent that a lot of the suicide victims are people who spent their whole lives struggling to get to "the top." But when they got there, there was nobody there and they were alone. These are often the beautiful actresses or the business tycoons. And they commit suicide having in hand the things the rest of us sometimes think would fulfill our lives and make us feel successful and truly accepted. They kill themselves rather than admit they were wrong in their life's search.

Remember how Adam and Eve hid themselves because they couldn't admit they were wrong? That's us. We are hiding now—a nation of hiders, often a church of hiders. But it is difficult, a real ego insult, to admit we've been wrong about the way we're handling our lives. And irrationally, rather than face ourselves and confess our wrong directions, we eat more, drink more, work more, long after these have lost their taste. We run in these and other ways until we reach the brink of destruction or an anxious abyss.

Evidently, as strange as it sounds, it is only when our own personal world is threatened with destruction and meaninglessness that many of us can be open to a radical change in our life's purpose and direction. Only at that point, when we need a whole new purpose and direction for our lives, *does Christian conversion become a live option for many people*. The change called for in one's life is that radical.

Of course, people can be converted without going through the experiences I have just described. But I am painting a right-brain picture of the inner dynamics of the way we human beings keep trying to be God and work out our own salvation. All this is to say that, however

we get there, finally we must know that we need a change of direction
in our lives before conversion becomes a viable option.[2]

Just joining a church, tithing, witnessing, and even becoming an
elder, member of the vestry, or ordained minister is *not* conversion
in the New Testament sense and will not necessarily change the basic
problems of our life—or give us that sense of being loved and accepted
for which we have been searching since childhood.

This is very difficult and threatening to talk about since Christians
have such strong—and differing—opinions concerning what constitutes
the whole matter of "conversion" and "becoming a Christian." So I
want to be perfectly clear. I am *not* saying here that a person cannot
become a first-rate Christian through having been raised in the church
by Christian parents and friends and gone through believer's baptism
or confirmation—even though the actual change in such a person's
life at the time may have been neither dramatic nor even very significant
emotionally.

But in the early New Testament church everyone was a first-genera-
tion Christian. No one had been "raised in Sunday school and church."
And since becoming a Christian was not popular with either the Jews
or the Roman gentiles, *anyone* deciding to follow Jesus Christ *had* to
face a *radical change in the direction* of his or her life. It is that kind
of "becoming a Christian" the New Testament describes. And in the
pages which follow I am going to try to describe Christian conversion
from the perspective of the New Testament church. But again, I am
not claiming that people whose experience is different from that which
I am describing are not Christians.

---

2. One might ask, "Well, if it's helpful to come to the end of your rope to get converted,
doesn't psychotherapy *keep* people from coming to the end of their rope—and so keep
them from conversion?" Although some people have made a case for that point of view,
the facts seem to be that by the time many people get to a therapist they are often so
blocked and filled with repressions that in their fear they are not even in touch with
their guilt and true feelings and thus can't even hear about God. Good psychotherapists
try to help people get in touch with their true feelings of sin and guilt so that they can
deal with them. And since I believe that conversion—responding to the gospel message—
is the best way to deal with our real sin and guilt, good psychotherapy which is not
prejudiced *can* become a great foundation for Christian conversion.

22

Christian Conversion—
What Is It?

SOME PEOPLE THINK Christian conversion was a special phenomenon which only happened to a few people in the early church. Others feel that conversion, when it happens, is a private and individual thing between a person and God that one really shouldn't talk about. Some people can only understand conversion as "walking the aisle" or "going forward" at a Billy Graham crusade or similar-type meeting. And other equally serious Christians think of conversion as the end product of a brain-washing technique!

But throughout the church's history, there have always been large numbers of those who have seen Christian conversion as a miracle of grace from the Holy Spirit. They've seen it as an individual encounter with God which saves a person from the misery, guilt, eternal lostness, and need for love which lies at the heart of the human adventure, an encounter which brings a person into the body of Christ—the church.

Conversion in the New Testament

But let's look at the Bible, because it gives us vivid definitive pictures of the radical change in a person's life which we've come to call Christian conversion. As I mentioned in the foreword to this book, I'm indebted to my friend Angus MacLeod from Christchurch, New Zealand, for some of the ideas about conversion, the church, and evangelism which will show up at places in the rest of this book.

Jesus said, "Except ye be converted, and become as little children, ye shall not enter into the kingdom of heaven" (Matt. 18:3, KJV). Peter said at Pentecost, "Repent ye therefore, and be converted, that your sins may be blotted out" (Acts 3:19, KJV). And Paul talked with excitement about the conversion of the Gentiles (Acts 15:3).

132

The problem is, there's no one Greek word in the New Testament that covers what we call conversion, so it's hard for us to get a handle on it. But the word which is used most often just means "to turn around." For example, in classical Greek the word *conversion* was used to refer to an army commander who, having forces going in one direction, wheels them in a new direction for a different way of attack. Or, say, a grizzly bear who is running away would "convert" if she turns and comes back toward you!

So when Jesus said, "Except ye be converted, and become as little children . . ." he could have said, "Unless you turn your whole lives around, and become as little children, you cannot enter the kingdom of God." (In fact, the RSV translates conversion as "turn" in this passage. See Matt. 18:3.)

The basic root meaning of conversion, then, is to turn or change directions. But in any turning *two* things are involved; a person turns *away* from one thing or direction, and in so doing turns *toward* something else. There are special words in the New Testament for both concepts.

Repentance

The word for turning away from something is *metanoia,* or "repentance." This is a Greek word which meant "afterthought," or "thinking again," or "having second thoughts." And when we have second thoughts, we usually have them with regret or sorrow. So, over the years, repentance came to mean a deep sorrow for sin, or a deep regret for an action, situation, or state we've gotten ourselves into.

It works something like this: we get so disgusted and discouraged with ourselves and the way we are behaving that we reach a point at which the regret and sorrow are so great that we feel we must stop. And when we reach this point and we *turn away* from what we are doing—we repent. For example, a person may be drinking, drinking, drinking for years, ruining his or her life. And all of a sudden a point is reached at which the regret, sorrow, and disgust is great enough that the person is willing to change the direction of his or her whole life and ask for help. This turning is an example of repentance.

Now this is more than a logical, left-brain "decision" to change. Unfortunately we in the church have often made repentance only a kind of intellectual exercise of changing of our minds. But in the Bible, repentance is a *turning of a person's whole life* in a different direction. When Jesus said, "Repent, the kingdom of God is upon you," he was saying, in effect, "Feel the sorrow and regret for the dishonest and harmful way you have lived! This life you're living is not satisfactory! Turn from your old way of coping."

Faith

If repentance is "turning from," the word for "turning toward Christ" can be translated "belief" or "faith." It takes faith to change the direction of our whole lives and follow Christ because, even if the past is awful, it's also familiar. Following Jesus is threatening and scary; we don't know where he may lead us and what our journey with him is going to mean. Because we fear losing control over our lives, it takes faith to turn to Christ.

The Philippian jailer asked Paul, "What must I do to be saved?" He was in the process of turning from his old way of life and he was panicky.

Paul replied, in effect, "Believe in the Lord Jesus Christ and you'll be saved. Turn your life around and put your trust in Jesus, as we have. Put your future, your security, and your family in his hands" (see Acts 16:19–33).

When the gospel is preached anywhere in the New Testament, the response called for is conversion—a radical about-turn, a reorientation of our whole lives. In summary, two things are involved: a turning away from sin or our old life—which is called repentance—and a turning toward God, toward Christ and his family and a new way to live—and that's called faith. My friend Angus MacLeod illuminates this truth with a little equation:

$$\text{Repentance} + \text{Faith} = \text{Conversion}$$

But how is conversion experienced in a person's life?

23

Some Ways Conversion Happens

THERE IS NO SINGLE WAY that conversion takes place. That's another thing that causes difficulty in discussing the subject with other Christians.

Many times a Christian leader assumes his or her own experience is the model for everyone. So this model is held up as the only way conversion is experienced. He or she dogmatically asserts, "This is the way conversion takes place—and therefore the way evangelism is done," and large groups of people may follow his or her lead. But a careful look at the New Testament doesn't seem to support the claim that conversion only happens one way. That's why it is so confusing to a lot of us. Conversion took place in many *different* ways.

One way it happened was at Pentecost. As a result of preaching, hundreds of people were converted and became Christians (Acts 2:14–42). Conversion also happened as a result of individual crises, like that of the Philippian jailer (Acts 16:11–34). Or it happened to people while they were studying the Bible—as in the case of the Ethiopian eunuch (Acts 8:26–39).

MacLeod tells a story about a man who was walking alone in a deserted area of the country. Suddenly he tripped and fell into a deep well. From way down in this well he yelled for help as loudly as he could, but nobody could hear him. Finally exhausted, the man realized he was going to die. So he prayed frantically, "Dear God, please get me out of this."

All of a sudden there was an earthquake, and the man was shot to the surface. He was profoundly grateful. A few months later, the same man was walking through the deserted area again with a friend. When they came to the well, he suddenly shoved his friend into it, so he could have the same experience.

135

You may smile, but a lot of Christians do a similar thing when they try to lead other people into and through a conversion experience. We try to force them into the kingdom through the doorway of our own experience, and we doubt the validity of a person's conversion if it isn't like our own.

But each of us reaches the limits of our own hopes, our own knowledge and ability in different ways—and I believe that most of us have to come to some personal limit before we will repent. Each person thus hears the gospel addressed to his or her own specific anguish or need. So each conversion is a unique encounter with God, because one of the components, the life we are turning *from* (and how we decide to turn) is different from anybody else's. Christ is the same, and conversion is always a gift of grace, but each one is different.

"Sudden" Conversion

Some people think conversion is sudden, like a lightening bolt. But Angus MacLeod insists this is not true. He says even a lightening bolt is not sudden; there has to be a buildup of atmospheric conditions or an electrical charge before lightening will strike.

The classic example of a sudden conversion usually cited is that of Paul. Remember his experience on the Damascus road, when it was as if lightning had struck him? But even that wasn't really sudden! Paul heard a voice saying, "It is dangerous and it turns out badly for you to keep kicking against the goad . . ." (see Acts 9, Amplified). A goad was a stick with a sharp point which was used to prod an ox to get it to move and change directions. The Lord was asking Paul why he fought God's prodding to get him to change the direction of his life.

What were these pricks of the goad? According to one tradition Barnabas was a friend of Paul's before becoming a Christian. Barnabus was converted, sold his land, and gave the money to the church (see Acts 4:37).

Another goad was Paul's teacher, Gamaliel, from Jerusalem's "Harvard." When Paul was persecuting the early church, Gamaliel told him, "Watch it, Paul. Don't put these Christians down too fast, you may be going against God" (my paraphrase—see Acts 5:33–40). And when Paul was holding the coats of the people who stoned Stephen, Stephen looked up as they were trying to crush his head with rocks and said, "Lord, do not hold this sin against them" (Acts 7:60, RSV).

I think Paul's own despair was a goad. He was a good Jew. He did everything right. He was going to earn his right relationship with God himself. And he tried everything he knew, but he was still miserable—his excessive anger and zeal against the Christians were evidence of his fundamental unhappiness.

All these happenings and frustrations were pricks of the goad which prepared Paul for the experience on the Damascus road. There, in a flash of awareness about himself and who he was and who God was, he turned to Jesus and surrendered his life. But it wasn't sudden. There was a lot of preparation.

Evidently it is never sudden. Conversion is not a twenty-minute conversation that leads to a decision for Christ, *even though the last step may be.* No, conversion is a complex process which involves our attempts through our whole lives to win love, to overcome guilt, to succeed, to find meaning, to be religious. One or more of these are apparently involved in the genuine Christian conversion—which will eventually permeate every area of the convert's life.

When we're sick enough of ourselves and our efforts at playing God in our own life situations, then we may be motivated to repent. That's our first step toward conversion. And at that point—when we are ready for a real change of direction—then we may be ready to turn to Christ. We can turn to him as our ultimate security, as our teacher, as the one who wants to give us the love, the freedom and the sense of acceptance and meaning we've spent our whole lives trying to get from someone, somewhere.[1]

---

1. Although this may sound as if we turn and instigate the conversion process, I believe strongly that our "turning" is a response to God's grace, which was focused on our lives long before we were consciously aware of it or could respond to it (see Rom. 5:8). It is also true that some people have been sincere and valid church members for years and have suddenly found themselves facing this radical decision to turn from an old life, an inherited faith, or a faith they never really grasped as a young person and to turn toward Jesus Christ in a whole new way. Many who come forward at large crusades are people like this.

24

The "Experience" of Conversion

WHAT IS THE CONVERSION EXPERIENCE LIKE on the inside of one's life? For one thing, it happens to each person alone. Preachers, evangelists, teachers, witnesses, books, and friends can all tell exciting stories about conversions or commitments to God. And they can inform us about the message Jesus brought. But in the final analysis each person reaches a point when only he or she, alone, can reply to God, even if there are a thousand people present when it happens. And although it's been described in many ways, the experience evidently is an attempt at a specific and total commitment of one's future (and past) to Jesus Christ.

Many ministers and teachers play down the necessity for a specific commitment of this magnitude, because they know that not every prospective (or actual) church member is going to make such a commitment. And that's true. But I'm not talking here about nominal membership in some sort of social or religious club. Rather, I'm talking about a way of living that leads to a new kind of courage which we've got to have to risk loving people, and which we must have to be open and to share our lives. That kind of experience and way of life does not come automatically through "church membership."

A Definite Step

Traditionally among Christians, sacrificial living and loving have come through this reorientation of life in which our whole futures depend on our willingness to risk trusting Jesus Christ. I believe the lack of this commitment is the primary reason the church is often flaccid and dull.

Ministers and church leaders often wonder why lay people are apa-

138

thetic. I believe it's because people who are not converted are not really walking in God's story *as their dominant adventure.* They have other, more important agendas for their lives, for the use of their creative time and their money.

The late Dietrich Bonhoeffer, the German martyr, said flatly that "unless a definite step is commanded, the call vanishes into thin air. And if people imagine that they can follow Jesus without taking this step, they are deluding themselves."[1]

This step is not just a left-brain process of saying yes to a proposition. It's a sense of being grasped, of responding and not instigating. In right-brain, dramatic language, people have said it's like "opening the door of your personal life to Jesus Christ and inviting him in."

Certain "sophisticated Christians" have at times made fun of that image as being naïve and simplistic, but if you look through your right-brain lens, it becomes deeply meaningful. "Opening the door" to our lives, to the place where the real person is, is like inviting God Almighty to come and live with us down inside with all the frightened, guilty, unacceptable feelings of a lifetime, inviting him to touch us and heal us deep within where no other healing touch can reach.

Running from God

But there is a paradox at this point. Almost everyone seems to seek God somewhere, somehow, at some time in their lives. We Christians believe that we're born to seek him and to seek ultimate reality. But paradoxically *we also run from God,* because we are afraid that God's going to judge us, control us, reject us and make us unhappy, as we've felt our parents would if they ever knew what was really inside us. Francis Thompson years ago wrote a marvelous poem called "The Hound of Heaven" in which he depicted his years of running—but also showed how God hounded him, tracked him through his life until he turned and embraced God.

I, too, ran from God for years. I ran in every way you can imagine. Every time he got close, I ran faster. Because I said to myself, "What about *my* agenda? Would I have to be some kind of puppet? Would I have to jump into God's agenda and be 'religious' and pious? What if he didn't want me to live life my way?" That sounds so childish and selfish as I write it, but that's the way I felt. I was so afraid I'd

---

1. Dietrich Bonhoeffer, *The Cost of Discipleship* (New York: The MacMillan Company, 1949), p. 53.

lose my identity if I tried to make a commitment of my life to Jesus Christ.

So I struggled and I ran. I made fun of people who talked about Christian conversion and I put them down. But there finally came a time when I had to stop running—and for me that moment came by the highway in East Texas.

I am convinced that, if a person is going to be converted, there has to be a moment in which this ambivalence about God is settled. I believe you must say, in any way that you can recognize as being true, that you're quitting the fighting and running from God. To do that is to say to him in some way, "I surrender. I want to live with you at the center of my life from now on." A conversion decision is as definite as a decision to marry.

We often make a commitment to God sound spooky, as if it couldn't be definite. Why couldn't it be? It's a real relationship. And one can certainly make definite commitments in a real relationship.

What Are the Proper Words?

What exactly does one say when making a commitment to Christ? There are no rules here. We've made rules as if one has to say this or make that specific faith statement—most of which are not from the Bible. Almost every evangelist has his or her own commitment formula. And the ones who have the largest exposure unconsciously set the tone, so that other people feel they have to make a faith statement the way the evangelists recommend. If someone has not repeated the accepted formula exactly, some Christians are skeptical and may say to the new Christian, "Are you sure you're a Christian?"

I can understand the need to preserve the faith and to strive for doctrinal purity. But at the point of conversion the repentant person is often simply trying to surrender to the God he or she has been running from. Once surrender has taken place, the new Christian will spend a lifetime learning about God and Jesus Christ and learning the various theological statements about the faith. But at the beginning I am convinced the exact words are not nearly as important as the inner act of surrendering to God.

At best we know so little about the way God works that I believe it is a mistake for any of us to try to put our brand of Christian experience on someone else. I certainly don't want to do that (on my best days). And I want to share with you several ways other people have experienced conversion. Here is a paraphrase of one statement of surrender from the life of a nineteenth-century Christian:

Here, Lord Jesus, I abandon myself to You. I've tried everything I could think of to manage myself and to make myself what I thought I ought to be. But I've always failed, and now I give it up to You. I give You permission to take entire possession of me.[2]

Sometimes the response is nonverbal. Some outstanding people have been converted this way. Frederick Buechner says,

Faith is here not so much believing this thing or that about God as it is hearing a voice which says, "Come unto Me." We hear the voice and then we start to go without really knowing what to believe either about the voice or about ourselves. And yet we go. Faith at this point is standing in the darkness, and a hand is there, and we take it.[3]

I'm not saying that what you believe isn't important. But I have never met anybody who, at the point of conversion, really understood much about the theology connected with what was happening to him or her. In fact, the older I get, the more I'm convinced that even the great theologians of the past have realized that they didn't really know all that much about God. And in any case the greatest of these were more interested in *knowing him* than knowing *about* him.

I can't remember any major theologian saying that, at the point of surrender, a technically correct theological statement is the thing that matters most. In whatever halting or beautiful way we can, we surrender to the God we've seen through the gospel, to the Christ we've had a glimpse of in some other Christians' lives. And we take a leap of faith with Christ into the future. The emotional experience following this surrender may constitute a vivid "peak experience" or there may be only a calm realization that one has come home to God. But whatever they are, the feelings connected with this act of surrender constitute what people call the "experience of conversion."

Do You Have to Be Converted to Be a Christian?

Loyal church members have asked me, "Are you saying that you must have the kind of conversion experience you are describing in order to be a *Christian?*" My answer to them is that if someone tells me he or she is a follower of Jesus Christ, I believe him or her—whatever

2. Hanna W. Smith, *The Christian's Secret of a Happy Life* (Old Tappan, N.J.: Fleming H. Revell Company, 1952, first printed 1870), p. 39—my paraphrase.

3. Frederick Buechner, *The Magnificent Defeat* (New York: Seabury Press, 1966), p. 42.

that person's particular experience may have been. I am convinced that I have not been called to sort out the validity of *other people's* relationships to Christ. I believe that God loves people deeply, whether they are converted or not.

But my own experience was that I had been a sincere and baptized church member for years, and had even gone to theological seminary, but I had never been converted in the sense I am describing here. As a matter of fact, I didn't believe in this type of conversion. But when I finally tried to consciously surrender control of my whole life to God on the roadside in East Texas, being a Christian took on a very different meaning for me. Christianity was no longer the "religious department" of my life. Trying to live for God *was* my life. I have failed many times and find I must surrender again and again. But the richness and relative peace in "being a Christian" came to me *after* that first conscious surrender.

So although I don't know what God has in store for people with different experiences who call themselves Christian, I can only say that I believe the inner act of surrendering to him is crucial—whatever the outward words or circumstances may be. That surrender, for me, has led to a much stronger motivation to love Christ and other people both within and outside the church. And through the experience of conversion I received some things I had not previously known about.

25

What Do We "Receive" When We Are Converted?

THE AFTERMATH OF CONVERSION differs greatly in different lives. But the thing "received," in some inexplicable right-brain way, always seems to alleviate the specific needs that were driving the individual through life at the time he or she got converted. Conversion seems to lay to rest some of the inner problems we've each tried so desperately and so unsuccessfully to solve on our own.

With me, the lifelong problem was "not being enough" for my father. Following my own conversion I realized that I was so much more of a man than I thought I was. And yet, realistically, I saw that I was not nearly the "knight in shining armor" I had hoped I would be. But to be able to look at myself, in spite of my imperfections, and to feel that—because of God's forgiveness and grace—"I'm okay," is a very peaceful experience. And I can do that now—some of the time. The desperate need I always had for love from my father—from someone who was above me and who was very important—somehow has been met by God.

Of course, in all honesty, some days now I wake up and am afraid or worried, and on such days I don't feel loved or even worthy of being loved. But as I keep trying to live for Christ, the sense of being loved and accepted has gotten stronger and is a more matter-of-fact part of my life.

The Big Win

Some strong businessmen and professional people have told me, "Listen, this Christian conversion thing is a cop-out; obviously, if you're surrendering, you're *defeated!* How can that lead to wholeness and courage? How can that be of God? It sounds like a loser's way."

But it seems to me that people who talk that way don't take into account the paradoxical nature of the right brain. In that instant when we seem to be surrendering in defeat, we realize at the deepest level in our lives that we have *won* in life. And we've won in the only way possible, because we can stop running from God, stop using all our energy to escape a God who is everywhere.

When I surrendered, I found that I could turn and embrace God, and that I could then turn and begin to embrace life—something I had always been afraid to do. When we have put the outcome of our lives in God's hands, we don't have to hide from people or to be as afraid to risk creative dreaming or loving. We know we're loved and cared for, even if we are rejected by the people we try to love. Subconsciously, in the moment of conversion, the lifelong fear of surrendering is transformed into one of awe and relief.

I saw that God had stood firm for years when I had tried to push him away. And he had done that not so he could make me pious, but so he could love me and help me find the happiness and the work I was supposed to do. It was one of the biggest, most wonderful surprises of my whole life. For years I had not believed that I was ever going to be basically happy. But I am. I had been afraid that, if I surrendered, God was going to make me do religious things that would be dull and endless, and that he would usurp all my creative time. Religious things, especially meetings, bored me to tears. But it has almost been funny to see that the surrender I thought would be stifling has actually freed me and uncovered a creativity I didn't even know I had.

The Nature of the "Conversion-Change" in Attitude

One of the fears of surrendering is that we will have to "give up" things, that with God we won't enjoy spending our money or our time. But here again is a right-brain paradox. And in my experience it's worked something like this.

When I was about fifteen years old, I was a kid who was really tight with a nickel. I took care of my money, and I spent most of my time playing basketball—that was about it. I played different sports in different seasons, but basketball was the main one. All my creative thought and energy were taken up practicing ball handling, faking, and shooting baskets, except for the time I spent studying, reading novels, and occasionally making model airplanes. But I was very selfish with my time and my money. My parents said about me, "That boy has the first nickel we ever gave him."

Then all of a sudden one day I met Lucy, a long-haired brunette with pretty eyes. And something changed. I fell in love. And on Christmas of that year I gave her a cross on a gold chain. It cost me twenty dollars then; it would probably cost about two hundred dollars now! My father—well, I won't tell you exactly what he said, but in effect he said, "My gosh, what's happened to that kid? He's gone crazy!"

I'd leave basketball practice early and go over to this girl's house and just kind of hang around like a puppy. I had plenty of time for her. All of a sudden *my whole life* changed. My parents thought I'd lost my mind, and nobody had told me I had to give Lucy anything or to change my life at all. I changed it because I was in love.

That's something like the way conversion feels. After surrendering to God you change your whole attitude and the focus of your life because you *want* to. You love God and are grateful to him! Our days are already full. God doesn't *take* anything out of our lives. He puts something new in—our awareness and love of him—and *we* decide what goes, what we want to eliminate. Sometimes the changes are not easy and may cost us a lot, but somehow the sacrifices don't really seem like "sacrifices"—because we are filled with love for God.

Being Filled with the Holy Spirit

At this point, when we have believed and surrendered to Christ as Lord, we're open to being filled with the Holy Spirit. The author of the fourth Gospel indicates that if we love Jesus and keep his commandments Jesus will "pray the Father, and he will give you another Counselor, to be with you for ever, even the Spirit of truth, whom the world cannot receive, because it neither sees him nor knows him; you know him, for he dwells with you, and will be in you" (John 14:16–17, RSV).

The church is divided concerning whether one can be filled by the Holy Spirit at conversion or whether this is a "second work of grace" that occurs later. I have known great Christians whose experience is very different regarding what this notion means and when it happens. But I believe God can give his gifts of grace any way he chooses. And it seems to me the important thing is to be open to being the habitation of God's Spirit in whatever form or at whatever time he wants to give it to us.

This is another right-brain concept. The Spirit, the personality of Jesus Christ which is present in the world now, becomes in some sense available to us. This is not rational, of course, but it is the experience of millions of intelligent, committed Christians.

I want to tell you a story that I think illustrates what happens. My friend Howard Butt introduced me to this analogy years ago and it helped me.

I play a little tennis—not much, but a little. I want you to imagine that I've been playing with my friend and pastor, Larry Hall, every Saturday for two years. And every Saturday he's been waxing me regularly, beating me soundly. Then, in some mysterious way, I find that I can receive the tennis ability of John McEnroe. And so I do, but nobody knows it except me, and I look the same on the outside.

So the next Saturday, we're on the court ready to play and ol' Larry's standing there saying to himself, "Oh boy, my patsy is here. I'm going to feel good this afternoon after I've beaten him again." Then he says out loud, "You serve, Miller. It's okay." (Because he knows he can return my serve—right down my throat.)

I just can't wait to serve. So I toss up the ball and hit it, and he doesn't even see it. He looks at me and says to himself, "It *looks* like Keith Miller, but it *serves* like *John McEnroe.*"

It's a fanciful, right-brain story, but the Bible indicates that, with the Holy Spirit in my life, I have the power to love with the effectiveness of Jesus Christ himself (see John 14:12–14). The mind's mine, the body's mine, but the spirit is the Spirit of God—when I have been converted and filled with the Holy Spirit. It's irrational, but that's our potential.[2] And with conversion and the awareness of the Holy Spirit comes a profound sense of gratitude that we have been found, turned around, and have a new inner world in which to live. It *is* like being born again!

The Motivating Power to Learn about Our Faith

As we began this discussion I suggested that conversion brings people a new motivation to love and to learn about their faith. The motivation to love comes from gratitude for having been accepted and rescued by God through conversion. But what about the motivation to *learn about* the faith?

At first, after I tried to surrender my whole future to God, I was elated and felt much peace. But gradually the enormity of what I'd done hit me. I had agreed to do whatever I could determine God wanted

2. There are certain traditional "gifts" the Holy Spirit may give to people, but according to tradition, his presence and power to love and to serve are available to all converted Christians.

me to. That was scary, because I didn't know much about God. And it became very important to me to determine which calls to action were from him and which weren't. Sometimes I was afraid of what God might ask of me. At other times, I wondered if I weren't just asking God to bless what I already wanted to do. And sometimes I got hurt or rejected when I tried to be his person. But I realized that in God's battle against evil and ignorance—my own and other people's—the enemy had real bullets.

Suddenly I found myself hungry to learn about God and to discuss this faith. I was willing and ready to do things I hadn't wanted to do before—such as going to meetings and reading the Bible and other Christian books. Whereas I had previously gotten very little out of the Bible and "Christian speakers," now I couldn't seem to read and hear enough about Christianity. I felt an urgent desire to learn God's Word and will.

I'm going to tell you a story which has helped me clarify why this motivational change regarding our desire to learn may happen, but I'm going to tell it a little backwards from the way it actually was reported to me.

Imagine that a group of tourists is in Italy outside a small town named Navoni. They're on a bus with a tour guide. They stop behind a large hill on the outskirts of the village. It's hot and they are served a refreshing beverage. Then the tour director tells them about this town which they're going to visit.

"This little village," he tells them, "is an ancient town. It has thick high walls running down the edges of many thoroughfares. There are trees growing up over the street—*big*, old trees. There is a cathedral at the end of the main street with slits in the walls out of which villagers used to pour boiling oil on attacking armies who were trying to sack the cathedral."

And after the guide tells the tourists these and more facts about the town, the people are given a questionnaire to determine how much they remembered from the lecture. They recall very little—especially the men—because they know they are going in and are going to have the tour guide with them.

Now, I want to change this situation slightly. Let's say it's during World War II. There is an American infantry force moving across Italy. One particular group of soldiers is supposed to clean out this same small village—which is reported to be full of enemy snipers. On the edge of town behind the hill, the officer in charge tells the American soldiers about the high walls down the streets, and about the big trees in which snipers could hide. He tells them other information, including the fact that those slits in the cathedral walls could hide a machine gun emplacement. And then, after the briefing and before the troops move out, they are given a little test concerning what they remember about the town. And in this case, the soldiers have almost *total recall!*

It seems somehow that we are motivated to learn and remember what we learn when *our whole lives and futures are at risk.* And that is what happens to a Christian when he or she is converted to Jesus Christ. Suddenly the stakes are high and the battle's real. Trying to learn God's will and his Word to us is no longer an option. In a spiritual sense, it's a matter of life and death. And so we are highly motivated to learn.

V

AN OUTPOST OF THE KINGDOM

INTRODUCTION

Real Life Is Stranger
Than Fiction

MY OWN EXPERIENCE OF THE GOSPEL would indicate that life for converted Christians is stranger than fiction. I would never have counted on this being an exciting, absorbing kind of life, an adventure that takes intellectual toughness and doesn't necessarily *feel* religious. And I had never before seen the church as a place where I could find real help with my personal and vocational dreams.

I had always thought that if I really got to be a Christian I would feel "spiritual." But as I read the lives of the saints, the great model leaders in the Bible and in the church, I saw that they don't seem *religious.* They seem *alive* and *happy* and *real,* and they got things done in the real world. The more I read and studied, the more my preconceptions crumbled.

The first time I can remember saying in a meeting that life as a Christian was very different than I'd dreamed it would be, I used that phrase, "stranger than fiction." When I finished speaking, a woman said to me that she knew what I meant. Then she proceeded to tell me this almost unbelievable story.

The previous winter her husband had been out of town for about a week, and had left her alone with their three children—aged two, three, and four. During the first part of the week it had snowed steadily every day. This meant that when the children went outside to play she had to put them in those multizippered snowsuits. She would get two of them in their snowsuits and then one would have to go potty. So, layer by layer, the clothes would come off for the trip to the bathroom, and then would come the struggle to put them all back on again. It was an exhausting, seemingly endless process, and it went on all day, day after day, until she thought she would go out of her mind.

Finally, toward the end of the week, it quit snowing and the sun

151

came out. So she said, "Kids, we're going on an outing! We're going to the Animal Farm!" The Animal Farm was evidently a place in the area where some of the animals wandered freely around. The kids could ride the elephant and could look at and pet the animals.

So she piled all these kids into her red Volkswagen bug, and they drove up the freeway toward the Animal Farm. But when they came through the front gate she could see that every mother in Connecticut had had the same idea—the parking lot was packed. But there was a little paved apron on the pathway which led away from the ranger station, so she pulled her little Volkswagen up and parked there.

Then they went out and had a great time. They wandered all over the farm for hours. Then the mother suddenly looked at her watch, because her husband was due in on a seven o'clock plane and expecting dinner. She said, "Okay, kids, we've had a fun day, but we've got to go home. Come on, hurry! Hurry!" So she herded them all toward the little red Volkswagen. But when she got there, in her words, "the front end of the car was just smushed."

Furious, she stalked up to the ranger station, and banged open the door. But before she could speak, the man at the desk said, "Lady, I'll bet I know who you are. You're the owner of the little red Volkswagen."

She said, "*You bet your boots* I'm the owner of that little red Volkswagen!"

"Don't get excited," he replied, trying not to laugh. "We're going to pay for the damage. Our insurance will pay for it. But you'll never believe what happened."

"Try me," she glowered, hands on her hips.

"Well, Millie, the elephant that takes the kids for rides was trained in the circus to sit on a little red tub. The manager turned his head, still stifling a laugh, as he continued. "When Millie saw your car, she couldn't resist. But we're going to fix it."

So they went out and inspected the damage. The motor, as you know, is located in the rear of a Volkswagen bug, so the car would still run. And apparently the wheel alignment wasn't seriously affected, so she got the kids in and started home.

The unexpected delay had made her really late, and she shot back out on the freeway, buzzing along as fast as she could. All of a sudden she came to a long line of backed-up traffic. Obviously there was a wreck up ahead somewhere. She sat there and sat there, and finally she said to herself, "I don't care what it is; I've got to get home." And she took off around all the cars on the left shoulder.

Right in front by the wreck there were two patrolmen on motorcycles. One was apparently writing down the details of the accident, and the other was directing traffic. He looked up as this little red car zipped by, then ran to his motorcycle and followed her with his siren blaring. When he pulled her over beside the freeway, he came walking up, put his glasses on his forehead, and said, "Look, lady, don't you know it is against the Connecticut law to leave the scene of an accident in which you've been involved?"

She said, "I haven't been involved in any accident."

He raised his eyebrows and looked at the front of her car. "What happened to your car?"

"An elephant sat on it."

He looked at her a few seconds and then reached in his pocket, pulled out a small package, and said, "Here, lady, I'd like for you to breathe into this little balloon."

". . . and that was when I suddenly realized," the lady told me, "that sometimes the truth does sound stranger than fiction!"

I think it's a funny story, but it's also a vivid illustration of the surprising turns real life can take. And that is especially true of living as a converted Christian. The changes that actually took place in my life would have sounded like fiction to me, too—until I experienced them myself.

In this section I want to take a closer look at what that life is like—and especially at how converted Christians live that life *together* in the body of Christ. I want to deal with three questions. One is: *How do we learn to live this strange life in God's story after conversion?* The second is: *How would the church have to change to accommodate itself to converted people looking for this open, creative way of living?* And third: *What would the marks of this kind of congregation be?*

But before we look at those questions in more detail I want to clarify just what I mean when I use the term, "converted Christians." I am aware that in ordinary usage it would not make sense and would be considered redundant. After all, if a person is a Christian, isn't that the same thing as saying he or she is converted? But the facts—which we often seem unwilling to face—are that many people have joined the church and are "Christians in good standing," but they have not repented, turned in a truly decisive way from their old lives, and turned to Christ as the practical Lord of their lives. These Christians have a very different inner experience, orientation, and motivation than those Christians who have been converted and intentionally turned from their former way of living and perceiving to a new life in Christ. I will refer to the latter as "converted Christians," not meaning "better" or "worse" Christians, but Christians who see walking in God's story as the *central purpose* of their lives (more important than the way they make their living, for example).

Not to recognize this difference when talking about the building up of a local congregation is to be naïve and to set ourselves up for bewildering disappointment and disillusionment. Many frustrated parish ministers are baffled when they hear about the vitality and sacrificial living which is apparently going on in a nearby church which outwardly appears to be like the one they are serving. The difference, which is "statistically invisible," is often that the "live" church has a core of converted Christian lay people at its center. Such a group of converted Christians trying to find God's will for their lives will give their time, energy, and money to further the cause of Christ in a way that a group of Christians who have not been converted can scarcely imagine.

26

Where Do We Learn How to Live in God's Story?

I'M CONVINCED THAT being aware of God's presence and trying to discover his will is the secret to beginning to walk in his story. Without this awareness of Presence there seems to be no atmosphere of life in a church, no living "spirit." So I believe that, if we want to stay close to God in our lives, the first thing we've got to figure out is where God's presence "hangs out" in the world today. That will be where his attention is focused, where we are most likely to experience him personally.

Now, people have said to me, "What do you mean 'Where does God hang out?' God is everywhere!" And of course that's true. But in the New Testament Jesus said that he would *meet us* in a couple of specific places or situations.

In the World

First of all, Jesus indicated that he would spend his "work week" basically where there is pain and lostness in the world. He said especially that he would be with the poor, the hungry and sick, the prisoners, and the people who were unwelcome in society—those whom he called strangers (see Matt. 25:31–46).

We in the church are often so self-centered we tend to assume (in our logical, left-brain way) that we *take* Jesus when we go out in the world and meet the poor and hurting people (the implication being that he won't be there unless we go and take him). But the biblical record seems to indicate that Jesus is *already out there* with the people in pain. He said in the twenty-fifth chapter of Matthew that out in the world is where we would *meet* him—in our contacts with the lonely

155

and needy people living on the outer edge of his kingdom, waiting in various ways to be brought in.[1]

In the Church

The second place Jesus indicated that he would meet us was in the church. One way he said it was, "Where two or three are gathered in my name, there am I in the midst of them" (Matt. 18:20, RSV) Certainly, he meets us through the many and varied worship opportunities in the church, but his presence is especially felt in the Eucharist or the Holy Communion service. When he instituted this sacrament, Jesus said, "Do this in remembrance of me" (Luke 22:19, RSV). In his book entitled, *The Shape of the Liturgy,* Dom Gregory Dix said that those words should have been translated, "Do this for the *recalling* of me." In the holy communion we re-call Christ into our midst now. We meet him and offer him our failures, sins, and joys; and we receive his love, forgiveness, and energy to go out again. It is a specific, concrete right-brain way of calling God into our life together again and again, as we walk in his story. And, for me, this "place" of meeting the living Christ regularly is the central aspect of worship.

So if Jesus lives on the front line of God's kingdom in the world, and if he is present in our worship in the church, then the church is like an outpost of love and caring on the frontier of the world's pain and separation. The Church is an *outpost of his kingdom,* a place where converted people walking in his story receive his love.[2] It's where we learn to love and to give away the life we are discovering. And it is from the church that we go out and meet Jesus Christ in the secular world as he roams the edge of pain, the threshold of his kingdom.

Harvey Cox, the writer and theologian, was evidently greatly impressed by Karl Marx Allee, a beautiful street in East Berlin that the communists built as a model of what they said all the world will look like when Communism takes over.

Cox's words reminded my friend Angus MacLeod that the church is also a model for the future—an illustration of future society as *God* has dreamed it. Karl Marx Allee is the description of a new order as the communists understand it, and the *church* is a description of the

---

1. I am indebted to Gordon Cosby for this insight on which he has based much of his ministry at the Church of the Saviour in Washington, D.C.

2. I am indebted to Angus MacLeod for this designation of the church as an "outpost of the kingdom of God."

new order as *Christians* understand it. Anyone can see what God is doing on the human scene if he or she comes into a church. (At least that is what it's meant to be—a model of the kingdom.)

Paul, in Moffatt's translation of the Bible, said "We are a colony of heaven" (Phil. 3:20). Just as the Philippians were proud to be an outpost of Rome, each local church today is an outpost of the kingdom of God, a colony of heaven, where we learn to walk in God's story. And according to the New Testament, God's kingdom will permeate society by means of us. Often this permeation will take place in "invisible" ways that call no attention to ourselves. Two terms Jesus used for this invisible penetration were salt and yeast (leaven), which change things without themselves being seen (Matt. 5:13 and 13:33).[3]

Years ago an old evangelist gave me a right-brain picture of this invisible penetration of the world. He told about a small village in France where there was a perfume factory that made lavender fragrance. At five o'clock in the evening, when the bell would ring and the factory day was over, the workers would all go home. And as they walked down their separate streets, the whole town would be permeated with the scent of lavender.

In much the same way, when the people of God leave the church and go to our work and to our homes, the whole community should be permeated with the kind of love and caring we are absorbing from our life together in the church. The world will be permeated by the scent of love as we move into its streets from our outposts of the kingdom.

---

3. I am aware Jesus also used "visible" metaphors, like light and fire for what Christians are to be, but I am struck by the fact that most Christian permeation of the world will probably *not* be as a result of the highly visible work of us professional writers and evangelists.

27

Marks of an Outpost
of the Kingdom

WHAT ARE THE CHARACTERISTICS of a congregation that is functioning as it was meant to—as an outpost of the kingdom of God? I could name many, but beginning in this chapter and continuing through chapter 29 I want to examine six of the basic characteristics I have found to be present in such a church.[1]

(1) NUCLEUS OF CONVERTED CHRISTIANS

First, in an outpost of the kingdom there is a small group of converted people who want to go on Christ's adventure with their whole lives. There may be only half a dozen, or four or five. But they will be meeting together regularly and, as they meet, they will pray, read the Scriptures, and try to determine God's will for their lives. At first their purpose may well be their own spiritual survival and growth. But they soon discover that they are also learning in a new way to love God, each other, and other people.

(2) OPENNESS AND CONFESSION

A second characteristic of an outpost of the kingdom is an open style of relating, and an opportunity for openness and confession. There are several reasons for this. First, as I mentioned earlier, we can't receive

---

1. I am not suggesting that the approach I am sketching out here is *the only* way to be a church. I am only trying to construct a model from my own study of the vital movements of the Spirit I've seen in the New Testament, church history, and my own experience over the past twenty-seven years in small groups of Christians. I know of many effective and vital congregations in which things are done quite differently. But here I am witnessing to what I've seen and heard which really seems to work.

love personally as long as we are hiding our real selves. So, if the church is to become a place where individuals learn to receive love, we have to discover how (in a sensitive, nonthreatening way) each person can be "seen and heard." We must learn to be open to one another—"unacceptable" feelings as well as hopes and dreams—so that we can each receive the love and cleansing of God through his people.

Because of the traditional Protestant fear of the abuses of Catholic confession at the time of the Reformation, and because of the unfortunate and bizarre examples of lurid public confession in certain kinds of Protestant meetings, many Christians are horrified at the notion of "confession" among Christians in small groups.

But although most Protestants don't seem to be aware of this, neither Luther nor Calvin wanted to give up confession in the church. Both of these great reformers felt it was a useful and necessary practice; they just were against selling absolution and indulgences.[2] And Luther quoted James (which book, I understand, he thought ought to be struck from the Bible): "Confess your sins to one another, and pray for one another, that you may be healed" (James 5:16, RSV). There is a deep healing which can come from confession. And to pray intelligently for each other, it is very helpful to know something of the content of our confessions.

The author of 1 John calls the open style of relating found in an outpost "living in the light":

> This is the message we have heard from him and proclaim to you, that God is light and in him is no darkness at all. If we say we have fellowship with him while we walk in darkness, we lie and do not live according to the truth; but if we walk in the light, as he is in the light, we have fellowship with one another, and the blood of Jesus his Son cleanses us from all sin (1 John 1:5–7, RSV).

A second reason for openness and confession in the group is that if we don't acknowledge our sin to ourselves, and if we don't bring it out and confess it, it is difficult to receive help—even from God. Jesus said to the Pharisees, in effect, "Even God can't help you if you don't know you need a physician. I came to call those who know they are sinners" (Mark 2:17).

Hiding our sins is a little like going to the doctor and saying, "Doctor, I need your help."

---

2. See, for example, Martin Luther, *Luther's Works* (Philadephia: Muhlenburg Press, 1959), vol. 36, p. 86.

And then when the doctor says, "Where do you hurt?" we answer, "I'd rather not say. I don't believe in discussing my pain."

When we call upon God, but don't confess our sins and difficulties, we are saying, "Help me, God, help me! Help me, fellow Christians. But I will not tell you where I really need help." Real confession is difficult because in our pride we want to be adequate, to solve all our problems by ourselves. And we are terrified that we would be rejected if we were really known. But I am deeply convinced that in the kingdom of God we must learn to see and confess who we really are in order to be healed by God and his people. This opens up the way for God to change us and make us new.

A third reason for this kind of open relating is that I believe we can *grow* spiritually only to the extent that we can deal openly with our sins and mistakes. Let's say I'm unknowingly making a harmful mistake in an important relationship, and I persist in doing it again and again and again. The other party is furious, but I don't know what is causing his or her anger. It is obvious, even to me, that a rift has occurred in our relationship, but I don't know what I'm doing to cause it.

Unless I *tell someone* I'm having a problem, there is no way I can get outside help. But if I confide in a group of loving, concerned people (who are aware of *their own* sinfulness and imperfection), chances are I will be amazed at how many of them are having—or have had—the same problem. They are probably going to be able to say something like, "Hey, listen, I really understand what you are saying, and what you are going through is no fun." Or, "When you say you always smile when she says that, I get the feeling you are making fun of her. Is that when she gets mad?" Or, "One of the things I have found is that when I do this [a concrete behavior], the situation changes." Amazing insights come out of groups in which one of the ground rules is to share feelings, insights, and experiences but *not* to *"give advice"* or try to *"straighten people out"* by criticism.

Many people think that only professionals can give this kind of help. But that's simply not true. As a matter of fact, in professionally led therapy groups, much of the help and many of the insights people gain come from the other members of the group who are themselves seeking help. Psychological researchers are now finding that in many cases lay people—when given permission—help just about as well as professionals in certain circumstances.

When the Holy Spirit moves in groups of converted people, things happen. I have seen men and women healed spiritually, emotionally, and physically in ways I would not have believed. The power of a caring, listening ear and God-based common sense in an atmosphere of nonjudgmental love is absolutely amazing.

Don't misunderstand. I am *not* saying that outposts of the kingdom should become psychotherapy groups. Not at all. But I do believe in the power of people really listening to one another, the power of sharing, the power of praying together. Sometimes just confessing and receiving forgiveness in Christ's name can allow a Christian to lay down a lifelong burden and go home healed and free. He or she has let the beach ball in the unconscious bob up to the surface, and is loved anyway. My doctor friends tell me that seventy or eighty percent of the *physical* ills which plague most of us could be cured if we had a nonjudgmental, understanding, and respected "audience" to hear us.

A Different Kind of Leader

Besides the commonly recognized leadership qualifications such as integrity, commitment, intelligence, and a grasp of the essence of the faith, the leader of an outpost group needs to have a special quality in order to be truly effective.

Outpost leaders must be people who understand their own sin and failure and who have the courage to lead in sharing, in confession, and in the receiving of forgiveness. They have a kind of matter-of-factness in dealing with God about what's wrong in their lives. They may agonize over their sins, but they realize that the only cure is repentance, confession, and forgiveness. And they do not feel that they are so special that they must hide their true lives. But by sharing the leader becomes the most vulnerable member in the group.

In the thirteenth chapter of John, when the disciples were at supper, Jesus took off his clothes and put a towel around him. Then he got a bucket of water and began to do the job of the most lowly and vulnerable household slave—he began to wash their feet.

Peter tried to stop him. It was an offense that the leader should make himself "nothing"—totally vulnerable—to serve his followers. It just wasn't done. But Jesus told Peter he would understand later. And after Jesus had finished, he told the disciples: "You call me Teacher and Lord; and you are right, for so I am. If I then, your Lord and Teacher, have washed your feet, you also ought to wash one another's feet. For I have given you an example, that you also should do as I have done to you" (John 13:13–15, RSV).

What would it mean in a small group today for the leader to be the most vulnerable, to serve the members of the group? At least one thing it could mean is that he or she could risk being misunderstood—being considered not leadership material—by being open about those failures and sins which would ordinarily never be known, in order to free the group to find forgiveness and help in overcoming their sins and failures.

In any case, Jesus' vulnerability and willingness to risk in order to free people has confronted me deeply. When I have seen such vulnerable leaders in action—being open about their lives and struggles—I have been convinced that the potential in this type of leadership for freeing others is awesome.

Not everyone will be able to lead in this way. Many leaders will be against this approach, fighting the obvious (and real) dangers and risks of being open. And what sometimes happens in an outpost is that someone who would not ordinarily be thought of as a leader at all becomes the group's leader in this aspect of its life.

Not Competitive Confession

And yet, this is not an attitude of "you show me your sins and I'll show you mine." A lot of groups get into an "easy" confession which can become a kind of exhibitionism or "competitive sinning." But what I am trying to describe instead is the deep understanding on the part of a Christian group that sin and failure are so built into the fabric of life, are so universal, that there is no question that we *all* experience them a lot. We all make a bunch of mistakes, not just a few. And this is not a *radical* view; I believe this is the New Testament view: "*All* have sinned and fall short of the glory of God" (Rom. 3:23, RSV, emphasis mine). Note that Paul doesn't say, "the average person," he says "*all*"!

And the author of 1 John is emphatic when he says,

> If we say we have no sin, we deceive ourselves, and the truth is not in us. If we confess our sins, he is faithful and just, and will forgive our sins and cleanse us from all unrighteousness. [But] if we say we have not sinned, we make him a liar, and his word is not in us.
> My little children, I am writing this to you so that you may not sin; but if any one does sin, we have an advocate with the Father, Jesus Christ the righteous; and he is the expiation for our sins (1 John 1:8–2:2, RSV).

It is interesting that for several hundred years in the early church, public confession of sin at Easter was a requirement before one could even join the fellowship of believers. As the church got more affluent and respectable, this practice was discontinued.

Confession Only in the Family of Converted Sinners

Again, please understand that I am *not* trying to get anyone into an honesty cult. Before people begin to be open in a group, a significant level of trust must be established. That's why I believe such openness *belongs deep within the fellowship of converted Christians,* those who understand *their own* sin. I do not believe the *average* church meeting or small group is the place for this kind of confession in the church. But in this chapter I am talking about a kind of openness which *can be* normative for small groups in an authentic outpost of God's kingdom. (This is a very sensitive issue, and we will discuss later in detail how a group might move toward such freedom.)

Actually, this openness about one's sins has been normative for many individuals in the Christian world for a long time; there have always been people of God who are open about their sins. Paul the apostle saw himself as the chief of sinners. In the seventh chapter of Romans he said, in effect, "I read about covetousness and immediately I wanted to covet and did covet" (see Rom. 7:7–8). And he also said, "I find that the things that I want to do are the things I don't do, and I do the very things I hate" (Rom. 7:15, paraphrased). That is not exactly claiming to be leading the victorious, never daunted, Christian life! [3]

Several years ago I was at a conference in Majorca, Spain. Our group, made up of ministers, medical doctors, psychiatrists, and others in helping roles, had the privilege of hearing a lecture by Dr. Paul Tournier, a psychiatrist who is one of the most sensitive Christians I have ever known. He speaks French and had an interpreter. During a question period an American doctor stood up and asked, "Dr. Tournier, do you know any phony Christian therapists?"

When Dr. Tournier's interpreter had translated the question for him, he responded, "Ah, oui. *C'est moi*" ("It is I"), and waited for the next question.

That is all he said. He didn't even qualify it or try to justify himself. I wanted to say, "Come on, Paul, tell them what you mean," because

---

3. When people use the term the "victorious Christian life," it seems to me that they must mean that the ultimate victories over death and sin are *God's.* But when they claim they personally don't sin, don't have to grapple with sin on a daily basis, or always win when they do battle sin, I have trouble relating that with the experience of Paul or of any of the other great saints of the church.

I knew him to be a scrupulously honest person. But he said only, "I am the one." And in the silence which followed we were awed by his matter-of-fact facing of the truth that he, like all of us, is sometimes not honest.

Churches are to be outposts in the community from which an honest and loving way of living can be shared in the world and in which real sinners will feel welcome. The sad fact is that the people we consider to be real sinners often *don't* feel welcome in our polite but sometimes psychologically closed churches, where no one would dream of confessing a serious sin or an unsolved personal dilemma.

Sin and Failure Part of Every Life

An outpost of the kingdom will be a place where failure and sin are seen not as interruptions to a righteous Christian life, but as *part of the very fabric of every righteous Christian's life.* So, if the first mark of an outpost church is a group of converted Christians meeting together, the second mark is a frank attempt to learn to be open and to confess our sins so that we may become whole.

28

Marks of an Outpost
(Two More)

(3) UNWRAPPING EACH OTHER

The third characteristic of an outpost church is seen in a surprising
way we can help each other toward creative wholeness and freedom.
Of course, there are many ways we can help each other, but I want
to list one particular thing members of the community can do for one
another—a specific act I have found to be truly creative and deeply
healing. One day my dear friend, Bruce Larson, and I were talking
about the story of Lazarus (found in John 11:1–44). And Bruce shared
an insight which was to change my life. He gave me a right-brain
picture of a very important aspect of Christian community.

As the story goes, Jesus received a message that his friend Lazarus
was sick and dying. Now, Lazarus and his sisters, Martha and Mary,
were all three close friends of our Lord. And so, when Lazarus had
become seriously ill, Martha and Mary had sent for Jesus, who was
in the country across the Jordan river. Their message was, "Please
come. Lazarus is dying and you can save him."

But Jesus didn't come. He stayed where he was for several more
days. By the time he did get to Bethany, Lazarus was dead. Martha
and Mary chewed him out a little for being late, saying he could have
saved Lazarus if he had come when they called.

Then Jesus said, "Come on, let's go out to the grave." So they all
went out to the tomb, and Jesus asked that the stone covering the
entrance be rolled back.

Martha said, "No, don't! He'll stink. It's been four days!" But, according to the story, when the entrance to the tomb was uncovered Jesus
shouted, "Lazarus, come out!" Lazarus came out of the grave, and
that is where the story usually ends. I've heard preachers and teachers

say, "You see? Jesus Christ can bring you back to life. Come forward, come out of the grave. You too can find new life."

But, as Bruce continued, I realized that the story *wasn't* over there at all. All Lazarus could do was to mumble through the bindings, "Hallelujah." He was still totally wrapped in graveclothes. And Jesus turned to the people standing by Lazarus and said, *"You* unwrap him!"

I think this is what we can do for each other in an outpost of the kingdom. Many of us have been brought to life spiritually by Jesus Christ through conversion. And yet we are psychologically tied up by the binding graveclothes of our parents' expectations, of society's demands, of the tightly constricting fears of being known and of being ourselves. What we can do in the name of Jesus Christ is to listen and care and help unwrap each other so our true persons can come out, so we can find our God-given vocations and discover who we are.

When I first became a converted Christian I became involved with a small sharing group made up of fellow businessmen. I was in the oil exploration business at the time, although for years I had secretly wanted to be a writer. I had a very foul mouth when I was converted; this was the way I'd heard my father talk in the oil business. So when I became a Christian, I didn't realize how profane I was.

One day when I was in this group, we were sharing some of our experiences with each other. I really wanted to say something to the group, but I felt too shy. Finally, with a stomach full of butterflies, I said, "You know, I'm kind of embarrassed, but I want to read you something I wrote down in my journal." And I cringed a little, but went ahead. I wanted to share my intimate thoughts about our Lord with these men who were my friends on the journey. So I read what I had written, and everyone was quiet.

Finally one of those rough old oil operators looked at me and said thoughtfully, "Good gosh, Keith. If you'd clean up your language, you'd be a hell of a Christian writer!" That is literally what he said. We all laughed as several of the men nodded, and I kind of shrugged it off—but I didn't shrug it off inside. And later I realized that those men unwrapped me and freed me to risk writing. I wrote a book not too long after that, ultimately I left the oil business, and now I am a full-time writer.

In the past few years I've seen a home builder become an artist, a car dealer become a priest, an attorney become a personal counselor. And I've seen other people realize that they *are already in* the place God wants them and that their present work can be their ministry. I could go on and on telling about people who have been unwrapped and freed to become what God made them to be.

(4) FINDING OUR BALCONY PEOPLE

A fourth mark of an outpost of the kingdom is a particular way of looking at the "communion of saints." [1] Imagine again the picture of our mind as being a circle, two-thirds of which is filled with the murky waters of our unconscious (see Figure 3, below).

Freudian psychologists have said that we have "basement people" down in our unconscious (such as our mothers and fathers, living or dead) who are controlling our lives. It's as if their heads and hands are sticking up in our conscious lives, as if we were puppets and they are running our lives without our wanting them to. Now this is rather depressing. But the late Carlyle Marney, Christian pastor, counselor,

---

1. In the Christian tradition to which I belong, the term "saint" refers to those who are committed to Jesus Christ as Lord and Savior. The "communion of saints" is that mystical community of Christians who are still living and those who have already died and are with God. In this view, all of us who are committed to Jesus Christ are "saints."

and theologian, said we Christians have a counteracting image for those introjected basement people. We have "balcony people."

Imagine that the room in which you are now sitting is the inside of your mind, and that over to one side is a balcony filled with people who are cheering for you. They are the people, living and dead, who have inspired you and made you feel you can be more than you are.

Some of the people in my balcony are: Paul the apostle, Andrea, my children, Bruce Larson, Paul Tournier, Elton Trueblood, Gertrude Behanna, Vester Hughes, Larry Hall, and several others, besides the members of the small group of men with whom I meet. These converted Christians in my balcony go with me wherever I go; I "take them with me" in my mind's eye. When I am standing up speaking and I am about to fail or back down in a confrontation and I am scared, they say in my mind (in a chorus, or one at a time), "Don't give up, Keith! Stay with it! You can make it. We know you can!"

Having an awareness of balcony people can also be a great help and comfort when you fail or find yourself alone in a painful personal situation. For instance, when going through a divorce, a death in the family, or some other personal tragedy, it is very helpful to know that our balcony people are "with us." And as they cheer us on and encourage us by the example of their lives, we are never left alone out in the world. We have the communion of saints with us.

The author of Hebrews calls such spiritually encouraging companions from the past and present "a cloud of witnesses" that surrounds us and follows us through history. But whatever they are called, these people who travel with me in my mind add to my life a strength and a courage I would not have dreamed was possible. In fact, I can't imagine how I could have made it through some of the hard times without my balcony people.

29

Marks of an Outpost
(Last Two)

(5) THE SEARCH FOR GOD'S WILL

A fifth characteristic of an outpost of the kingdom is that the Christians in it are trying to learn God's "way of doing things"—and specifically, the direction and actions which are best and fitting for their own lives. Usually this search is called "seeking God's will."

We Christians believe that the biblical drama shows how God chooses to operate in the world. We believe that we can see, in the Bible, patterns for how he wants us to relate to himself, to each other, and to the material world he's given us to tend. But the converted Christian's question is, "How can I find God's will in the *specific* situations in which I find myself *today?*"

Learning God's Will Through Personal Prayer

Personal prayer is perhaps the most common way Christians use to try to determine God's will for their lives. Paul advises the Ephesians to "give yourself wholly to prayer and entreaty; pray on every occasion" (Eph. 6:18, NEB) and he tells the Thessalonians to "pray continually" (1 Thess. 5:7, NEB).

Prayers for God's guidance range from quiet listening and receptivity to frantic entreaties—and such praying is as old as the church. Sometimes the "answer" to a specific prayer seems to be "no" or "wait," but sometimes in various ways Christians through the ages have felt sure that God was talking to them in no uncertain terms, that their answer is "yes—go" and do a certain, specific thing.

For example, when Paul was en route from Greece to Jerusalem, groups of fellow Christians in Tyre and at Caesarea as well as the prophet Agabus from Judea all warned Paul and begged him not to continue his journey. But Paul felt that God had told him to go. He was, he said, "under the constraint of the Spirit" (Acts 20:22, NEB). And so Paul, going against the advice of the Christian fellowship, went where he felt God had told him to go (see Acts 20:6–21:17).

Reading the Bible

One of the most common ways Christians have sought to discover God's will is through reading his "Word" or message in the Bible.

Some people read the Bible by simply opening it anywhere and starting to read, seeing what God may say to them. It is true that some outstanding people have had life-changing experiences doing this.[1] But if you are in the kingdom for life, I recommend reading the history of Israel and the message about the nature and purposes of God as these things unfold in the whole Bible. I use commentaries, atlases, and a concordance for help in understanding the context and the meaning of the content to the writers. The Bethel Bible Series[2] is a terrific way for an outpost group to get the sweep of God's story. You study, yes, but you also learn to "think story."

There are times for reading the Bible *devotionally*—just letting God speak to us as we use our imagination to put ourselves in the story and to see how it relates to our lives today. But there are other times for *hard study* about the content in its historical context. I believe every serious Christian needs *both* kinds of Bible reading—*but they are very different.* Studying is left brain and often doesn't touch the intuitive, decision-making part of our lives. Devotional reading is right brain and can often get the truth in where our inner person lives and can help us make decisions about our behavior and relationships.

Many scholars study the Bible one way professionally, then they read it through the lens of story in their devotion times. By putting

1. Augustine was almost at the end of his rope in his inner struggle when he was in a courtyard of his house. He heard a voice which he took to be a child playing outside. The voice said, "Take up and read." Augustine picked up a New Testament and read where it had fallen open: "Not in rioting and drunkenness, not in chambering and wantonness, not in strife and envying, but put ye on the Lord Jesus Christ, and make not provision for the flesh, in concupiscence." He put down the book and committed his life to God—to become one of the outstanding Christians in the church's history. See Augustine, Bishop of Hippo, *The Confessions of St. Augustine* (New York: E. P. Dutton and Company, 1951, p. 187.

2. For information write the Reverend Harley Swiggum, Bethel Bible Series, P. O. Box 8398, Madison, WI 53708.

yourself into the drama in a noncritical way, you can learn to think right brain. You can learn to think as the Hebrews who wrote the story thought. And in doing that, you can more nearly learn how God operates as Lord of his story in all kinds of situations.

After years of studying and "soaking" in the scriptures this way, as well as studying the content and context, Christians have found that they more nearly "know" God's will, because they more nearly know *him*. And at some point in this journey their unself-conscious decisions begin to be more and more in accordance with God's will.

Learning What God Might Have Us Do in Specific Situations

No one seems to know exactly how God may decide to communicate his will in any given circumstance. Sometimes there is an almost audible sense of a "Voice" saying words. At other times it is more a sense of what is "right for me to do." But new Christians often know so little about God or his story that they don't know what to expect that God might say to them. There is often, however, for the Christian who is willing to stick with it over the years, a growing sense of the way God speaks in prayer.

But some Christians can't understand how this could be. I've heard people who are mostly left-brain-oriented say, "There is no way you can find God's will for specific situations. What is God going to have a television factory worker do, since there weren't any televisions when Jesus was around?"

But I'd like to give you a right-brain way to look at the problem of finding God's will in specific situations. First, think back in your childhood to the time when you were about nine years old. Let's say you are coming home from school one day and you see that one of the kids down the street has left his new pair of roller skates right out on his front steps, where you could pick them up. No one is around, so you look both ways and then grab the skates, slip them under your sweater, and walk home.

Now, having brought the skates home, you hide them under your bed. That night your father finds them and discovers you have stolen them. Do you know what he would do when he discovered that you had stolen the skates? I know *exactly* what my daddy would have done. He would have sent me back with the skates to confess what I'd done and to say I was sorry.

When I have asked this question of groups, a large percentage of the people seem sure they know what their father's reaction would be. I then ask (of those who felt sure they knew what their fathers would do) how many of their fathers are no longer living. Then I always ask those who raise their hands in answer to that question, "How in the world could *you possibly* know what your father's will would be regarding a situation that never even happened during his lifetime?" And yet people are almost sure they *do* know what their father's will would be. How?

Of course, the answer is: We know because we lived with our father for years. We know his will because we know him. We watched him do all kinds of things, and we feel sure that we know what he would do, even in imaginary situations.

Sharing the Adventure with Other Christians

We can learn God's will in a similar way. We learn it as we read his story in the Bible *and* as we live with him in a "family" of other Christians who are also trying to learn about him and his will. If those of you who are reading this book are trying to be committed to God, and if I am trying to be committed to God, and if we are all in touch with him through prayer and worship, then all our experiences will be touched by the Holy Spirit. And over a period of time as we search for his will separately and together and share what we are learning— the failures and successes—we will begin to grasp some things about God's will for our own lives that we could never learn by ourselves. Also, when we think we have been told by God in a prayer time a specific thing to do, we can check with the fellowship and often learn more about what it is we are hearing in our prayer. This is important because many times what we think we hear is, upon reflection, clearly not from God. So one way to learn God's will is through sharing the adventure with other converted Christians.

Resources of Worship

A fourth—and often neglected—way of getting to know God better and becoming more aware of his will for us is through corporate worship—and especially through the sacraments of the church.

It is almost incredible to me to realize how we Christians have failed to take advantage of the rich, life-giving power available to us through the sacraments. For years the services of Baptism and Holy Communion or Eucharist (the two sacraments almost all Christian bodies believe were given to us by God) bored me. They always seemed long and tedious. And many people seem to feel the same way; as a matter of fact, some denominations have moved Baptism outside the main worship service times into a private corner of the week so it won't interrupt the regular worship of the people.

But Baptism, if done in the midst of the congregation's worship, allows *all* Christians present to review and renew their own relationship with God as they say the words of commitment with the new member of Christ's body.

I now see the sacraments as rich, essential parts of each Christian's life. They are special "places" to meet the living Christ. The liturgy tells God's story of the life and death and resurrection of Jesus every week. And when we have strayed from his path it gives us a right-brain way and a "place" to step back into his story and to identify our stories with his.

My own experience has been that when I have done what I can but am still filled with grief or anger over a death or sin, with failure or agony over a broken relationship, I can confess these real feelings and bring them to the altar to leave with God. I sometimes imagine that the communion rail is a conveyor belt which goes directly to God— taking all the things we bring to him as we come into the service. I feel as if he takes these things and washes me in a silver light so that I can start the week clean and new inside.

Then, when I receive the bread and wine, symbolizing the body and blood of our Lord, I imagine that his actual life and spirit are coming into my body and going to the furthest corners of my personality— conscious and unconscious—through my bloodstream.

The sense of power and presence which can come through the experience of the Holy Communion can be a constantly renewing fountain for us individually and corporately. And often people find that as they bring their sins and burdens to God in this service, their minds become clear and they can again hear God's voice and see his will for their lives.

This is such an important and neglected aspect of walking in God's story that I'd like to write a whole book about it. But for now I just want to say that examining and participating in the sacraments *can be* an enormous help to the lives of those in an outpost of the kingdom.

A thousand years before Freud, Eric Erickson, and Daniel Levinson, Christians became aware of certain common crisis points in life. And the church has been given services for many of these experiences—

for birth, for adolescence, marriage, vocation, sickness, and death. We gather together when people are going through these important passages and crises, and support them by offering ourselves and them to God. And yet, in the contemporary church, we seldom use these sacramental services in the supportive way they were intended.

A Road of Boundless Mercy

In these ways, then—by praying, by getting to know the Scriptures, by immersing ourselves in a group that shares and prays, by getting to know the Scriptures, and by participating fully in personal and corporate worship—we can learn God's will about how to grow up, how to live, and how to die creatively. This is a very tough and fascinating course. It is not sissy; it is not soft. Life as a converted disciple of Jesus Christ in an outpost of the kingdom of God deals with real pain— and real joy.

The late Dietrich Bonhoeffer described our search this way: "If we answer the call to discipleship, where will it lead us? What discoveries and partings will it demand? To answer this question we shall have to go to Him, for only He knows the answer. Only Jesus Christ, who bids us follow Him, knows the journey's end. But we do know that it will be a road of boundless mercy. Discipleship means joy." [2]

(6) JOINING CHRIST IN THE WORLD

The sixth mark of an outpost community is that sooner or later the Christians there find themselves being impelled to join Christ in the world. At the time of conversion, Christians are not just freed *from* something painful or constricting in order to feel good (although there is some popular evangelism which implies that). Rather, we are freed *for* something. We are freed to *participate* in God's will as it unfolds in the world, and to share his life and message that we are trying to live out in our own experience. In chapter 34 we'll look at some of the exciting ways outpost groups have found to make a difference for Christ in the world around them.

Actually, everything we may do in an outpost of the kingdom— from praying, to worshiping to witnessing to feeding the poor to helping change the structures of society so that "the least of these" can have

---

2. Dietrich Bonhoeffer, *The Cost of Discipleship* (New York: The Macmillan Company, 1961), p. 32.

a chance—is part of finding and doing God's will in the world. So is each individual's search to find his or her true vocation as a business person, priest, teacher, welder, or homemaker. As we each continue to search, with the fellowship and support of our brothers and sisters, we gradually discover our own particular role in the chapter of the kingdom-drama that is being lived out in our time.

SUMMARY

These, then, are a few of the characteristics I have discovered in churches that are trying to become outpost congregations in the kingdom of God.

(1) First, a few converted people begin meeting together.

(2) Then, as they learn to become more open, they find that they love each other and can pray together about the real issues of their lives.

(3) As the members of the group come to understand each other more deeply, each learns to help unwrap the others so that everyone can find the creative potential God has placed in him or her. And as scary as it is, people almost invariably discover that it's fun and exciting to try to find their creative potential.

(4) With an awareness of their balcony people, the outpost Christians find that they feel less alone and more courageous in their commitment. They discover that their group and their balcony people constitute a Family that transcends ordinary human relationships.

(5) As these things are happening, each person is getting to know God himself more personally through prayer, the Scriptures, the sacraments, and the group's life together. All of the insights and freedom the outpost members are gaining individually help them to begin becoming aware of what it means to know God's will.

(6) Then they invariably move in some way to join Christ in sharing his message of hope and in loving the bruised and broken people around them in the world.

30

Beginning an Outpost Community

HOW WOULD A PERSON begin a tiny outpost of the kingdom if he or she were starting from scratch? Let's say one of you who is reading this book really took this idea seriously. If you are a minister or layperson thinking about starting an outpost group (either a nucleus group within an existing church or a sharing group that may grow into a church), or if you are studying this book as a group, let me offer you some practical suggestions out of my own experience.

First, if you haven't "surrendered" to God and offered him the keys to your future (realizing that you can't commit totally), *do it* before you begin an outpost group. You don't have to be *"totally* committed" (I don't know anyone who is that), but the group's *intention* must be to try to put their futures in God's hands and find his will for their lives. This type of group is for converted people.

Second, if you are the leader, *don't* begin a group unless you want to go on the group's adventure for your *own sake.* If you are a minister, for instance, don't do it as a "good program for the church." In beginning this sort of group, you are forming a family. And I am convinced that you can't do that successfully the first time without being a totally involved participant in the group—in terms of *your own personal inner journey.* Such a commitment may seem a little frightening, but I believe that's what it takes to begin an authentic outpost of the kingdom.[1]

Third, ask yourself if you are willing to learn to be more open about sharing your own life. You are gathering a family of people who want to learn how to be open to God and to each other. And if you are

---

1. After a person has started one group, he or she can help other groups to start, but an outpost leader needs a home in a group, too. He cannot merely flit from one group to another without a group somewhere in which he is a vulnerable member.

not willing to try to be open, the group will probably never get off the ground. Your silence or lack of openness will be taken by some as judgmental—whether it is or not. I have seen church leaders sit in the corner of a group, saying, "I don't want to interrupt the meeting by contributing input," with the result that everybody began editing his or her remarks for the silent person sitting in the corner. In situations like these it is very difficult for any spontaneous honesty to develop.

Even as I write this I realize I am suggesting some pretty threatening standards for a leader. One minister, when asked by one of his members why he was never personal with his people said, "Oh, they'd kill me if they knew me." And I know it's threatening. But after twenty years of being a part of all kinds of groups, I know that a half-hearted leader who is only involved "for the good of the group" will in all likelihood fail to form a healing and creative outpost of the kingdom. I wish it were easier, but in my opinion a failure to realize this cost is one reason there are so few vibrant and healing outpost churches.

If as a group you're willing to learn to share your lives, to repent and confess (so you can stay open), you can become a healing nucleus in the church, a place where God can use you to heal people, so that they can be unwrapped and sent out to live again and to love. It will be like forming a pool of love into which you can dip the people you bring in from the world.

Fourth, commit and be loyal to the new group. If you are a pastor, this may present a problem. What about the rest of the people in your church who are not converted or who think this whole way of being together is not the proper approach to Christian living? Obviously, if you're in that position, you've got to minister to all the people—that is your job. But if you want an authentic outpost group in your church, *you must "go with" the group emotionally and spiritually.* You can keep ministering to the others, but you've got to choose within your own heart whether you are going to give priority support to the outpost group.

One of my best friends, who is a minister, got turned on to the outpost idea. But at first he said, "Well, I'm just going to minister to everybody. I'm not going to choose." And as a result the budding outpost group floundered, because they had no real leadership among the clergy.

Then this minister went to another church. He started an outpost group there, and this time he said, "I am with you." And the whole church grew! He had been afraid that, if he openly stated to anyone the approach to living the faith he was a part of, some of the old-timers (who provided a large part of the church budget) would leave—as they had threatened to do. Well, in his new parish some of the old-timers *did* leave. But he was relaxed and free, and within a few years the giving in that church had almost doubled. People were coming from all over and were being converted and growing in the faith.

I once heard John Powell, who is a writer I really recommend to you, telling a story about the fact that you can't be everything for everybody, that you have got to make choices. He told about some people traveling on a German twin-motored airliner during an overseas flight to England. They were out over the water in rough weather. All of a sudden one motor conked out and the people got kind of nervous. Then the other motor conked out. They were at a pretty high altitude and were coasting down when the loudspeaker came on. A male voice with a thick German accent said, "Ladies and Gentlemen, do not be concerned. Ve have everything under control. Ze motors are out, but ve are going to make a crash landing in ze vater.

"Now vat ve vant you to do is, vhen ve land, all of you who can *svim* line up on ze *right* side of ze plane. Those of you who *cannot svim,* line up on ze *left* side of ze plane. Ven ve land, ve vill open ze door at ze front of ze aircraft. Those of you on ze right side, file out and svim toward doze vhite clifs, und zat will be England. Those of you on ze left size of ze aircraft . . . thank you for flying Lufthansa."

Sometimes there is nothing you can say to people that will make them like what you are telling them.

And this is true when it comes to starting an outpost group. Sometimes (and this is very tough), you've got to make choices about what you think the gospel of Jesus Christ says—choices which will not please everybody. Somehow in our fear of hurting people's feelings, we have (amazingly) forgotten a crucial fact: that the kingdom of God Almighty as represented in the church, was not *intended* to be a social club—like some sort of fraternity or sorority—where we want everybody to be happy and to vote together.

We Christians have a way of living that we believe is a manifestation of *the truth incarnate,* and it is life-changing, but frightening. It breaks through social taboos of not discussing one's problems or admitting failure or sin. And *no one* really knows either how to live the life perfectly *or* how to lead people neatly into being the family of God. The leader and people must learn what *each* outpost will be as they go along together. This is hard for everybody—for leader types (like me) who always feel they have to be in control, for shy people who feel uncomfortable in groups, for people (like most of us) who are afraid of being known.

I would go so far as to say the outpost approach is not for everyone—at least not all the time. God deals with each of us differently and on different schedules. But if you are ready to try this exciting approach to living in God's story with other Christians, know that it will be an uncertain path you'll have to carve out together. Your group may get discouraged or angry, or even dissolve or leave you. But if you are convinced it is the right approach for you, you will find another group and go on . . . and on.

It makes me a little nervous to write all this, because I know from my own experience that I can't give you a "plan" which is guaranteed to work. I know that you will have to begin this journey of walking together in God's story, not knowing where it will lead or what it will demand of you or the people who go with you. But I can promise you an adventure with incredible learning and growth potential—and the possibility of discovering something of what Christian love and sharing the gospel are all about! [2]

---

2. Appendix A is a case history of how I started my first outpost group.

31

The Doorway to Openness—
On Sticky Hinges

THE FEAR of learning how to be open and the misunderstanding of what constitutes creative and healing openness seems to block more outpost groups than anything else. So I'd like to discuss openness here.

Some people have said to me, after hearing my story or hearing me talk about openness, "Listen, there is no way I could be as honest as you are. I just could not start out and be that open about my feelings."

Well, you're not supposed to. In the first groups I started, we certainly were not very open about our feelings—except in a few rare moments.[1] In fact, twenty years ago this would have been a different book; I would have been so afraid of rejection that I could not have risked saying some of the things I am saying.

"Being open" is an attitude, an intention to share real feelings because one believes this is the healthy and renewing way God made us to live. This loving openness is the way he wants us to share our lives as converted brothers and sisters in order to move toward creative wholeness as persons. And it's something that usually develops slowly and hesitantly in an outpost group, as the members of the group get to know and trust each other.

When we share something about our lives and are not rejected, we discover that the thing shared no longer has power over us—and that particular truth is never again as threatening as it was the first time we hesitantly shared it. As time goes on and more things are shared without rejection, a person who is committed to sharing can have greater and greater freedom from the fear that personal experiences might not be safe to talk about. And open people in outpost groups can become more and more able to share their experiences when it would be helpful

---

1. See Appendix A.

to another suffering person. I can testify that, for a closed or insecure male, this freedom to share is a remarkable experience.[2]

Start Slowly

I would advise you, if you are just beginning an outpost group, to start slowly with the business of openness. Don't begin by asking members to blurt out strong negative feelings, current hatreds, crimes, or sex exploits.

That's the kind of thing many people are afraid we concentrate on in these groups. But outpost honesty is about hopes and dreams as well as fear and sin and pain! And the right-brain paradox is that, even when someone does confess a sin or reveal a painful situation, there often follows a great feeling of relief for the person who has made himself or herself vulnerable. Then, sometimes within a few minutes, the whole group will find itself laughing uproariously about something. Paradoxically, confession and openness often bring joy.

(Sometimes people who are new to groups are surprised by the laughter that is often a part of group sharing. But many of them soon realize that seeing the humor in our ridiculous sin and pride is a healing gift from God—a gift that frees us from the tyranny of our own failures.)

If I were beginning an outpost group right now, I might start by saying something true but fairly nonthreatening, such as "I have always been afraid to pray out loud, because I've been afraid my voice will crack." (Which is perfectly true—for years I was reticent to pray out loud for fear I would sound foolish and naïve.) Then I would ask others in the group to share something equally nonthreatening that tells something about them as a person. From there, we would hopefully progress to deeper levels of openness and honesty.

What I have found in twenty years of being involved with small groups is that, strange as it seems, people are not usually as interested in lurid revelations or "big sins" as they are in hopes and dreams and ordinary problems—things we all have. Hearing about those kinds of issues frees other people to share their own hopes and dreams and ordinary problems.

---

2. To remain healthy psychologically one does need an inner area of privacy. And each person must decide the nature and extent of the sharing he or she will do. But with converted Christians, the sharing of sins and pain can lead to receiving the forgiveness and freedom of Christ through the members of his Body. This is liberating—if somewhat threatening—news.

A Door Opener

How does the kind of openness we've been discussing begin in an outpost group? It usually takes someone who will dare to take the first step and to risk being vulnerable.

Let me tell you a story about a woman who was part of a group in which I was involved some years ago. We had been meeting for a while, but somehow had not been able to reach a point where we could talk about the real issues of our lives. (We were all members of the same church, and paradoxically that sometimes makes it more difficult to share real feelings.)

But one night I had discovered a new method. I asked each person to take five minutes to tell anything he or she wanted to about his or her past life. If anyone failed to take the full five minutes and there was any time left (one member of the group served as a timer), then we could ask that person *any* question we wanted to about his or her personal life. And he or she was supposed to answer honestly. Those were the ground rules.

Needless to say, everybody took the full five minutes. And it was really fun. Then we went around the group again, and each person was supposed to tell the happiest experience in his or her life. When we started around this second time, the first woman who had spoken said, "The happiest day of my life was my wedding day." There is nothing wrong with that statement, but the way she said it and then looked at her husband with raised eyebrows gave him only one choice. She had just made her husband an offer he couldn't afford not to follow. So his happiest day, of course, was his wedding, too. And from there on we had the happiest bunch of weddings you ever saw going around that circle.

And I thought, "We've done it again. Here we are, faking it with each other," because I knew that several of the couples had really been miserable in their marriages. I was feeling very frustrated and discouraged, and I was just about to close the group for the evening, when one of the women said, "Wait a minute. I haven't said anything."

She was a shy-looking woman, not quite as well dressed as the other ladies, and she had the air of clutching her clothes close to her at the collar. She'd been so quiet all evening that I had not noticed that she hadn't spoken the last time around.

She said, "You know, I don't really belong in this group. You're all college graduates and I didn't even get through high school. You are all successful socially, and I don't feel that way at all. You talk easily about your childhood, but I had a miserable childhood. I remember one night when I was three years old and I heard my parents arguing. I can still see their angry eyes and twisted faces. Finally my mother shouted at my father, 'You get out of our lives and don't you *ever* come back!'

"That was the last time I ever saw my father. That night I went to bed scared and anxious and cried myself to sleep. I have been scared and anxious when I've gone to bed every night since . . . and I'm thirty years old.

"You were talking about the happiest moment in your lives. Let me tell you about mine. After my daddy left, we didn't have hardly anything—we were really poor. One December night several years later, my little sister and I were coming home late. It was Christmas time, but well, Christmas had become just another day at our house.

"When we got home, we discovered that the front door was locked and all the shades drawn. My mother had the only key, but she had taught us to pry open a window on our long front porch so we could crawl in. So I opened the window and pushed the shade up so I could climb through into the living room.

"Then I just stared. There in the corner of that bare room was a scraggly Christmas tree with lights on it. And underneath, in the soft glow of those lights, were two doll bassinets with live-skin dollies in them. We couldn't imagine where our mother had gotten the money for such gifts." She paused, remembering the scene, and then concluded, "And that was the happiest moment in my life."

We sat there, deeply moved. And then the young woman said, "But I don't belong with you. You have so many things and you are so successful socially." She paused again and looked at us frankly as she said, "I guess I just want what you already have."

Nobody said anything for what seemed like five minutes. In that silence I realized it was *we* who needed what *she* had—the ability to be open about her life so that we could love her (which we did). And her honesty freed the rest of us to begin being open about our own lives.

I am convinced that this is something of what has to happen before authentic outposts can develop into places where real sin and pain can be dealt with. Someone has to begin by being vulnerable first, by sharing something about himself or herself. Vulnerability is the way people have been led into God's kind of love since Jesus first got up on the cross without defending himself.

The Need to Be Sensitive

I can't emphasize enough the need for the members of an outpost group to be gentle and sensitive with each other. This is good to remember especially when we are talking about open sharing, because there is always the possibility, when we are vulnerable to one another, of doing each other harm. Sometimes, when things seem to be going slowly, it's tempting for the leader to try to chide the group or push it toward openness. But if you feel the group is ready to go a little further toward being open, then a better way is for *you* to be open about some specific feeling—even the fact that you are feeling impatient.

Many of us are not used to expressing real and deep feelings unless we are motivated by strong rage or passions. Then, because such feelings have been repressed so long, they sometimes come out too strong and hurt people. Strange as it sounds, many of us have to *learn* how to be honest in a way that isn't harmful. (For most of us this can come from practice in talking openly about less volatile aspects of our lives.)

Bruce Larson tells about a Christian friend who was trying to learn to express hostility. This man had never let his anger show, and he knew it was just eating him up. So he decided the next time he was mad he would express it. One morning he woke up with a grim look on his face and his wife said, "What's the matter?"

The man replied, "I HATE YOU!!!!" (Pause.) "Of course, I hate everybody . . ." (Another pause.) ". . . but if I start loving anybody again, you'll be first."

The best way I've found to avoid the harm that can come from long-repressed feelings emerging too strongly is to begin by having each person be open about *his or her own story.* As time goes on, each person can begin to share needs, problems, sins, and pain. Honesty about *other people's* sins and failings has its place in an outpost community, but only much later, after love and trust have been firmly established.

Another aspect of being sensitive in the group is taking care not to make members feel guilty for *not* being open about something in their lives. I think most people on and off the church rolls feel guilty enough already; they don't need to hear another message of "guilt." With time and love—and with the example of other group members who are willing to be vulnerable—most "closed" members who really care about being part of an outpost community will open up.

(This practice of being sensitive to the needs of others and avoiding laying guilt trips on them also applies later, when you go outside your group to witness or preach. I believe it's important not to make people feel guilty and pressured because they don't want to be converted— most people *won't* want to be! It has helped me to remember that the Hound of heaven will continue to track them, even if they don't respond to me.)

I was speaking to a ministers' group one time, and I had said about what I have written here. When I had finished speaking, one fiery young minister stood up and said strongly, "Listen, I'm not going to worry about what people think! I'm going to witness wherever I am!"

Somebody said, "They'll crucify you, buddy."

And the first man, with what seemed like a rather smug expression, said, "They crucified my Lord, too!" And there was a pause of a few seconds.

But then a white-haired minister over in the corner said, "Yeah, son, but don't forget. They crucified three that day, and *two* of them deserved it." If you are not sensitive to people's feelings and are rejected by them, they may have a point!

32

Some By-Products of Outpost Living

AFTER THE FIRST GROUP in which I was involved had been meeting for about fifteen months, the minister of our church called me and asked, "What are you telling them about tithing?" On my end of the line, where I knew he couldn't see me, I cringed and thought, "Oh, no," because the subject had come up only obliquely as we had talked about Paul's sacrifices in prison. For some reason I suddenly felt guilty, as if I *should* have talked about tithing. But I asked nonchalantly, "Why do you ask?"

He said, "Well, I have checked the records and it's obvious that your whole group is tithing. Not only that, but out of that group we've gotten two Sunday school leaders, three vestrymen, and a president of the church women's organization." As he recited the list, I recalled that we had not talked about leadership responsibility or time stewardship, either, and yet everyone in the group had become involved in the church. And at that moment I discovered a secret about motivation. The things that we have always tried to get people to do in the church by arm-twisting and other kinds of pressure *are natural by-products of living in an outpost of the kingdom!* When people are walking in an exciting, life-changing story, they want to share what they are finding. And they want to give back to God and his work some of that which they have discovered came from him in the first place.

Moving Beyond the Outpost Walls and Joining Christ in the World

Out of a growing outpost group often comes a natural desire to share, a desire to get out in the world and do things to express the love one is receiving. At one point the members of our group decided that we were going to find out how to get out in the world to love people for Christ's sake. So we agreed that the next week, instead of reading our Bibles, we would read the newspaper "through Jesus' eyes." Our assignment was to "find out what is happening in our city which causes you pain to read about. What catches your interest? Which stories or articles tell you something about the pain and lostness in this community?"

Well, the next week one woman named Bebe came back and said, "Hey, you know what? We've got a lot of starving people in this town. And we ought to help feed them."

Everyone looked at the floor. And all we said was, "Let us pray." We didn't even know how to begin to help starving people. We were just a nice little group of fourteen ordinary Christian folks. Finally, out of the embarrassing silence, I said to her, "Bebe, why don't you pray about feeding these people and see if you can come up with a way we might help—we don't seem to have any ideas."

The next week Bebe came back and said, "I've got an idea." She and her husband owned a hunting ranch in our area of the state. In Texas there is a good bit of range where deer and various other kinds of domestic and imported game can be hunted for a daily fee. There were a lot of deer on her husband's ranch.

So Bebe said, "I figure that most hunters shoot deer, tie them over their hoods and take them home. They freeze the meat, and then leave it there so long that it gets freezer burn. The next year they dump the old meat out and go do it again. So if we worked it right, I don't see why we couldn't get a lot of this deer meat and feed the poor with it."

It didn't seem very probable that our group could make a real impact toward feeding the poor, but Bebe was so enthusiastic we decided to give it a try. The women in our group figured out a system. (If you really want creative power, get a bunch of sharp women motivated. They often really understand how to get things done in a community without a lot of cost.)

These women went to a man in our church who owned a locker plant. I don't know exactly what tactics they used—they may have reasoned carefully with the man or just batted their eyes a couple of times and said, "Would you give us free locker space so we can feed the poor?" (I am not suggesting that "batting eyes" is the best approach in such situations, though that may in fact have been what they did in this case.) But whatever approach they took, these women got free locker space.

Next, they agreed to give a butcher the hides and horns if he would agree to grind the meat into hamburger and package it free. Then they told their story to the radio stations and newspapers and they got ads out everywhere. In the hardware stores they put up posters with information about how to donate deer meat to the poor. Now the system was in place—ranchers or hunters could donate their deer and the meat would be processed and stored, ready for distribution.

But then we hit a problem, because we didn't *know* any poor people personally. So we went to the Roman Catholics, because we thought *they* might. They directed us to an outfit called Caritas (who did know the poor). We got them to agree to deliver the meat if we could get it to them. So we introduced the Caritas people to the meat locker folks and hundreds of poor families were fed protein that year who wouldn't have had it otherwise.

Not too long after that I moved to another city. I didn't hear anything more about the project, so I just assumed that it had been dropped. But seven years later I happened to run into the man who was in charge of the whole charities program in that area for the Catholic Church, a priest named Fr. Richard McCabe. I said, "Dick, whatever happened to that deer-meat deal our group started seven years ago?"

He said, "Oh, you wouldn't believe it. It's still going strong. We've given meat to tens of thousands of people, and it hasn't cost a dime."

There is a group of Christians in another city doing a similar thing. They discovered that the grocery stores throw a great deal of good food away every day because by law (and competition) they have to. (The labels have been defaced, the cartons damaged, or vegetables wilted but are not yet really spoiled, etc.) This group has developed a system to gather this food from the stores and distribute it to the poor from a defunct school building they rented. All at very little cost (other than time and effort) they have been able to help hundreds of needy families.

Potential for Healing Society's Problems

As a result of a book I wrote several years ago with Bruce Larson (*The Passionate People*), I have received letters and calls from outpost groups all over America who have started ministries to the poor, the sick, and the elderly; to prisoners and ex-prisoners, to battered children, women trying to get started again after a divorce, and people in many other pressing areas of need. The possibilities are endless—each group will have to go to Christ to find the form and angle for its own ministry.

It can be exciting and gratifying to think and act creatively toward meeting real needs and alleviating suffering.

Having said that, I must add that when outreach projects are going on, they often don't feel either religious or "successful." Most likely there will be frustrations and problems which may tempt everyone to give up and forget about those who are in need. Like other acts of Christian love, outreach to the suffering just doesn't always feel loving!

I personally have never felt at ease dealing with people at the lowest end of the economic totem pole, and so outreach to the very poor has always been difficult for me. I've felt guilty about these uneasy feelings from the beginning of my life as a Christian. But I have discovered that part of my problem is ignorance and the fear of rejection, and knowing this has helped me overcome my uneasiness to a certain extent. But I have also found that there are things I can do for people which are more natural and effective for me than ghetto outreach.

Whatever form it takes, reaching out beyond the group to love other people for Christ's sake is an important part of being an authentic outpost of the kingdom. As I have seen outreach ventures develop out of the concern of loving, growing Christians, I have realized that there is in the church the ready potential to solve many of the problems in this country and around the world. We've got enough power and influence to make immediate local inroads on the suffering that is all around us—if we put our creative energies to it. There is enormous potential in this way of living in God's story with a group of fellow adventurers.

33

The Inner Process Which Makes
the Outpost Work

HOW CAN WE DARE to start an outpost of the kingdom of God, when we know we are vacillating, off-and-on-again creatures, and that we will fail—again and again? The bottom line of why I would even consider risking failure this way is that God has given us an ongoing *process to handle failure and sin.*

The Healing, Revitalizing Process

The process works something like this: First, a person goes out to try to do or be something, anything—it might be a moral effort, a physical effort, any kind of effort. We try, but sooner or later, if we keep growing, we are going to fail and sin. Reinhold Neibuhr said that even though it may not be technically *necessary* that a Christian will sin, it is *inevitable* that each of us will. And since we human beings can always envision in our imaginations *more* than we can accomplish, some failure is built into the fabric of life.

But because of our pride, when we fail or sin, the first thing we generally do is deny it. We blame our failure to be righteous or perfect on somebody else. "It's my wife," "It's that kid," "It's my boss." "So why am I cross? You'd be cross too, if you had my boss [or my wife or my kid]."

Repentance

But pretty soon, if we are converted and committed to trying to live Christ's truth, we get sick of our phony defensiveness, of denying our sin, and we *repent.* We *turn from* that behavior and we confess. "Yes, it is *my* problem. Yes, I've got a bad boss, but I'd be bad too

if somebody were doing to me what I'm doing to him [her]." Then
we *turn to Christ,* just as we did in the beginning. (In fact, this whole
process is like the beginning steps which lead us to conversion.) And
when we confess, he forgives us.

Sometimes we may need to confess before a brother or sister in Christ,
or more formally before a minister, before we can accept God's forgiveness. Sometimes we don't *feel* anything different after confessing, and
must confess and receive God's forgiveness on faith alone. But whether
we can feel it or not at the time, an outpost group can help us know
we are forgiven as they continue to love us.

A Clean Slate

This process produces a miracle. Imagine that there is a blackboard
on the wall of the room where you are reading. It is as if three classes
have written on this blackboard and no one has erased it. That is the
way many of our lives look—cluttered and confused by our sin and
failure. And when Christ forgives us, it is as if he takes a damp cloth
and wipes the cortical slate of our minds clean—like a blackboard.
Then he takes a piece of chalk, hands it to us and says, "Here, *you*
write the next chapter of your life. You are free and the blackboard
is clean." Wow! *The blackboard is clean!*

How many times will he forgive us? The Christian answer here is
really illogical, but is an absolutely essential right-brain truth. In fact,
it is perhaps the *crucial thing to know* about Christianity if one wants
to risk trying to live an open, vulnerable life.

Peter was walking along with our Lord one day. They were talking
about forgiveness, and Peter asked Jesus, "Lord, how often shall my
brother sin against me, and I forgive him? As many as seven times?"
(Matt. 18:21, rsv). (I figure Peter had fouled up six times, somehow,
and was hoping that the number of forgivenesses was going to be seven.)

But Jesus looked at him and said in effect, "No, Peter, seventy times
seven" (v. 22), which is the Hebrew way of saying, "an infinite number
of times."

Wait a minute! Think this over. Really think about it a minute.
My father told me when I was a young businessman, "If a man cheats
you in business, forgive him once; the 'cheating' may have been an
accident or a rare moment of weakness. If he cheats you a second
time but you really like him, talk to him straight about what happened
and forgive him a second time. But if he cheats you three times, *never
have anything to do with him again!* You are a fool if you do." And

at the time I thought my father was being soft and lenient in suggesting *three* chances.

Seventy times seven? Andrew Greeley has said that if a person forgave another person the way Jesus Christ forgives us all, we would say the forgiver was mad. But this "madness" of God is the answer to the basic problem we've been discussing—the fear of risking rejection in being open about our sins with God and other people. We can risk failure and rejection an account of our sins because we can always be forgiven by God and provided with a totally new start when we fail, sin, or make fools out of ourselves.

Does This Mean We Have a "License" to Sin?

People have said to me, "What do you mean, God forgives us again and again? Are you saying that we don't have to try *not* to sin?" No. The right brain paradox is that the very opposite is true. If we love God and are grateful to him, then we want very much to *quit* sinning—we don't like to hurt someone we truly love. So we begin to try harder not to sin. And when we are committed to confessing our sins and to coming to him again as we fail, then the more he forgives us the harder we try to quit sinning. What this continuing process means is that with God's help—and with the help of some of our fellow sinners in an outpost group—we can begin to whip some of the really big sins of our lives *now*.

How Do We Overcome the "Really Big" Sins?

I think there is a great misunderstanding afoot among Christians about how we overcome a really deep-rooted personal problem or sin. Popular folklore—supported by sparkling witnesses—would have us believe that all one does is repent, confess, accept God's forgiveness *once*, and zap!—that particular sin and attendant temptation disappear forever. And of course, sometimes that's evidently the way it happens.

But if they are honest, most Christians will admit that even after conversion and the "gifts of the spirit," sin and failure do not disappear. Most of us (my conviction says *all* of us) find that some temptations come back to plague us over and over. And we may fail again and then again; it may take five or ten years for someone to quit a specific crippling sin. But as I understand the gospel, God is not going to give up. He wants ultimate freedom for each one of us. And it is incredible how long and how faithfully he has stayed with his people. When you hear some Christians' stories, you can almost see the Hound of Heaven continuing to stalk them for years, until they come to themselves and come back to their Father for good.

History has shown that God sometimes wins us back from the edge of the abyss again and again—long after others have given up on us. His way back is tough; it involves repentance, confession, and restitution when possible.

But this continuing process allows us to have real freedom, openness, and strength. For one thing, it is only after we've *been* forgiven a few times that we really learn to forgive others as God forgives. And it works the other way, too. As we attempt to forgive people who have really shafted us, we learn to understand a little about the cost of the grace we have been given by God.

Another thing God's persistent forgiveness does is free us to try some helpful but risky things to help Christ in the world. We can tackle problems at which we know we may not succeed because failing publicly is not going to destroy our egos. As tragic as it sounds, in many churches—as in America generally—*failure* is treated as some sort of *sin*. (That is, we feel guilty when we fail and feel the same sort of emotional worthlessness we feel when we have sinned.) But as Christians, we know that whatever we have done, we can come clean and come back again to God, and he will accept us and give us a new start—and that a group of loving balcony people in our outpost group probably will too.

This has been true in my own experience. In the past, when I sinned or failed at something, my tendency was to get as far away as possible from the people who knew about my failure. For instance, if I failed at a church project, I'd find myself withdrawing from the church. But now, when I am in an outpost group, I am usually able to confess my sin or failure to them almost at once, to ask God and the group for forgiveness, to try to make restitution, and to go back and try again.

How Could God Honestly Do It?

"But how *can* God bear to forgive us again and again if he knows we committed the same sin before—and may very well commit it again?" That's the question I am often asked and one with which I have wrestled in my own life. I want to close this chapter by telling you a story that is going around the Catholic church and that helped me grasp the nature of Christ's kind of forgiveness.

A famous story is told about a bishop of the Roman Catholic church, Bishop Sin. A young nun in his diocese claimed to have had a vision of Jesus. As was the custom when someone said they had experienced such a vision, she was called before the bishop for an interview.

"Sister, did you speak with him?" he asked.

"Yes, I did."

Then after talking to her further, he decided on a test which would indicate whether she had had a real encounter with Jesus. Pointing to himself he said, "All right, if you ever have another vision of our Lord, would you ask him this question: 'What was the bishop's primary sin before he became a bishop?'" (He knew that only God and his confessor would know.) "I'd like for you to come and tell me what he says."

About three months later, the nun made an appointment with the bishop.

When she came in, he asked her, "Sister, did you see our Lord again?"

"Yes sir, I did."

The bishop's expression was suddenly very serious, with just a trace of apprehension, as he said, "Did you ask him, 'What was the bishop's primary sin before he became a bishop?'"

"Yes, I did," she replied.

Hesitantly, he asked, "What did he say?"

The young woman looked up toward the corner of the room, remembering her Lord's face. Then she replied to the bishop, "He said . . . 'I don't remember.'"

There is a sense in which the forgiveness of God is so complete that it is as if we had never sinned before. So he *can* forgive us again, because after forgiveness each sin is a "new one"! Because we have a Lord who loves us this much, some of us just may turn and be converted. And if we do, we can begin to risk failure and rejection as we savor and share his love with him and his people from an outpost of the kingdom of God.

VI

PASSING THE CUP OF FAITH

INTRODUCTION

Some "Bad Press" About the Word
Evangelism

WHEN I FIRST BECAME a Christian, the word *evangelism* really turned me off. I came from a tradition in which evangelistic efforts were considered to be meddling in other people's lives—and this was considered poor taste and a valid cause for personal rejection.

Then I made a commitment and met some long-time converted Christians. And they all seemed to talk about the importance, the *essential nature,* of evangelism in the life of the church. However, as I met people who had regular evangelistic programs in their churches, some of them admitted that it was hard to detect much *long-range* change or growth resulting from the usual annual evangelistic efforts.

The only ones who appeared to me to be succeeding in reaching people through evangelistic efforts actually operated outside the established churches. To a newcomer reading the New Testament, this seemed almost like a contradiction in terms. And in any case the churches or the evangelists which did bring people in didn't appear to be doing much with them in terms of helping them be healed and become mature in the faith. And instead of addressing this issue, everyone I talked to seemed to be looking for a "new evangelistic program" which might "work."

The whole subject seemed pretty discouraging. Half the church appeared to have dismissed evangelism as not being a valid enterprise. The other half seemed to believe in evangelism but admitted privately that what was happening in their churches was ineffective and short-lived. And it was hard to find *anyone* who really enjoyed taking the time and effort to engage in evangelism personally.

Evangelism isn't a turn-off word for me any more (that's one reason I'm writing this book). In fact, I'm convinced that evangelism is a very important aspect of being involved in an outpost of the kingdom.

But I think if we're going to talk about "evangelizing the world" with any sense of reality, we in the church had better understand clearly the extent to which a lot of people outside *and inside* the church still have very negative feelings about the word *evangelism.*

Why Should We Care?[1]

I think anyone who takes the New Testament seriously as a source book regarding Christian living has got to ask, "How does authentic evangelism take place?" and "What's supposed to happen to people after we evangelize them?" Christians must ask this because in the New Testament story, it seems very clear that everyone who was a Christian shared the faith. The people who were converted as a result of that sharing were taken *into* the church and nurtured (see Acts 2:43–47), with the result that the church grew and blossomed incredibly.

But as far as I can determine from studying the New Testament, "evangelistic programs" *as we know them today* were never heard of. People often cite the multitudes Jesus spoke to as clear examples of "evangelistic mass meetings" like the modern ones. But that simply is not accurate. Anyone who is familiar with contemporary mass evangelism knows the enormous effort and expense and the intricately organized advance planning it takes to go out and get the audiences who fill the stands. Months ahead of time, in the area where the meetings are to be held, dozens of churches commit to bring so many busloads of members (if necessary) to fill an agreed-upon number of seats so the meeting place will be filled.

I'm not saying that there is anything wrong with this approach. But that just wasn't the way things worked in the New Testament. The people *chased* Jesus down and *followed him and his friends* around. They asked questions and watched the healing changes in people's lives. As I suggested earlier, it was as if there was a beautiful aroma or scent which followed the little bunch of Christians around Palestine as they lived together with Jesus. And it was evidently this scent of love which brought the people out by the thousands. It was something about the way they lived together, as well as the message, which brought out the people. And it wasn't just the unique charismatic speaking

---

1. The author of Luke records Jesus' saying to the disciples "Thus it is written, that the Christ should suffer and on the third day rise from the dead, and that repentance and forgiveness of sins should be preached in his name to all nations, beginning from Jerusalem" (Luke 24:46–47, RSV). So Christ's injunction should be enough to make us care—but so far it hasn't usually done the job.

ability of Jesus which brought out the crowds, because they *kept coming out* to hear Peter and the apostles after the crucifixion and ascension.

And when people heard about the kingdom, they wanted to be *a part of its loving family*—even if it might cost them their friends, families, or even their lives.

As I see it, the "success" we often struggle so hard for in our evangelistic efforts today was the *natural by-product* of the way the early Christians lived. They had strategies—which we'll discuss in later chapters. But they were passionate to tell what they'd seen and heard. Unlike many of us who strain to make evangelism happen, the *focus of their whole lives* was on the Kingdom they were announcing and on living out the healing adventure of God's story in their life together with Christ.

A good many years ago, an outstanding surgeon got converted at Laity Lodge. As I recall, we'd been talking about a "successful program." He said, "I'm beginning to understand the problem with the church's usual programs of evangelism." Then he went on to tell about his experiences as a physician who supervised younger doctors and interns. It seems that one time he was in charge of a bunch of sharp young interns, one of whom was a very brilliant and competitive person who wanted to get his hands on the toughest cases he could find.

A really sick man checked into the hospital one day. His temperature was up, his blood count was down, his fluids were out of balance, and he was generally in very bad shape. This young doctor said, "I'll take him." And so the patient was assigned to this young intern—under supervision, of course.

He started working on the sick man, and sure enough, he got his temperature down, his fluids in balance, and his blood count up. Everything was going very well. Then all of a sudden, inexplicably, the patient died.

The supervising physician was walking down the hall and came to the room where this patient had died. The intern was just covering the patient, and it was obvious from the expression on the young doctor's face that he was furious. As the supervisor watched, unobserved from the hall, he saw the young doctor start to stalk out of the room, then stop and look around at the chart, which was kept on the foot of the bed. He stepped back and picked up the chart, took a pen out of his pocket, and scrawled something across it. Then he stormed angrily out past the supervisor without even speaking.

The older physician said he just couldn't resist going in to see what the young man had written on the chart. It said, "This patient was in better condition when he died than when he first came to me."

When he finished the story, the old doctor looked at us and said, "I think it's time we quit congratulating each other on what a good evangelistic program we've had, and ask the question, 'Are any of the patients still living?' "

I would like, in the final section of this book, to look at Christian evangelism in the light of that question. Specifically, I want to discuss three things. First, *what did Christians in the early church do to evangelize? And why was their evangelism effective?* Second, *how would we structure a church that could really evangelize a community on a continuing, year-round basis?* I want to suggest a possible model for such a church today. And third, *how could one person help another to be converted?* If you have a friend or someone in your family to whom you'd like to talk about getting converted, how could you do it?

First, what did evangelism mean to the Christians in the early church?

34

Evangelism in the
New Testament Church

IN THE NEW TESTAMENT, the word used for "evangelize" simply means "announce good news." For example, if I said to you, "I've been at a meeting with the chairmen of the banks in Houston, and they've decided to lend to those of you who are Houston residents, for a twenty-four hour period, all the money you want up to $500,000 per customer at 3 percent interest for five years," that would be evangelizing you. That would be announcing some good news.

Evangelism is a simple idea. During New Testament times, the people had no radios or televisions, but they did have heralds on the street corner. And these heralds would, in effect, yell out the five o'clock news: "Hey! This is what happened in the wars in Poland. Listen to this! The emperor's coronation is going to be next Tuesday at ten o'clock in Rome—and his wife's getting over the measles, by the way." (News commentators couldn't have changed that much.) These sorts of announcements by heralds were a part of everyday life in the Roman empire.

So think of Jesus in Galilee as a herald announcing some Good News to the people. And it was news for which they had been waiting a long time. For hundreds of years, as I've suggested, the prophetic voices among the Hebrews had been saying, in effect, "There will come a day when God will step onto the stage of history with the other current events and will be in charge of things as a king. He will bring about honesty, openness, and fairness [which they called justice], and the freedom [which they called peace] to live without the fear of being ground under from the outside or torn up inside by guilt."

Having been a politically controlled nation off and on for hundreds of years, the people had held very deep in their hearts the hope that God would send his King. His coming would really mean a change

201

in their lives. Imagine if the people in Poland today had hopes that a loving ruler would come and free them from their oppressors. Now, by comparison they've just been under outside rule for an instant in time. But imagine if they had had *hundreds of years* of this expectation and yearning for one who would come to free them. The excitement of their anticipation would be high!

This was true of the Jews at the time of Jesus. Jewish tradition said that the coming herald or news announcer would be a man designated and marked by God for this important role. In the Old Testament, someone who had been designated by God for a specific job or task was anointed with a little oil (poured on his or her head by a priest). The Hebrew word for one who had been so marked or "anointed" was *Messiah,* which literally means "anointed one." The Greek translation of that Hebrew word was *Christ.* In other words, the people of that time were looking for a Christ, a herald annointed by God, to come from him and announce a message to all the world.

That was what Jesus was, and the Good News he brought was that the kingdom of God had come. Somehow, at long last, God was near and approachable again, as he had been in the Garden of Eden. Suddenly God's children were to have permission and power to live as free people.

How Did Evangelism Happen?

Here's a little right-brain scenario about how that first bit of evangelism got started. Imagine John the Baptist coming out on herald's corner one day and shouting, "Hey, look out, he's coming! He's coming, everybody! And there's good news and there's bad news. The good news is that he wants to love you and free you, and it's going to be a fantastic time in the kingdom. The bad news is he's *very* upset. He's upset at our playing church and at the way we've been dishonest with each other and with him."

And the people were excited at this announcement—Luke says they were on tiptoe with expectation. Next, imagine Jesus coming out on herald's corner at the five-o'clock-news time on Saturday. (Actually, he came out as a lay reader in the local synagogue.) He looks around at the crowd, and reads something out of Isaiah.

Then he says, "Listen, today, right now in front of you, the kingdom you've been looking for which will straighten out the world's basic problem is here. The age of God has arrived. The hope that's been in your hearts is now a reality. You don't have to look for it through a telescope any more. Just open your eyes; it's here! And *I'm the one* who's bringing in this new program for the world!" (see story in Luke 4:16–30).

It's pretty hard to imagine how that announcement sounded to the people who heard it. But you're going to find out, because I have a similar announcement for you now: "The reason I've put this book together is that I've got some good news—news you've been waiting years to hear. I, Keith Miller, am the second coming of Christ. I'm deadly serious about this. And I'm going to tell you in the remaining pages of this book what I would like for you to do."

How do you feel about me now that I've told you this? Angry? Offended? Shocked? Irritated? Of course, I'm *not* serious about this. But just imagine, what if I *had* been? It would explode your mind! No wonder they were astonished when Jesus stood up and made his announcement! From a left-brain perspective, I would seem to have more background to be the Second Coming of Christ than Jesus did *when he* announced that he was the first coming. He was a carpenter from Nazareth. And he'd never even led a religious meeting or written a book (see the story in Luke 4:14–22).

Can you feel in your stomach what they must have felt—the anger, the disbelief? What he said really blew their minds; they took Him out of that meeting where he was speaking and tried to throw him over a cliff. And that's how the first Christian evangelism went over.

During the next three years, Jesus evangelized or announced the Good News in an unusual manner—a way that "rang true" in a right-brain way. He not only talked about it; he *lived out examples of it* with his disciples everywhere he went. He healed the emotional and physical ills and the brokenness of the people. He fed the hungry, was loving and intimate with people, and he prayed to the Father with them in a very personal way.

Actually, he spent most of his time with a very small group of men and women who tried to live the life of the kingdom. And people were drawn to this small group from all over by the quality of that life. The love they were experiencing overflowed into the streets and highways of Palestine. And the almost irresistible aroma of that love attracted broken people who were trapped in their lives—as many of us have been trapped—and who came and found hope.

Three years later, when Jesus died in agony, it was hard for his followers to believe that God's kingdom had really arrived. For two days they were near despair and felt they had made a terrible mistake. But as I've suggested, Jesus' return from the dead on that first Easter

Sunday was like God's personal endorsement stamped across the bottom of his life. Only God could have brought Jesus back from death. Now they knew the Good News was true!

Gradually, it dawned on them that they had misunderstood the kingdom, or the reign of God (they'd been left-braining it). The "kingdom" was going to be *inside* them and in their fellowship. The Greek word, *basilea,* translated as "kingdom" does not refer to a geographical area. It more nearly means "rule" or "reign." The soil of the kingdom was wherever God *reigned in people's hearts.* And gradually the followers of Jesus saw in amazement that the day of liberation and salvation had come, on a grander and more universal scale than they could have imagined.

Men, women, black, white, rich, poor, Romans, Jews, could all become members of a *family,* the family of God. They'd be brothers and sisters, given to each other to love. And Jesus was not only the news commentator or the evangelist. He himself was the *King*—or the Crown Prince—of this surprising inner kingdom or family of God!

But as Angus MacLeod reminded me, the Good News was not just for individuals—and I forget that sometimes. The good news was a force for the renewal of *all of society,* a leaven, a ferment for change!

So evangelism in the New Testament meant sharing Jesus' announcement of the Good News that the kingdom or reign of God had come, and that the King was more like a loving father than a harsh despotic oriental ruler. Evangelism was not just a program or a theological statement; it was the living account, the story of Jesus as he lived out God's message through concrete acts and words of love. And it was news not only for individuals, but also for all of society.

This Good News called for conversion, a turning away from the old meanings and life they'd had, and from sin. It called for a turning *to* Christ in faith with one's whole future. The new Christian was to be a disciple, a student, learning how to live and to share his or her whole life for God—nothing less.

35

Evangelism after the Ascension

WHAT HAPPENED TO THESE FIRST CHRISTIANS after Jesus left them? That's an especially relevant question, because that experience pertains more nearly to our lives today. We are told that, after Jesus ascended into heaven, God sent the Holy Spirit, as Jesus had promised. Christians experienced the Spirit's presence in vivid ways and described their experience in powerful right-brain images. (You may want to stop and reread the exciting story found in Acts 2:1–35.)

When these Christians, filled with the Holy Spirit, got together, they formed tiny outposts of the kingdom throughout the Roman world. They opened their lives to each other, and they helped each other with personal problems, financial problems, and all kinds of difficulties. They prayed together, read the Scriptures, and regularly shared the thanksgiving meal which developed into what was later called the Lord's Supper or Holy Communion. This became their central worship service; in it they met their living Lord in his spirit as they received spiritual food and strength for their journey with him and each other in his story. The Holy Communion became known as the Eucharist (which means "the thanksgiving" in Greek) because the Christians were so happy they'd been forgiven. Their lives and times of worship were characterized by real joy.

These outposts of the kingdom were exciting places into which the early church members brought people to meet their Lord, to be healed, and to be made new. And when pagans made a deep contact with Christians, they became different. They found a new way to live in a world which had been a frustrating chaos for them. They too were faced with problems like high interest rates, deterioration of family, anxiety about the future, and death. But now they could deal with these and other problems with a peace and sense of fulfillment they

never dreamed they could have. And they felt loved and forgiven—
free to love other people and tell them this news.

Two Groups of Evangelizers[1]

The New Testament Christians evangelized in two basic ways.

Specialists. The first was that of the five o'clock heralds. These were
specialists, or "evangelists." The apostles were a part of this group of
specialist-proclaimers, and there were also some gifted lay people like
Philip and Timothy who could speak well. And then there were bishops,
priests, and deacons who weren't usually traveling evangelists, but were
the local boys holding down the fort and proclaiming the gospel from
specific localized outposts.

Ordinary Converted People. The second group of evangelizers was
made up of people who were not specialists, and this was a far greater
evangelistic force in the early church. They were the everyday lay people
who witnessed. The Greek word for "witness" is *martis,* a legal term
meaning to testify to the facts you've seen or heard. For instance, in
a lawsuit, a person might be asked to describe an accident he or she
had seen. If you went to court and were a witness, you could *only*
testify to the facts you had personally seen or heard. You wouldn't
be allowed to make any judgment about the facts or try to influence
people's decisions concerning the facts. You were only called on to
say the truth about what you personally had seen and heard.

A Christian witness was one who told what had happened *in his or
her life.* The first witnesses had seen the living Lord. Later the witnesses
told what had happened in their lives because of having believed, repented, and committed their futures to God. A witness did not (does
not) have to be a theologian. The biblical witnesses in the early church
told about the life they were in the midst of living.[2]

This kind of evangelism was very powerful. People could identify
with these untrained lay men and women. The power of the theologically
uneducated witness is a real paradox. From the beginning lay people
must have thought, "Who would want to hear about me and what
I've seen?" I thought that for years. I wrote *The Taste of New Wine*
wondering, "Who would want to hear about what I've experienced?"

---

1. For the strategy here and in Chapter 37 I am indebted to Angus MacLeod.

2. Paul was certainly a specialist-evangelist. But when he was in real imminent danger
and had one shot to make a case for himself, he often seems to have dropped his theological
arguments and told the story of his own conversion. (See Acts 9:20–29, 22:1–16, and
26:2–24 for repeated accounts of what Paul "saw and heard" as he was converted.)

And I couldn't believe the response. The right-brain fact seems to be that the clods out of our own backyard which we hold up in God's light can become like diamonds to other people because they verify their own existence. This was part of the power of the personal testimony of lay people which helped evangelize in the Roman world in the first century. And this power is still very much alive in the twentieth century.

36

A "Witnessing" Case History

As a young Christian, occasionally I was asked to travel and speak with three other Christian businessmen. Three of us were in the oil exploration business and one was in the wholesale clothing business. One of the men had an airplane, and we'd fly to different cities and speak to men's meetings. Actually, we would just share what had happened to us as a result of trying to commit our lives to Christ. We talked simply and directly about what was going on in our daily lives, and each of us would tell some of our own story.

I remember one particular meeting of several hundred men at a regional denominational gathering. I told about my conversion, and a little about what was happening in my adventure with Christ. Then I got an urge to say something more, and I added, "You know, I've got the darndest feeling that I've come to this meeting to talk to one of you guys. I don't know who it is, but I just have that feeling."

When I sat down I thought, "You stupid jerk! Why did you say that?" (Have you ever done something on an impulse that you later thought sounded really awful?) As I sat there, I cringed inside. I felt like everything I *don't* want to be. (I just want to be dramatic, not melodramatic.)

When we all had finished speaking, people in the audience were very polite and came up on the stage to shake our hands and meet us. While I was visiting with some of them, a man walked up to me in the line—a really muscular guy with a shock of black hair and big, thick glasses. He had a tear coming out of his eye, and he said, "I'm the one. Could I talk to you?"

I said, "Well, uh, yeah. Can you wait a minute? There are a few more people here, so if you'll just stand over there by that curtain, I'll be there in a minute."

When the line had dwindled, I went over to the man and said, "What are you doing here? How did you get here?"

And he said, "You're never going to believe this, but I'm an attorney, and I travel a lot. And I'm married." The words just tumbled out of his mouth as he continued. "This is not where I live, but I have a mistress in this town. She lives right down the street.

"I was going to see her and had pulled up and parked my car in front of her apartment. As I got out, I ran right into these three guys from my home church. And they said, 'Hey, what are you doing here, John?' Well, inside I panicked but tried to look cool.

"I didn't know what to say, so I shrugged and said, 'Just passing through.' So they said, 'Fine, come on down to the meeting and hear these Christian businessmen.' I said, 'Sure, haven't got anything else to do!' So that's how I got to this meeting.

"And I heard you talking about being frustrated and pushing your life too hard and not handling it well, and you said that God was helping you with this. I realized that my life is really out of hand. It's in bad shape and I'm scared."

As John was saying these things, the men I was traveling with were looking at their watches and signaling to me that it was time to leave for the plane. We all had to get home. I started to go with them, but then I said, "Wait a minute," and I turned back to John. "Would you like to commit your whole life to Christ—turn away from this woman and try to start learning to live again?"

He said, "Boy, I sure would!"

So I suggested to him, "Okay, here are a couple of things to do. One is just to confess. Tell God where you've been and who you are. And tell him you're sick of yourself. And the second thing is to turn to Christ and say, 'I give up. I want you to come into my life and help me clean it up and to learn how to live again, because I don't know how to live anymore.'"

He said, "Well, I'm not sure I can do that."

I said, "Can you tell him you *want* to want to do that?"

"Yeah, I really can. I want to do it." So we prayed together, and in a prayer John confessed and asked Christ to be his Lord and show him how to live.

I was very green and not used to doing that sort of thing, and I really hated to be leaving John alone with no more training to begin to live for Christ. So I said, "Listen, I'll tell you what. I'll pray for you every day for a month if you'll pray for me. At the end of the month, write me a letter and I'll go on praying with you a month at a time until I don't hear from you anymore."

He said, "Okay, I'll do it."

Then I added, "Remember, don't try to force yourself to be a 'great Christian.' I'd suggest you go easy for a while about telling people what's happened to you. Go home and just try to adjust your life and get started praying and learning to read the Bible."

Well, over that next year John grew like a weed. I never saw anything like it. I'd send him a book and he'd devour it; two or three days later I'd get a note back from him. He evidently read a number of books along with the Bible. He was doing all kinds of loving things at his church and in his community. And his life was really changing. In his letters he kept telling me about people he was talking to.

John lived in a small town of about ten thousand people.[1] He wrote one day and asked, "Would you come and talk to some of my friends? There are so many people who want to talk about Christianity and I really don't know what to tell them now. I'm out of my depth."

I thought, "Sure, I'll go." At that time I hadn't written any books, so I'd just be a friend of John's who was coming to town.

The little commuter plane was delayed getting in to John's city, so I was running late that evening. John met me at the airport and said, "Am I glad you're here! Listen, some of these people are saying, 'I want to know specifically how you became a Christian.' I don't know what to tell them."

I just said, "Well, fine, John. I don't know what I can do, but I'm glad to see you." I didn't know what else to say. When we got to the church, we were really late. We came up in the hall near the altar end of the sanctuary because we were going in where the pulpit was. I could hear the muffled sound of singing. The minister met us at the door and said, "Listen, I want to tell you, Mr. Miller, I don't know what you men did for John, but this guy's changed my life."

I was surprised at such strong words, but not nearly as surprised as when I opened the door to the sanctuary. As I stepped through that door and looked inside, I just stared for about fifteen seconds— into the faces of eight hundred people who had come to find out what had happened to John.

When people see those they've known changing and finding hope,

---

1. John's name, his vocation, and the size of the town have been changed.

they want to know what's happening—just as they did in the early church. Throughout the New Testament we read accounts of witnesses like John in my story—men and women who brought people to the specialists, and the specialists told them the Good News of Jesus. And non-Christians got unlocked inside and joined what looked like a joyful historical party.

After a time, in fact, the Roman authorities began to get uneasy about the growing number of Christians because these people who had accepted the Good News were refusing to participate in the pagan rites that were fundamental to the Roman state. So the Romans made it a capital offense to be a Christian, and they killed quite a few. But the Christians refused to break up the church. The outposts held, and the tougher the Romans and the Jews got, the more the church grew. Hundreds of people in the Roman world believed what the specialists and the witnesses had to say because their *lives* fairly shouted, "This is *real* and *very important* to me!"

But the early Christian communicators knew a basic strategy many of us overlook as we try to present the gospel message.

37

Translating the Message

THE EARLY SPECIALIST-PROCLAIMERS would adjust the *way* they made their announcement of the kingdom's coming according to *the group* with whom they were speaking. Paul, perhaps the supreme specialist-evangelist, was a genius at this "focused" communication. For instance, as Angus MacLeod has pointed out, many of the people to whom Paul talked were slaves or slave owners. So when he talked to these people he called the kingdom-gift Jesus was bringing from God "redemption." *Redemption* was a term used when a slave was freed by being bought out of slavery. When one had been redeemed, he or she could never be put back into slavery again. So using the word *redemption* made it very clear to these people that Jesus came to make them free forever.

But when Paul talked to people in the business world, and to those who were involved with the law, he used a different term altogether. He used the term *justification* for God's gift through Christ. Justification meant that a judgment had been rendered in court in favor of the defendant. Having been justified, the defendant was free and could never be tried again for the same offense.

When Paul was talking to the ordinary people who were interested in personal relationships, he talked about Jesus' bringing "reconciliation" with God—bringing people back into an intimate relationship with him and with each other. And when he evangelized the Jews, he talked in terms of their expectation that the kingdom of God was coming to bring righteousness and peace. He announced its arrival in Jesus. It was brilliant!

This was a brilliant strategy. But what we often do today is to talk indiscriminately to non-Christians about "redemption" or "justification" or "reconciliation" or "the kingdom of God" without asking ourselves what the person we are witnessing to *feels* in terms of specific needs. We use terms like *redemption* because Paul used them in his New Testament teachings. But how many people do you know who are *actually* sold into slavery right now and are looking for a way out?

We use Paul's specific words instead of *doing what he did*—which was to translate the gospel in terms of the specific needs and language of each audience.

What I've been trying to do in this book is what Paul did—to *be* biblical rather than just to repeat the words Paul used. I believe we can translate the gospel in terms of contemporary needs. And I believe we *must* do it if we hope to reach a biblically illiterate world.[2]

Paul and the other early evangelists couched their message in the shape of the *emotional and spiritual needs* of the people. For years I have been trying to relate the gospel in terms of loneliness, broken relationships, the search for identity, and the need to be loved unconditionally because I believe these are common problems with which many people today can identify.

But it's the same gospel—the gospel of Jesus Christ, of God Almighty who created us all. And it deals with *all* our needs, all the problems from which we long to be liberated in all kinds of ways. And if this is true, the gospel can be related to anyone.

Different Roles for Different People

One of the striking things to me about Jesus' dealings with the disciples has always been the fact that he did not try to destroy their uniqueness, but worked *through* their God-given differences. For example, Peter was always headstrong and impulsive. Andrew was homespun and loyal, and the Bible indicates that God respected and used these different personality traits and inclinations. And when it came to evangelism, the early Christians evidently did not all try to imitate each other the way we often try to do.

Today, a church might decide to "become evangelistic" with the goal for "every member to be an evangelist." That certainly *sounds* like a worthy goal. But the New Testament picture is very different. It indicates that Christians are to receive *different gifts*—"that some

---

2. I want to add quickly that I think we should teach the Bible more than we ever have in the church. Unless he or she really *knows the Scriptures well*, the chances of a specialist-proclaimer's translating the message accurately may be very slim.

should be apostles, some prophets, some evangelists, some pastors and teachers" (Eph. 4:11, RSV).

But in our anxiousness to spread the Good News, we who are in leadership positions sometimes try to get everyone to do what *we* do. We teach *everyone* how to knock on doors and have them memorize a certain gospel presentation, (or teach them to do whatever the person does who is running the show in a particular congregation or movement). We create a "trumpet corps" or a "horn choir" out of the whole congregation—everyone is supposed to do the same thing.

But I don't see the process working like that in the New Testament outposts. Instead, I see an "orchestra" in which each person plays a different "instrument"—a different role—in the evangelistic process. When I first became a Christian, I was a "piccolo player," but I was trying to play in the tuba section where the saints played the deep notes. Can you imagine anything more ridiculous than a piccolo player trying to play in the tuba section?

Or let's say you're a spiritual triangle player for God. Your only job is just not to be out to the restroom when it's your time to ding. But your job, whatever it may be is a crucial job in God's eyes, and neglecting it—or trying to do someone else's job—will result in real loss for the kingdom.

And I believe that in a church where authentic evangelism flourishes, there are Christians with *different gifts* doing *different* but *complimentary things*. All of the problems and joys of life are being faced and dealt with by someone who knows about them firsthand. And some people are specialist-evangelists, but most are probably witnesses.

This is the example I see being given us by the New Testament church. The members supported each other in risking as they tried to *live* the gospel. They loved and helped the members of their fellowship who were doing different things (like being evangelists, prophets, teachers, etc.). The witnesses supported the specialists and vice versa. They prayed for each other, helped with problems, forgave failures and sins, and extended themselves for each other's spiritual nurture in every way they could. And these outposts became miracle centers, where evangelism took place every day as an overflow, a by-product, of their life together.

Where Was the "Scene" in Which Evangelism Took Place?

Where did it happen? It happened everywhere. It happened at big meetings, as at Pentecost. It happened in synagogues, in prisons. It happened out of doors and in homes. As a matter of fact, it happened *mostly* in homes, because for over a hundred years there evidently weren't any church buildings.

We're often so big-time and so "logical" that sometimes we can't see the silent power of the Holy Spirit working through ordinary people who are, from a left-brain perspective, insignificant. Angus MacLeod quotes Professor Gordon Rupp, the British historian, who visited Russia and reported that there is a revival of Christianity there.

People asked Professor Rupp, "How come, despite years of persecution and communist propaganda, the church still survives in Russia?" And his answer was this: "It's largely due to the grandparents."

It seems that the old people kept coming to the churches, and they were dismissed by the communist leaders as nobodies who would soon die out. People would come back from visiting Russia and would say, often disparagingly, "There are only old people left in the church." (I can remember when people said that.)

But those old grandparents took their grandchildren under their wings and passed on the faith to them. And the strength of the church in Russia today is largely due to the witness of grandparents and old people who quietly cared for the coming generations. It's amazing.

Why Do We Evangelize?

Why do some ordinary people evangelize, even at the risk of their lives, (as some are still doing today in different parts of the world) when they get no public recognition or acclaim for doing so? I've sat on church committees, and have heard reasons for embarking on evangelistic programs like, "Look at the statistics. If we don't evangelize, the church is going to die." Or "We Christians have no voice in society any more. If we don't evangelize, the communists will take over with their atheistic ideology." But I see nothing like this kind of reasoning in the New Testament.

The Christians in the New Testament evidently evangelized *because they couldn't help it!* They were excited and grateful. Instead of reporting about Christians sharing out of grim duty, their epistles have an enthusiasm that sounds more like a Texas businessman talking about the Houston Oilers or the Dallas Cowboys.

I read a book a year or so ago that really turned me on. In fact, I liked it so much that I bought five copies to give to friends for Christmas. Nobody *told* me to do that—I wanted to! And when I saw a movie called *Chariots of Fire* and another called *Ordinary People* a while back, I must have called half a dozen people about each movie and told them they "had to see" it. This is what New Testament evangelism was like—people sharing what they were finding because it had affected them personally.

38

How Would a Contemporary Church Become an "Evangelistic" Outpost of the Kingdom?

WHAT WOULD THE NEW TESTAMENT MODEL look like clothed in the structures of a contemporary church? I realize that no doubt there are many such models across the country, and that some churches have great things going. But some don't. Many people have told me that they don't even know how they would begin to structure their church to include a concrete, specific, continuing kind of evangelism. So in this chapter I want to try to translate and combine some of the New Testament elements into contemporary terms and structures.

An Evangelizing Church Must Have a "Warm Center"

First of all, I believe that an evangelizing outpost has to have a "warm center" of converted Christians meeting together in small groups, trying to learn to live for Christ and to love each other. I'm convinced there has to be a place in the church to bring people when they have been converted—a "pool of love" where they'll be accepted regardless of the trauma they live in, and in which they can learn the almost lost art of being who they really are. *And until a church has such a center, I don't think that congregation should even try to put out an evangelistic hand to the troubled people in the world.*

This may sound hard, *unless* one really believes that the purpose of authentic evangelism is not just new names on a roll, but lives actually being healed and transformed by the Holy Spirit into the whole image of God. If there is no center of healing warmth and love into which new people can be brought, why go out and get them at all? They will only feel lost and out of place on one hand *or* realize that we are unconsciously caught up in a strange game of *talking about* life in Christ in one way in our evangelistic services—with no real intention of trying to live it that way on a continuing basis. And those who stay in the church will soon grasp the situation, make the adjustment, and join us in the "talking game." And the subtle effect of this way of being the church is that, over the years, a spiritual numbness often (probably usually) sets in, and the sharp clarity and wonder of the gospel seems distant and unreal. I have been a part of this unconscious and silent conspiracy all my life—and still am. Only when I am in an outpost group where I can see real life changes *continuing* to take place, can I even *see* the lethargy and relative deadness of so much of my Christian life in the congregation.

However, there are many churches today that do not have a place for honest sharing and love at a gut level—and don't want such a place. But how can people who are not caught up in the gospel process of giving and receiving love and forgiveness *with each other* become able to love the world in a healing way? And when people from the world do come to such churches, they soon sense whether or not there is any real love for them. And if there isn't, they will not stick around long after the meetings. (Fortunately there are often some individuals who reach out to new people, but it is often in "friendliness" and not to provide a place where the new Christian can find love and growth in the body of the congregation.) These are some of the reasons I'm convinced that the place to start evangelism is *inside* the church, building a "warm center" that will be the base for all other evangelistic efforts.

A Specific Time and Place Set Aside for Evangelism

If new conversions are not going to "die out" in a congregation's ongoing life, it seems crucial to have certain "evangelistic doorways" built into the church's calendar structure.

Some churches have found it helpful to have a regular time that is set aside for evangelistic presentations, an evening where people can come, or be brought by members to hear what is involved in being converted. Now, how this is managed will depend on the structure the church already has. There are contemporary churches which already have many evangelistic services—sometimes once every three days. Some denominations have an "invitation" and a time for "decision" built into every worship service. But there are also many churches in America today in which there is not one place in the entire year's program for people to get converted.

For churches that don't already have a structured time or place for evangelism, I would suggest that one night a month—perhaps on a Sunday evening—the church could have an all-church evangelistic meeting. Someone who is trained to present the gospel message and to give inquirers an opportunity to get converted could speak. Individual witnesses could also be present to tell what's happening in their lives and to describe how their lives have changed with regard to hope and meaning since their conversion to Christ. And then inquirers from outside the church or "nominal" church members who are interested in being converted would have a chance to ask questions and to make a commitment.

With this simple structure there would always be a "place" in the life of the church where interested people could be brought for exposure to the gospel message and to hear people witness about their specific turning to Christ.

A system like this would also mean that the preachers who are assigned to preach on Sunday morning could concentrate on areas of growth and nurture without worrying that there is no evangelistic message being presented on a regular basis. (Many ministers have rebelled against a system in which no teaching comes from the pulpit because every sermon is an evangelistic pitch. But sometimes they have overreacted and eliminated evangelism altogether. The system I have suggested would guard against either extreme.)

Most churches have services or sacraments—confirmation or "believer's baptism"—which traditionally are supposed to signal conversion. But all too often these services, which were meant to mark a commitment to the living Christ, have become puberty rites. The kids (or adults) who become Christians through these services often are not confronted with the fact that they are saying publicly *that they are going to try to live in a different way, for a different purpose, in every area of their lives.* And that they are *seriously* and *actually* turning *to* Christ as *Lord of their whole futures.*

In the first place, most of the younger people being confirmed or baptized in early adolescence probably don't even have well-defined lives of their own to turn from. They are too young to know who they are and where they are going. In getting confirmed or baptized, they may be very serious and sincere, but in early adolescence, at one level many are "doing what they're supposed to do," and others are only intending to "join the church," which is not the same thing as conversion.

Again, I don't want to be misunderstood. I'm not saying confirmation and believer's baptism cannot be authentic vehicles of conversion. And

I'm certainly not advocating that they should be eliminated or that young people should not be confirmed or baptized! But realistically I am convinced that by the way we often treat the preparation of people for these services we have (in actions louder than words) unconsciously trivialized the gospel and the radical nature of conversion to Jesus Christ—and we don't seem to be aware that we are doing it. The point I want to make is that to have an authentic outpost of the kingdom there must be a place for a clear and serious turning of one's whole life to Christ with a reasonable beginning grasp of what that means. That is why I like the idea of separate, regular evangelistic services.

Three Ongoing Ministries of Evangelism

In conjunction with ongoing "warm centers" of honest sharing and evangelistic services, I believe that there are three types of continuing evangelistic ministries which can be orchestrated in the *same church* (instead of choosing which kind of evangelism your church will have). There are special places for the *specialist-proclaimer,* the *midwife,* and the *witness.*

The Role of "Specialist-Proclaimers"

As I've suggested, I believe the New Testament church used a sort of orchestra model for evangelism. And I think a church which is trying to be an authentic kingdom outpost can benefit from this "orchestra" approach in which the members have different but equally important roles in the church's evangelism.

The "specialist-proclaimers" or evangelists would be trained to speak about Jesus' story at evangelistic meetings. This would of course include professional preachers, but it could also include trained lay men and women. Some of these specialists would make a lifetime vocation out of getting so immersed in the story of Jesus Christ and the announcement of his kingdom that they can relate it to any situation. They would be able to speak in terms of redemption, justification, reconciliation, justice, peace, loneliness, agony, the search for purpose or identity— be able to couch the gospel in any terms which may meet an audience at the point of its experienced needs.

The Role of "Midwives"

Another kind of specialist besides the evangelist who would speak at large meetings would be that kind of person who can, in a private conversation, help guide someone else through the process of accepting Christ as Savior and Lord. These specialists would be spiritual "midwives," who would learn how to lead people through the steps of repentance and faith to conversion in a nonmanipulative way. Lay people, members of the outpost community, could be trained to fill this helping role (and many people really would love to learn how to do this). I'll give some suggestions about one approach to this sort of helping in the next few chapters.

The Role of "Witnesses"

The rest of the members of the outpost church—the ones who aren't specialists or midwives—would be honest witnesses who could spread the gospel by sharing their own personal experiences of repentance and conversion with those they meet. They could evangelize by telling some ways in which they have begun to find new hope and meaning or love since surrendering to God. This is not bragging nor claiming some special kind of goodness. As D. J. Niles's classic statement puts it, "It's like one beggar telling another where he found some bread."

To begin to witness, a person who is not a specialist can simply talk about living in the outpost group, describing the aspects which are exciting and real to him or her and which have helped toward finding peace or purpose. Witnesses should be free to talk about whatever is making them happier and more fulfilled—in spite of new problems— and made them want to join the church. This might be something as serious as "a place to share my hurts and frustrations, where I feel sure I'll be heard and not judged." Or it might be that the thing that is *really* important to a certain witness is the fellowship he or she has found on a bowling team called "The Holy Rollers." The important thing is that the witness be *authentic.* If a person fakes it in order to be considered more pious, his or her witness will almost invariably smell of unreality.

For instance, if a witness starts talking about deep theology and trying to lead people to Christ when the bowling team is where his or her heart is, that person will probably come across as a phony. But if that same Christian tells about how a group of warm people on the bowling team accepted him or her and offered love and a place to be accepted, then the listener—who may feel lonely and rejected— may be drawn to "come and see." And *then,* at some later time, the enquirer may want to hear what an evangelist or "midwife" has to say about the Lord of these people and his Good News about life.

This would mean that the Christians who aren't specialists simply would talk to people about what's going on in the outpost group that has meaning for them. Then when somebody says, "You know, I'm really interested in the kind of Christianity you seem to have found in your church, the Christian witness could call a "midwife" on the telephone and say, for instance, "Hey, Henry. How about coming over for dinner? I've got some people who want to talk," and in that relaxed setting the interested people can hear the gospel in terms of their own lives. Or perhaps the witness could bring interested people to one of the regularly scheduled evangelistic services for exposure to someone proclaiming the gospel message and to the stories of others who are on the adventure of living with Christ.

With a structure for evangelism such as the one I've been describing, everybody can take part in the church's evangelism as a member of an "orchestra" in which each person plays a particular role and the sections all work together toward the goal of sharing the story of Jesus Christ. But how would one person—an evangelist or a "midwife" or a witness who is interested in learning to talk about the faith—go about choosing an approach for helping other people become converted to Jesus Christ?

39

Selecting a Way to Talk About Our Faith

As SURPRISING AS IT MAY SOUND, I used to be against the idea of talking about my own faith (or anyone else's). Where I came from, this was considered to be rude. So when I became a Christian, I used to say to myself, "I'm going to *live* my faith and not talk about it."

But then one day I was thinking about what it meant to be a Christian and several things struck me. In the first place, my attitude was nothing like that of the Christians in the New Testament outposts of the kingdom. They evidently loved to share their faith with other people.

In the second place, in one awful moment, I saw that my attitude was all wrong and unloving. I realized that as a new Christian I was like a person in a dread disease ward of a hospital who was being healed of an awful malignancy. I was walking around in the ward comparatively healthy, helping the other patients to die more comfortably, and *not introducing them to the physician who might heal them, too.* By "acting but not talking" I was unwittingly calling attention to what a great strong guy *I* was. That really got to me.

This business about living the faith is good. But not talking about it can be a real cop-out. In a sense, when I do not admit to others what a difference God and the process of conversion have made in my life, it's like pretending I did something *for myself* which changed my life, when the facts are that by myself I hadn't been handling it well at all.

But if we are to talk about our faith, how do we begin? I suggested in the previous chapter some ways a person might witness to his or her own experiences of being converted and being involved in an outpost community. In this chapter and the next, I want to get more specific, considering some ways an individual might begin sharing the gospel and helping other people be converted.

Proclaiming the Gospel

Traditionally, there are certain elements in an "evangelistic sermon." And some ministers and lay people have let their ignorance of the "proper form" keep them from preaching about conversion. But since conversion is basically a facing of one's true separation or sin and a turning from it toward Christ in surrender, any talk which tells part of God's "saving" story and leads to these results would seem to be a valid evangelistic sermon.

Over the years I've found that for me it's more effective to begin by communicating about the Good News describing *personal* needs that I sense my audience shares with me and then relating the needs to the gospel. Over the years I have uncovered these needs while listening to my own heart and to other people in counseling sessions and outpost groups, through studying psychology, and from reading the Bible. But dealing directly with such needs is often threatening. So to *begin* making contact, a speaker or "midwife" needs to find something familiar but not personally threatening to the listeners that can serve as a "bridge" into the audience's lives.

Billy Graham frequently starts his evangelistic sermons with a newspaper article or something that's familiar in the lives of the people— something which is on their minds. Many other preachers and speakers have found this helpful advice—but it pays to be sensitive when choosing the topic.

Some years ago Norman Vincent Peale was speaking to some of us who were interested in learning how to spread the gospel, and he gave us this advice: "Be careful when you use information about people's personal situations. Think through what you're saying about a local place or circumstance before you start trying to win them by 'understanding' their situation. Don't just fake it."

He continued, "One time I was in Bloomington, Illinois. They have two small suburbs there. One little town is called 'Normal' and the other is 'Oblong.' I was reading through the paper the night before I was to speak, to get something current about the local situation for my sermon. On one page I saw a small headline that read 'Normal Boy Marries Oblong Girl.' I thought that was hilarious. But when I said that from the pulpit, nobody laughed. It was just too familiar for them to 'see' in perspective."

Many problems people have are that way. They have been involved with those problems so long they don't even see how they appear to an outsider. So, in speaking about personal needs, I've found it helpful to begin by describing a real difficulty I have *in my own life*—something I suspect may also be a difficulty for many people in the audience. For instance, in Chapter 1 I began by talking about the franticness of life in America today. I told about noticing the signs of aging on my hands as I was shaving, about a friend whose suicide reminded me starkly of the fragile nature of life. And I spoke of concern about my relationships with my children and about finances. These were all true problems I was facing as I began making the films on which this book was based—problems I suspected many in the audience also shared.

Talking about the Need for Conversion

There are many ways of actually approaching the subject of being converted. Some approaches center around a theologically loaded question, like "Where would you go if you died tonight?" Well, that question may very well get the listener's attention. But if the immediate effect is *fear,* and the gospel which follows is seen as a parachute to wear through life to be used at the time of death, then the long-range results may be very inhibiting to the church's life. I am aware of the absolute centrality of the "salvation" aspects of the Good News as they relate to the overcoming of death, and of our unhealthy tendency in this country to repress any thoughts about our own death. But I am a little leery of approaches to evangelism which don't *also* relate strongly to that search for love and fulfillment which we all carry on *during* our lives.

I want to be very careful about this distinction. I am *not* saying that a commitment resulting from a question about death or other theological issues cannot lead to a genuine conversion commitment. But I am saying that, as absolutely crucial as the death question is, there is much *more* to Christian conversion. I think the old evangelists were referring to this difference when they said, "Have you only accepted Jesus as *Savior?* That's not enough! He wants to be *Lord* of your life, too!"

Conversion, the kind seen in the New Testament, is a turning away from an old life and a turning to a whole new life under the lordship of Jesus Christ (see Matt. 22:37). If we want God to "save us from death" (and I do), that's one thing. But the New Testament Christians accepted Christ as also being the *transforming* agent regarding the way they lived in *this world.* Paul says this change is so great that we are to "be transformed by the renewal of our minds" (see Rom. 12:1–3).

It's easy to misunderstand this. I hasten to add that many people who start their evangelistic efforts with a theological question, end with the business of helping folks try to commit their whole lives. And I'm not saying theological commitments are invalid. I'm just saying if you leave out the part about turning and reorienting your whole life, conversion as I am describing it isn't completed.

The risk of "theological question evangelism" is that as a result of a "successful" evangelistic program you may get a turned on "rescue squad" ready to save people from death, but no "hospital"—no warm center for healing lives. There will be no place into which new Christians can be taken to learn to love and share the pain of life with its disappointments, insecurities, and broken relationships. And the New Testament church always seemed to be such a "hospital."

But if we don't use theological issues such as facing death as the center for discussing the need for conversion, how can we go about it? I will be making some suggestions in the next chapter. But first I want to look at some basic attitudes and presuppositions that have been helpful for me to recognize in leading people to conversion.

Everybody Needs God

Behind the approach I am going to present is a presupposition which must be taken on faith. The presupposition is that behind the adequate-looking facades we see all around us, *everyone needs God.* Everyone needs the freedom to love and live which Jesus' announcement of the kingdom promises, as well as the freedom from sin and death. We are *made that way*—for the love, direction, purpose, and freedom God has for us in a relationship with him and with each other.

But in our normal life outside the faith we are separated from God, from each other, and from that inner freedom God intended us to have—regardless of how fine a person we may be. This separation is called sin, and traditionally people have felt a vague but deep sense of guilt which came from a feeling that we are actually sinning or at least "not being what we should be."

But many modern people don't sense this basic separation as guilt. Many have rejected the idea of feeling guilt for anything, and so they have repressed the guilt feelings they do have. The old-hellfire-and-damnation sermon is often ineffective for evangelizing many modern men and women because the listener says, "I don't feel guilty. (I'm just a little nervous, that's all.)"

But people today do often feel a sense of loneliness, of incompleteness, a chronic feeling of anxiety. The failure to find intimacy and a sense of identity is a commonly expressed need. Underneath calm exteriors there is an indefinable restlessness. And so I would suggest that these feelings constitute a place to start when approaching people about their need for God, because to repent, or turn to Christ, a person must have some notion of what he or she is turning *from*—or at least a strong sense of need for "something." As I suggested earlier, one has to be highly motivated to turn to Christ as Lord. It is helpful if a person is so sick of his or her life—whatever it is like—that he or she is willing to take a chance on God and his story. But some people only sense a vague but undefined need.

The Way We Think about Conversion Makes a Difference

Because conversion is such a big step in a person's life, the way the one who is evangelizing *thinks about* conversion has a lot to do with the way people receive his or her message.

I've been present during the negotiations that led to the merger of two corporations. There was no question that something serious was happening. The way people carried the papers and the way they talked and watched and listened to each other—all indicated the importance of the proceedings. Even a casual observer would know right away that whatever was happening was very important to the parties involved.

But if I walk up to a theater to buy a ticket, sometimes I hardly even look at the ticket seller. I usually just give her or him the money and go on in. From my behavior, it would be obvious to anyone watching—including the person with whom I'm dealing at the ticket window—that we are involved in a superficial transaction.

I have known evangelistic approaches that seem to make entering the kingdom of God just such a quick, unencumbered transaction. The process of conversion is treated as just another twenty-minute conversation. But when we talk about conversion, we are talking about *the most important commitment* a human being can make.

Because this is true, unless we take the evangelistic encounter seriously, unless we take some time to establish a relationship and to hear the other person's needs, our efforts will probably come across to sensitive, thinking people as bizarre and inappropriate. If we treat the transaction as if it were a membership to a social club or college alumni association, people will sense it—and they won't be likely to listen to what we say. But if our attitude and words say (and if we believe) something like, "This Christianity is very important to me. It is changing my whole life," then I am convinced that almost no one will laugh at us or think we are being simplistic. And they just may want to hear more.

I know it may seem that I have almost worked this point to death, but if we are talking to people about *conversion,* we are not just leading them to make some sort of verbal response to Christ. We are discussing a profound decision which may wind up costing them their jobs or their current friendships, and which will definitely change the direction and purpose of their lives. And to *push or manipulate people* who have not considered the deep nature of the changes that can happen as a result of conversion seems very unfair. Christians have said to me, "Yes, but if we don't put the pressure on them they may get away." From God? Or from us? Don't worry, I do not believe God will desert them just because we may have to move on.

40

Cultivating the Soil for Evangelism

IN SEARCHING FOR A MORE REALISTIC APPROACH to telling people about how they might make a commitment, I came up with a few guidelines which have been helpful to me.

First, since I was not a part of a church which had an evangelistic structure, but was only operating out of a small group outpost within a church, I began my attempts at evangelizing by just making friends with people. I started looking around at men and women already in the routine pathways of my life. When I did this, I discovered that all sorts of people began to step out of the shadows—the guy at the gas station where I regularly bought gas, the elevator operator at the Petroleum Club, and some other people with whom I had routine contacts over the months. Also there were business associates and all kinds of people connected with my work whom I had noticed "on the edge of my consciousness" but to whom I hadn't really paid much attention. I began to speak to and listen to them on coffee breaks or after business conferences. And with some of them I eventually found opportunities to talk about my faith.

Making Friends for Christ's Sake

This kind of evangelism begins by listening with real interest. And I discovered that sooner or later, in the atmosphere of sincere caring, some of the frustrations and the problems in people's lives are going to come out in conversation. When we listen in a caring way, we are sort of feeling along the rim of someone's soul for a crack—for some hurt or frustration lying below the surface of their lives.

This kind of listening often moves the conversation to what is going on inside our lives—behind our facades. And it seems like almost every-

229

one today is yearning for a nonjudgmental ear. Certainly in my experience, when I began listening intently with encouraging words and looks, I found that people would share an amazing number of fears and uncertainties which had been crouching just inside their hearts.

This might be easily misunderstood. When I suggest that we listen this way, I do *not* mean we are to trick people into making some sort of religious commitment. It is more like honestly making friends for Jesus Christ's sake—friends who may or may not end up being recruited by us as eternal companions on the adventure of walking in God's story. And since we are not "selling" or trying to convince them (at least I am not—on my best days), we've got all the time in the world. We don't have to rush up and try to get them to do or say something. We can just try to get to *know the people.* In the process we often learn what they feel they need to turn away from. That way, if they do become interested in being converted, we can help them turn from whatever that is to Christ and his church.

One thing I have to remind myself is *not* to think of the people I'm listening to as "prospects" for the kingdom. Just our *thinking that* can change them from persons to objects to be manipulated. They may begin to sense that "something is not real here" if we're thinking, "How am I going to get this 'message' in?" And the sensitive ones will look at us and say to themselves, "This guy's not listening to me. He's only interested in himself and what he wants to tell me."

Just as I was writing these words I realized it was trash day, and I hurried out to the street with the trash bag. A stranger came walking up our street and hailed me as I was going back toward the house. He had mistaken me for my next-door neighbor (who moved last month). Since I was writing about making friends for Jesus Christ, I was especially conscious of paying attention to this man—even though I was anxious to get back to my writing.

After we got the identity mix-up cleared, I asked him where he was from, and he said that he and his wife are visiting our town in Texas from out of state. He asked me if I'd "tried the churches here." I said yes, and told him where we go. It was obviously not the one he had chosen, and he changed the subject and began talking about the poverty and prostitution along the Mexican border, describing in some detail the abhorrent practice of having nine- to eleven-year-old girls dance nude in the night clubs in border towns. His conversation was so sprinkled with evangelical Christian terms that, smiling, I finally said something like, "I perceive that you are a Christian."

He said, "Yes, I know the Lord." I told him that my wife and I are Christians too and that, as a matter of fact, "we both write about Christianity." He nodded and went on talking about something else. In the course of our conversation, I found out about this man's retirement, and that he originally came from a Scandinavian country (family tree 150 years old, etc., etc.). Finally, when he turned and walked off down the street, I realized he had apparently not cared about me at all. I felt that he really hadn't listened to anything I'd said. The only question I could remember his asking me was if I had "tried the churches here." And as I came back in and sat down to write, it occurred to me that right now the man might be telling his wife over coffee how he had "witnessed to" the man in the small, tan house down the street. I realized how put off I was by his Christian words and phrases—because he never listened to me or seemed interested in me as a person.

This encounter a few moments ago made me want to emphasize again here the *great value* of just listening to people and getting to know them not just because we want an evangelistic "feather in our cap," but because they are important people in God's eyes.

Bridges and Doorways

Another ingredient in this approach to people is to identify honestly with their sins and problems. That doesn't mean to fake it. But there's not a personal problem I've heard so far that I can't identify with at least in my imagination. If I've never actually had the experience someone is describing, I can usually say at least, "Yeah, I really think I know what you mean. I've never been there, but boy, I sure have thought about being there"—or whatever is authentic for me. Such identification forms a bridge across which other people can walk into our lives and we into theirs—and new and deeper relationships can be formed.

I have found that each person I meet has a whole adventure or personal story he or she is living out. It may be exciting or boring or terrifying. It may be going well for them or they may be bogged down. But since I am convinced that everyone is created to need a relationship with God, I believe that each person will sooner or later experience a deep dissatisfaction in their life without him.

If this is true, then God is always waiting for the right time to meet people and to show them a new experience of life. And you or I, as a Christian friend already in their lives, may become a doorway through which they can someday step into the kingdom. In the meantime, we are not trying to spout answers to all their problems. Instead, we are praying quietly for these people (being careful not to parade this in front of them). And in each case, we are continuing to find out who these people are and what problems they are facing.

Jesus did this—he listened to people and took their problems seriously. If they came to him with withered hands, he healed their withered hands. Then they followed him all over to find out about the kingdom of God. He talked about taxes, about business (see Matt. 21:33–41), about prodigal children (see Luke 15:11–32), about adultery (see John 8:3–11)—problems not exactly foreign to this generation.

When we take the time to listen to a person and identify with his or her problems, there's a good chance the relationship may grow. And in time that person may acknowledge that life is not complete, that in fact it is pretty awful. Then there may come a time when we can "witness"—tell how our own lives got to the place where we were scared or lonely and miserable, and we decided to try God seriously. We can tell how he has really made a difference in our own lives— not how God made us "good," but how he made us more joyful or hopeful. (If we're *not* more joyful or hopeful at some level *in spite of* the new problems that a commitment to God has brought into our lives, I'm convinced that we need to check our own faith, because we may have missed something important about conversion.)

This business of telling about our own experience is hard for many people to do, especially at first. But if we are telling how we are finding some peace and hope through a commitment to Christ as our primary loyalty, and not bragging about the way God has made us good, most people will hear us thoughtfully.[1]

But if that doesn't happen; if the other person changes the subject and says, "Hey, did you hear how the Houston Oilers did this weekend?" then it's time to back off. Instead of saying, "Listen, friend, I'm about to save you, why are you running away?" I'd recommend saying something more like, "No, how'd the Oilers do?"

In this approach to witnessing we don't have to *convince* anybody. Jesus indicated that it's going to be the Holy Spirit's job to convince (or convict) people concerning things like sin and righteousness (see John 16:7–10). So often we Christians feel that we must *argue* with people about the necessity of their making a commitment. But there is a sense in which every person must decide for himself or herself.

---

1. Jesus was pretty emphatic in telling people *not* to call him "good" (see Mark 10:17–22). I don't think Jesus was denying his identity. I think he was saying that the point is not "being good," but rather (as the continuing passage indicates) having God as our number-one priority.

Many of us would have followed the rich young ruler all over town to get him into our church—imagine what we could do with his tithe! We'd have nailed him, and yet Jesus let him go. And as far as we know, Jesus never followed him (see Luke 18:18–25).

But let's say our friend *is* interested in what we have said about our experience and indicates a desire to consider Christian conversion. How would we help such a person to make a beginning commitment?

41

Helping a Seeker with Repentance and Surrender

As I DESCRIBED IT IN CHAPTER 22, conversion consists of two movements: *repentance* (turning *away* from sin or the thing which represents sin) and *faith* (consciously turning *to* Christ as Savior and Lord of one's life).

If this is true, then we can help the process of conversion to happen by (1) helping the seeker to discover what it is that represents the sin or separation from God in his or her life (the thing which is keeping him or her from being able to make a clear commitment of the future to Christ), and (2) helping the seeker to confess and then walk through the process of actually making a specific surrender or commitment of faith.

Exactly how we go about this, however, will depend on just where the seeker is in his or her life. Each person comes to the point of conversion through a unique series of circumstances, and part of listening and "making friends for Christ" is becoming aware of those particular circumstances. But it seems to me that basically there are two kinds of seekers with whom we might be dealing, and we would approach each one in a slightly different way.

A Seeker in Crisis

One kind of person who might approach us about being converted is the person who is in an obvious crisis situation. This person may have reached a point of despair or discouragement with his or her life and be ready to turn from that life (repent). Often there are certain blatant, dominant sins or desires that represent the old life, and the seeker in crisis is ready to turn from these, too.

To help this type of seeker through the doorway of conversion (assuming, of course, we have listened and shown caring and become aware of the elements and intensity of the seeker's conflict), we can start by explaining the two movements ("from" and "to") that make up conversion. We can urge the person in crisis to confess the specific sins and self-centered ways that are keeping him or her from the Lord, naming them out loud or silently and telling God that he or she wants to turn from that old life toward Christ. Then, after this person has confessed and repented, we can help him or her to make a commitment of faith by simply saying something like, "Lord, I surrender. I commit my life, my future, into your hands."

In the next chapter I will suggest what we might do to help such a person *after* he or she has repented and made a commitment in faith.

The "Something More" Seeker

But besides the person who comes to us at a crisis point in his or her journey, there is another type of seeker. This person may already be an active member of a church—or even a church official. He or she is not necessarily at a crisis point in life and may not be aware of any blatant, conflicting sins or desires that are keeping him or her from making a personal commitment to Christ. And yet this kind of seeker realizes that he or she is not really "converted" and asks for help in understanding how to enter into an intimate relationship with God.

As an example of how we might begin to talk to this kind of seeker, let's imagine you, the reader, are at this point in your life. Let's say you and I are sitting across the table in a restaurant. We've known each other for some time now, and you've found out about my life and about my Christian conversion. I've told you some of the things about me that I've written earlier in this book, and you're curious about the changes that have happened in my life.

So you say to me, "Keith, I'm really interested in becoming converted to Jesus Christ. But when you say I should repent, I'm not sure what sin or separation I may have which I should turn from. Can you help me?"

What follows is what I might say to you. I hope it will serve as a helpful model for explaining conversion to the "I Want Something More" kind of seeker. And if you are this kind of seeker yourself, just answer the questions I'll raise and follow me through this process to see how it would feel on the inside to be talked to in this way.

How to Repent When You're Not Sure What to Repent Of
(A Sample Explanation)

One way to begin to find the focus for your repentance is by looking inside your life. You don't have to tell me what you see when you ask yourself these questions, but just be specific with yourself and with God.

First, what's the most important thing or person in your life right now? Think a minute. There is often a tendency for people in the church to say, "God" or "Jesus Christ." But if you do say "Jesus Christ," then what is the *second* most important thing? This is very tricky. We who've lived around the Christian church are trained to say that Jesus is most important—and he should be! But sometimes our behavior shows that other things are really more important to us. And often it's hard to get at what these things actually are.

Where is the Focus of Your Life?

How do you decide what is the most important thing in your life? There are different ways, but here are two that have been helpful to me. One, when people read the newspaper, they usually read the same kinds of stories every day. Some people always read the sports section. Some read the business section next. Some people even read the paper in the same order every day (I often scan the front page, then start at the *back* page and work forward). What kind of books do you habitually read? What your mind selects unconsciously to read in a recurring fashion tells you a lot about where the true focus of your life is and what is important to you.

A second way to determine what's the most important thing in your life is to ask yourself what you think about when your mind is free. There are recurring thoughts in our minds that are like a small ball tied on a rubber string to the middle of our minds. We throw them out and get busy working or doing things around the house, and then, when it's quiet, these thoughts come bounding back into the center of our attention. Sometimes they are fantasies about the future or memories of moments in the past. Sometimes they are "good" thoughts and sometimes "bad" thoughts. But ask yourself now: "What are these recurring thoughts I have when no one is around and my mind is free?"

I realize that sometimes there are situational anxieties concerning a sick child or a crisis at work, and the tendency is to think about such problems all the time. But I'm not talking about crisis situations. I'm talking about *recurring* thoughts over periods of months and even years.

Do you spend most of your spare time thinking about your wife and your relationship with her? Do you think about your husband and/or your children? Your loneliness? Do you think about being great in your vocation? Do you think about sex—or food? Or about your weight, or your beauty—or lack of it? Do you think about some sin or guilt from your past? Do you think about yourself?

Whatever you think about or focus on in this recurring fashion when your mind is free may be what you worship primarily instead of Jesus Christ. And the love of anything or anyone more than God is a sin, a sin which needs repentance in order to be in the right relation to God.

People say to me, "You mean it's wrong to love a child more than anything?" You bet! People have said to me about a runaway son, "I just worshiped that child. I don't understand what happened to him." How many children of "good Christian families" (in which the mother or father loves the child more than anything) have run off and gotten drunk or pregnant, or taken dope, or gone to prison? When this happens, the child is sometimes using the unacceptable behavior to say to one or both of the parents, "Listen, you're trying to make me something I can't be. You're making me your god—making me responsible for your happiness." And although this awareness may not be conscious, the child may feel that "impossible demands" are being placed on him or her.

If you try to make a husband, wife, or child responsible for your happiness, that person may run away from you. People can't stand the role of being someone's god; they know they can't fulfill such expectations. It is very easy to ruin your relationship with whatever you love, if you love it more than you love God. People who ruin their marriages in this way are often bewildered and say, "I don't know what happened to our marriage. I loved this man [or woman] to distraction."[1]

A minister can love his or her ministry more than God. People say, "Wait a minute. Could it be wrong for a minister to love a ministry more than anything?" But if a minister loves a ministry more than anything in the world, he or she will often manipulate the church to

---

1. Of course there are many other reasons for the unacceptable behavior of children and mates, but sometimes this "over-focusing" on a child or partner can lead to real tragedy.

make that ministry whatever he or she thinks it ought to be. Subtle changes in direction can be made, votes can be loaded—whatever it takes to make the ministry work.

Many ministers become unloving manipulators when, consciously or unconsciously, they love their ministry more than God. And they are often bewildered when people no longer respond to them or want to follow their leadership. (It's bewildering because the minister feels "truly dedicated".) But this sort of situation is a far cry from an outpost of the kingdom in which the confessional community listens together for the voice of God in their midst, and in which the minister is simply a guide, a leader, and a fellow participant in their confession and their listening.

We need to know at some level that we all love ourselves and our agendas more than we love Jesus Christ and his way, and that this is our human condition, our spiritual condition in the world. *All of us* have sinned and fallen short (Rom. 3:23). The sins that keep us from conversion are not always bad things. They may be good things that God has given us but which we have put before him in our lives (like children, mates, vocations, etc.). These preferred things or people become idols or little gods. And the Bible is very clear about the fact that we are not to worship anything besides God (see Exod. 20:3). So we need to repent of this out-of-balance love or idol worship.

A very intelligent minister once said to me, "You can't compare the love of a child with the love of God—that's comparing apples and oranges. That's like saying, 'Do you love God more than you love jamocha-almond-fudge ice cream?' " And for two days, I believed him. And then suddenly, I thought, "No, it isn't apples and oranges!" I realized that minister was looking at a right-brain truth through a left-brain lens. The Bible is full of statements comparing people's love of material things to their love of God, saying that the Lord is a jealous God (see Exod. 20:4–5 and Luke 16:13). He wants people's primary love and loyalty. And when the Hebrew people loved their greed and material things more than they loved God, prophets such as Amos and Hosea railed at them and called them to repentance. In a right-brain way you *can* love something more than God and put him in second (or last) place in your priorities.

Helping a Seeker Confess and Surrender

I know that was a rather long discussion on this issue of putting God first—and I certainly don't recommend giving it as a speech to someone who is interested in being converted! It is just an example of some things which might be said to clarify a person's thinking about sin and separation from God.

Now, it's important to realize that this prospect of turning away from what one loves most and turning to Christ instead as the central focus of life can be terrifying for the seeker. He or she may wonder, "What will happen to me if I surrender to God?" "Will my child or wife still love me?" Or, "Maybe I won't have any identity if I commit my life to Jesus Christ."

If we're trying to help a seeker through the process of conversion, we can reassure the person we're talking to that such fears are normal. We can share some of our own experiences that show life after conversion doesn't mean giving up close relationships losing our identity, or becoming bland and boring. But, in the last analysis, we can't make the decision for him or her; there will come a time when the seeker will just have to go ahead and take the plunge of confessing and surrendering to God.

Taking the Plunge

The basic steps are the same ones the seeker in crisis took. I will describe them here as I might to a person who has indicated that they might like to make a commitment of their future to Christ. (Note to the reader: If you would like to make a new commitment to Christ to settle the question of conversion in your own life, you may want to take these steps as I describe them.)

First there is confession. I might advise the one seeking to "tell God simply in a prayer that you don't love him most, and what it is you can't turn from." The person might say, "Lord, I really don't love you most. What I really love most is my child [wife, vocation, sex, etc.]. I can't seem to turn from this child [etc.] because in spite of my best intention to love you best, I still love this child [etc.] more. But I *want* to love you most."

Such a confession is an outward sign of repentance. Sometimes we can't honestly say we are prepared to change everything and to put God first in our life. But we can still come to him, honestly confessing, and I believe he'll take us as we are. In fact, in a very real sense, that's all any of us can do, anyway, because we can't change what we really want most by a simple decision. But we can express our intention by saying, "Lord, I *want to want* you more." And if a seeker can't honestly say he or she loves God most, I ask them if they can say to God right then, "I *want to want* you most, Lord."

After confession and repentance comes the moment of surrender, when the seeker tells God something like this: "Lord, I know I'll ruin myself and this person or thing I love (perhaps everything else in my life) if I keep trying to run the show and the relationship to please myself. So I surrender to you. I ask that you come into my life with the Holy Spirit and show me how to live for you and your purposes, one day at a time." And these words become the outward signs of the inner commitment of faith.

At this point, when a seeker we have been talking with makes a commitment of faith, we can ask the person to pray with us. I generally pray something like this:

> Lord, thank you that you create doorways all over your world for us to walk through into your kingdom. Help us to know how to trust you with the most important people and things in our lives and to be your person, and not to be afraid to live the life you've set before us.
>
> In Jesus' name, Amen.

42

After Conversion—A New Beginning

A PERSON WHO HAS repented and made this commitment to Christ in faith is not *promising* God anything. He or she is not "swearing to God" to be righteous or good. (Jesus was against such statements; see Matt. 5:34–37.) Instead, this person has only repented and confessed and by intention turned the keys of his or her future over to Christ.

One of the striking surprises of walking in the Christian story is that we can't keep our promises perfectly—even to God. That's why we need continuing forgiveness. We are not as strong as we would like to believe. But our Lord knows this. As a matter of fact, we are not even the ones responsible for keeping this relationship with him. That's why the Good News of the gospel is so fantastic. *God* is going to keep the relationship. He's going to stay with us forever. Even if we run away, he'll be there when we get back!

What Happens Next?

After having helped someone make a commitment to Christ, the next thing I try to do is take that person along to an outpost group so that he or she can experience the love and support that comes from being intimately involved with other Christians. In this group the new convert can begin to learn to pray and to read the Bible and to share life with other believers.

If the person who has just been converted has never been baptized, he or she will probably want to seal the inner commitment he or she has made with the outward sacrament of baptism. And he or she will also want to learn about the strength and renewal that comes from the corporate worship of the church—especially the Holy Communion.

241

The members of the outpost group can guide the new convert in becoming involved in these things.

Newly converted Christians are starting out a whole new life with Christ as Lord, and they need help as they learn to love other people and themselves. The Christian life from the beginning has been something of an apprenticeship arrangement. Paul, for example, always had some younger Christians with him (such as Mark, Aristarchus, and Timothy), and he taught them how to live and to share the gospel.

That is why I believe it is very important for a person involved with helping people become converted to have a group into which new converts can be brought. I'd strongly advise anyone who is not part of such a group to pray about it, to try to find another converted Christian or two and to *start* an outpost group before he or she goes out to evangelize.[1] Of course, you may have to form a group (as I did) from the people you help into the faith. But the main thing to remember is that Christianity, walking in God's story, is not a solo deal, particularly for people who have just surrendered to God.

Beginning to Witness

A newly converted Christian may someday be called as a specialist— a proclaimer or a "midwife." But most likely he or she will be a witness who just may learn to say things like, "Hey, I met this great bunch of people down at the church. Why don't you come down there with me to meet them?" Or, "Recently I met some people who really believe in God. And through them he is changing my life in ways I wouldn't have believed." Such witnesses can be very effective contributors to the church's evangelism effort by just loving people and inviting them to come to church.

Remember, witnesses do not have to be theologians. The amazing truth is that many of the greatest saints were not very good theologians at all. Many of them didn't know much about systematic theology and probably couldn't have passed a modern seminary examination if their lives depended on it. But they had gotten acquainted with the living God, and they had learned how to walk with their Lord in his story. And they saw that all of life was different through the lens of that story.

---

1. The film series on which this book is based, *New Wine: Evangelism as a Biblical Way of Living* might be helpful to some people who are thinking of beginning an outpost group. Or Keith and Bruce Larson have a course for groups seeking to begin the Christian life as an adventure; it's called *The Edge of Adventure*. For information on the films and the course, contact a Christian bookstore or write Word, Inc. in Waco, Texas.

In these last few years I have found that in an outpost of his kingdom, God can even be with us in our mid-life crises—helping us to face everything from the need for diet and exercise to the reality of our own death . . . to the brown spots on the backs of our hands.

Years ago I wondered what God might do with me if I made a really serious commitment, attempted to surrender my life totally to him. (And as I've suggested, the *process* one goes through in conversion is not just a one-time thing. Most of us have to go through it again and again when some new idols come along and capture our imaginations.)

My fear was that God was going to have me buy one of those big, flappy black Bibles, go down to the Petroleum Club, stand up and bang on a glass to get everyone's attention, and then say in a loud voice, "I've got Good News for you guys and girls . . ."

And now, years later, I have to smile when I think about most of the things I was afraid God would have me do. A lot of them I've done. But the unexpected thing is that I've done the things I had been afraid to do because *I couldn't wait to do them.* The last thing I wanted to do was become an evangelist. And yet here I am, writing this book about what may be involved in commiting one's life to Jesus Christ. I didn't imagine then that I'd be doing this now.

The thing I was most afraid of was that, if I surrendered, God was going to send me to Africa or India or some other far-off place as a missionary. And when that idea occurred to me I thought, "Oh no, Lord!" I knew it would be somewhere way far away, because Jesus said, "You shall be my witnesses . . . to the end of the earth" (Acts 1:8, RSV).

A few years ago, I realized that the reason I thought the end of the earth was going to be a foreign country was that, to me, the *center* of the earth is wherever *I* am. But where then is the *end* of the earth from God's perspective? Where might he send us to be witnesses if we commit our lives to him?

If the heart that beat in Jesus Christ is in any sense the heart that throbs at the center of the universe, then the end of the earth from God's perspective may be wherever the influence of that heartbeat stops. That might be in your house or apartment, or at your office or church or city hall. And it may be that God is calling those of us who've caught the scent of his love to go home right where we live, to be wholly his people there. And maybe for the first time in our lives we will have truly come home.

EPILOGUE

IF YOU HAPPEN to take what I've said in this book seriously, I want to make one suggestion. If you have read something here that really turned you on, and if you feel that you have heard what I am trying to say, *don't go out and tell everybody about it.* Instead, go ask them, "How have you been the last few days?" And then listen to what they have to say. Then they'll *know* you've changed. Basically I do not think the world is waiting for advice about how to solve its problems. I believe it's waiting for somebody to listen to it and love it.

I pray that you will "start small" in simply learning to live one day at a time with and for your Lord. Just imagine his presence with you as you go about your daily work and play. *Find* some Christians to love you and guide you, and learn all you can about living and loving for Jesus Christ.

Lord, give us the courage to believe you. Give us the courage to help heal the people around us and to extend ourselves for their spiritual nurture. And Lord, also help us to have the courage to extend ourselves for our own spiritual nurture, in spite of what people may think, so that we can love them and you and ourselves better. Help us somehow to find a way to create small outposts of your kingdom, so that we can dare to go out and bring people in, because we've got a place to bring them.

And now, Lord, when we close this book and go back into our lives, help us to stay close to you and to listen to the people around us and love them.

In Jesus' name, Amen.

APPENDIX
A Case History Regarding the
Beginning of an Outpost Group

THE IDEA OF forming a small group had never been attractive to me. I am basically a loner and had seen most groups and committees as being ineffectual and cumbersome. But I came to a place in my adventure as a Christian where I was miserable and discouraged.

After a couple of years of studying the Bible and the lives of the saints and praying, I felt I wasn't changing any more. I had no one in the church I attended to whom I felt I could talk about what was happening in my life as a Christian. In any case I was too shy to broach the subject of my inner feelings. But as I'd read the New Testament, I had noticed that where lives were changing there were almost always *groups* of people. So I decided to start one.

The first thing I did was to clear the idea with the minister. If you are a lay person starting one of these outposts in a church, I strongly suggest that you do this, too. The minister is responsible for the spiritual growth of the flock and needs to know what is happening so he or she can either take part in it or help other people in the church understand what's happening.

To recruit members for my first group I went to the power people in our community and in our church. My thinking was, "Boy, if *these* people got in a group and went on the adventure with God, we could change this whole town." But as is often the case, most of them were too busy. So I began to search for people who really seemed to want to be committed to God. And I found the most unlikely group you ever saw. They were not the combination of people you would have chosen for a dinner party or a power caucus. I had gone to each one personally and talked about conversion. And those who became converted were the ones I later invited to meet with me in a group. (As I stated earlier, I think this is an important principle.)

One of the people I went to was an older lady from our Sunday school class who wore funny little hats and must have been about sixty-five at the time. I'll call her Mrs. Smith. Mrs. Smith was the coffee server every week in the Sunday school class, and she never missed. I never saw her say a word to anybody. She just moved silently around the church near the edge of the halls.

246

Then there was a woman who had just left a Roman Catholic order of nuns and become an Episcopalian. There was a young geologist and his wife. And there was a retired couple who had just lost their only son in a car wreck and were devastated by the tragedy. These are some of the ones who come to mind as I'm writing this, but there were several others—twelve in all. And each one of these people had made commitments of their futures to Christ.

Some people close to me said, "You can't get that group together. Their interests are too different. They'll never make it socially." And I said defensively, "Well, if the group breaks up, look at the time it will save. And at least we will have tried it." But I still went into the first night's meeting a little shaky about the outcome.

The First Night

I was so shy and afraid to fail that I planned the first meeting very thoroughly. We met on a Tuesday, I believe. That night, I told the group, "We're going to pray, read the Scriptures, and try to find out how to live for Christ in our personal lives. That's it. No other agenda. And I hope we'll get to know each other in the process."

I also said to the group, "Let's commit for eight weeks." I had just picked this number arbitrarily; I didn't know how long it might take, and eight weeks seemed like a good number. But I did feel it was important for the group to set a definite time limit.

(My experience with that group and with others since then has shown this was a good idea. I've discovered that people avoid making open-ended commitments—those with no set ending time—because they fear they may have trouble getting out later. Or if they do make a commitment and then want out, they may "sabotage" the group by their behavior to the point that they kill the group and *everybody* has to leave. I've actually seen this happen. So I suggest, if you are starting a group, that you begin by deciding on a definite ending time. This may sound overly structured and mechanical for the beginning of a "family." But then, have you ever attended a wedding?)

Once we had decided we would meet for eight weeks, I added that, if they wanted to give the group meeting social priority one night a week for eight weeks, they should come back the next Tuesday. I said that I realized some of them might not see the meetings as that much of a priority, and that was fine. But if they did come back, we would count on their being present at all the meetings unless they were sick, had a business conflict, or already had a commitment on the calendar.

Prayer

Once we got started in our group, the meetings went something like this. We would come together and go around the circle and pray. None of the people in the group had ever prayed out loud except in the worship services. We were all Episcopalins, and in those days in our parish, it was hard to pray if you didn't have a book. So I said, just to avoid embarrassing periods of silence, "All right, we are a bunch of nice thoughtful people, so if you don't have anything to pray about, just say 'Thank you, God,' so the next person won't panic waiting to see if you're going to pray. If you don't say something, they won't know if you are *ever* going to pray and won't know when it's their turn."

Well, at first, the time of prayer sounded something like this: "Thank you, God; thank you, God; thank you, God," right around the circle. And then I prayed a long prayer in which I probably said oblique things *at everybody*—probably telling God how nice it would be if everybody would pray. (I don't recommend *ever* trying to "straighten people out" during prayers—or at any other time. But I sometimes still forget and am tempted to give people "hints" and advice they haven't asked for.)

Getting Involved with the Scriptures

Besides praying together, we read the Bible in a certain way which I hoped would help us see that God could speak to us specifically through the Scriptures. The following is a description of the way we approached Scripture reading.

Basically, we would take a small passage of Scripture in one of the authorized translations (for instance, RSV, KJV, NIV, or NEB—not a paraphrase translation). Between meetings, each of us would: (1) rewrite the passage in our own words (the more down-to-earth and informal, the better); (2) ask ourselves, "What point is the author trying to get across to his readers?"; (3) ask, "What do I think God is saying through this passage to *me* about *my own life?*"

We were "not allowed" to read a commentary until the week *after* we had discussed the passage in the group (to keep people from avoiding their own feelings and making a left-brain head trip out of the experience). And everyone was to *write out* his or her answers to the questions—not just come up with an answer in their heads. The blocks of material were small enough that the whole assignment could be done in thirty minutes or less. That way the group, many of whom had never studied the Bible, would not get discouraged. In the meeting, we would go around the circle and share our responses to each question. I know that the whole exercise may sound simplistic and boring to a scholar. But what happened was that as we went through Philippians, half a chapter a week for eight weeks, people began to see and hear things about Paul, about their own faith, about the Scriptures, and about Jesus Christ—things which they had never heard or thought. We had a sense of discovery.

And when there were issues on which we weren't clear or about which we disagreed, the people most interested in the issue would be assigned to read up on the passage in the commentaries and report back to the group the following week. That way people were motivated to find something specific when they studied in the left-brain way. (As leader, I avoided looking things up for other people, so that the interested individual could get in the habit of studying for himself or herself.) And we found that we were becoming more open to the Holy Spirit as we came to the Scriptures together with our personal seeking.

By the end of the eight weeks several group members had shared ways they felt God had spoken through the Scriptures to their lives for the first time. They had made some decisions on the basis of what they had learned. And their experience quickened the hearts of the rest of us in the group.

As people learned to handle the Bible in a natural way, it became a book they could relate to personally. And they learned how to use various kinds of study helps (for instance, concordances, commentaries, Bible atlases; Bible Dictionaries, etc.) to enhance their understanding.

Closing the Meeting

At the end of each meeting we would talk about what we were going through in our lives as we were trying to live for Christ. In a period of silence we would ask ourselves if we wanted anybody to pray for us. And then we would tell the group our needs and we would pray for each other at the end, going around the circle again.

Then I would give instructions for the next week's study.

Privacy and Integrity in an Outpost

Before leaving our group the first night, I had said to them, "There won't be any new members allowed after next Tuesday when we start the full eight weeks." I felt that behind our personages we were all so shy about our faith and our true feelings—such a bunch of fawns— that we might jump away at the first hint of a new personality coming in and not being known. What often happens is that a group starts meeting together and being open. But if a new person comes in, everybody kind of "edits" to him or her. And the group gets self-conscious and silent again, or superficial and no longer personal. (I've watched it happen dozens of times over the years.) So I felt that, if we had eight weeks without new people, maybe we could begin to be able to talk with each other about our personal experiences.

Another thing I said that first night was, "Don't tell anybody what goes on in these meetings. That's a ground rule if you want to be in the group." I said this because one of the reasons it is so hard to share our inner persons is that we're afraid someone may tell our secrets or personal thoughts and expose us to ridicule or censure. I wanted to (1) protect our group from the threat of gossip, and (2) not put any pressure on them to have to defend the faith they were barely discovering. Besides, I remembered that Jesus told people "not to tell" about the healings he was involved in.[1]

Setting Limits

I decided to send the group home after two and a half hours. I felt we had to have a time structure to the meetings, since the members were very busy, hard-working people and I didn't want them (or their families at home) to get burned out about our time together. So the first night, after two and a half hours, I sent them home. But some of the group spent another two hours outside under the lamppost. They just didn't want to go home.

After about three days I started getting calls from people saying, "I would like to get in your group."

I said, "I'm sorry, we're full. But we'll put you on a waiting list."

One of the church officials called me in a couple of days and said, "Hey, we've got some people who want to get in your group. We'll

---

1. I have no idea why Jesus told people "not to tell." But the effect of his telling them this was fascinating. We in the church today often try to get people to go out and tell—and people resist doing so. Jesus told them to be quiet—and they told everyone. For instance, when he had healed the man who was deaf and had an impediment in his speech, "he charged them to tell no one; but the more he charged them, the more zealously they proclaimed it" (Mark 7:36). And when Jesus had finished talking to the woman at the well, he did not instruct her to tell what had happened to her. And yet she brought out a crowd of people, and many from that city believed because of her (John 4:7–38).

Now, I don't think for a moment that Jesus was a trickster, but I do believe he knew that sharing with integrity needs to be spontaneous and voluntary.

send them over for your next meeting."

I said, "I'm sorry, but they can't get in for eight weeks."

He said, "Listen, this is a church. Where's your authority for that?"

I said, "Jesus." (Jesus evidently spent about two-thirds of his time with twelve people forming the first outpost of the kingdom. And he shared his life and his dreams with them. Later, the members of that small group shared their lives with the world.)

After his initial negative reaction, this minister who'd called me was very understanding, and he said, "Okay, that's neat. We've never had a waiting list in this parish!"

What we in the church have done sometimes is to make the gospel and the Christian life "cheap," when it is only "free." There is a great deal of difference between "free" and "cheap."

I remember an incident which took place shortly after we had moved to a new neighborhood in Austin, Texas. After living in this neighborhood for about a year, I came home from a trip and there was an invitation already opened and lying on my desk. I read the invitation and it said, in essence, "You have been one of the special people chosen for membership in a new country club."

I was young and impressionable, and I said to myself, "Hey, it's kind of nice that they recognize me." Then I picked up the envelope and saw that it was addressed to "Occupant." And the invitation which had sounded so gracious suddenly seemed cheap somehow.

I think that is what we have often done in the church. We *say* a very personal thing to people. We say, "We love you, Jesus loves you," and yet we don't even go to the trouble to learn their names. And I was determined that since our group was making a sacrifice and time commitment to come, I was going to protect our privacy to see if we could meet each other on an intimate level. By the end of eight weeks, we not only began to learn the others' names, but we started to have real love and concern for each other. And I realized that, at least for our group, the "privacy" had paid off.

The Problem of Discouragement

But the group's beginning to be open and loving almost didn't happen. And many times during the first few weeks, I was tempted to quit and give up. I can't emphasize this enough: When starting an outpost there is much resistance to be overcome—from within the group as well as from outward pressures. All I know to tell you is to go on in faith if the group will go along. This kind of community goes through long periods when things seem to be bland and not particularly exciting for the leader. Then there will be sudden insights or breakthroughs—often coming from the most unexpected sources.

For example, for five weeks when we prayed, it had continued to be, "Thank you, God; thank you, God; thank you God." And I was tempted to give up about our ever getting personal in our prayers. I could hardly stand being the only one who prayed about personal concerns. I even began to feel that the group wasn't really interested in learning to pray (and thought I was an oddball for doing it). Finally, after the fifth meeting, I was having thoughts like, "Man, Keith, you have blown it somehow. These people don't even want to *be* here. They have committed to come, but they just can't wait for the eight weeks to be over."

Now, looking back after years of experience in groups, I would know to share my fears with them and to ask them to express *their* feelings about what was happening in the group. But in those days I was afraid they would criticize me or what I was doing.

You may think it strange that a group leader would have so many fears about failing, but I'm convinced that the lack of recognition about how scary it gets—and about how often a leader is tempted to quit—tends to make new group leaders feel they are failing when in fact they are having a normal group leader experience.

Anyway, in our group at the sixth week, the prayer time went: "Thank you, God; thank you, God; thank you God." Then it became Mrs. Smith's turn to pray. And Mrs. Smith, who had told us she had never prayed out loud before in her life, said her first personal prayer. She prayed very quietly, something like, "Dear God, this has been the most wonderful six weeks of my life. I have never felt loved before." As she prayed there was a tear in her eye. No one could speak, we were all so moved by her sharing her feelings with us.

And I decided to go on for the next two weeks.

We discovered that there is great power available in a group as we learn to release ourselves in trust to each other—because we are putting our ultimate trust in God.

At the end of eight weeks this group made the decision to go on. (This is always an option for groups that commit for a specific, limited period of time.) We continued to meet together for two years, eight weeks at a time, and we found that the learning was so natural we weren't even aware how much had happened to us until it was over.

There is much else that Jesus did in our group. If it were all to be recorded in detail, I suppose no publisher could print all the books which would be written.